DIGITAL SUPPLY NETWORKS

"In a digital economy, connected by the cloud through ubiquitous smart devices and data-enabled actions, understanding and implementing a digital supply network is the lifeblood of the system. The authors elegantly illustrate how major advances in technologies must be orchestrated in new ways to power the rapidly evolving and real-time demands of supply chain management. The insights are both provocative and actionable, providing the reader with a road map for implementation."

—BRAD D. SMITH, Executive Chairman, Intuit

"An important and timely subject that most companies are grappling with!"

—YOSSI SHEFFI, Director, MIT Center for Transportation and Logistics, MIT

"Exciting times ahead—the digital transformation will unlock new opportunities and hence needs to be the key strategic topic for organizations. A fascinating read for executives who intend to drive the digital journey using the emerging technologies."

—DIANA VOLKS, Head of Supply Chain Management, Bayer

"Over my 40-plus years of global supply chain experiences, I have become an ardent convert in the pursuit of end-to-end digital connectivity. Often the journey of a reimagined integrated supply chain will enable cross-functional collaboration and surface new insights and surprises. Defensiveness and pushback from the operational floor and across functions may occur. It is important for the organization's leadership, from the shop floor to the boardroom, to embrace the new end-to-end intelligence and focus on how to accelerate results. The rewards are well worth the endeavor. *Digital Supply Networks,* by Sinha, Bernardes, Calderon, and Wuest, provides a valuable transformational road map for your organization's journey."

—BOB GORSKI, Former Executive Vice President, Kraft Foods, former Vice President Global Supply Chain, Procter & Gamble

"The COVID-19 pandemic shows us that in times of increasing complexity and speed, we depend on transparency, fast reaction, or even prediction to reduce the vulnerability of our entirely globalized supply chains. And digitalization is key to gaining this required level of transparency and anticipation. This book provides helpful insights, explaining more technical details in a digestible manner."

—**STEFAN WASKOW,** Partner, Head of Procurement & Quality, Volkswagen Consulting

"Everyone involved in executing a supply chain is keenly aware that digital technologies will completely change the way we do work. As consumer and customer expectations drive the requirement to deliver goods faster, receive real-time information on their orders, and provide a superior customer experience, supply chain practitioners must evolve and transform. *Digital Supply Networks* provides a practical, hands-on playbook to help your organization transform both your systems and processes as you build your road map to take advantage of the new digital technologies that exist and are still to come."

—**JEFF FLECK,** Chief Supply Chain Officer, Georgia Pacific

"A must-read for manufacturers and anyone entering the Industry 4.0 workforce. If you want to know where jobs of the future are heading, *Digital Supply Networks* is an expert guide to understanding the infrastructure, processes, and behaviors that exist within our new cyber-physical reality. At its core, this is a critical resource for decision makers in every sector who face the enormous challenge of staying competitive while navigating and adapting to a rapidly changing marketplace."

—**THOMAS LICHTENBERGER,** President and CEO, Festo Didactic

"Predicting the future can be challenging but preparing for it becomes manageable with this thorough guide, filled with insights on the functional and technical capabilities behind DSN. Let this playbook aid you in taking active control of where your business is headed and ensure that the inevitable disruption of the supply chain will let you emerge stronger and more prosperous as opposed to trapped in one of the many pitfalls on the way. The holistic and easy-to-follow approach of this book makes it relevant to a broad audience of business professionals, executives, and students."

—**JACOB MUNCH SJELDAN,** Senior Business Solutions Architect, Novo Nordisk

"*Digital Supply Networks* is a valuable resource for understanding the disruption taking place across the globe as digital technologies transform supply chain management processes. Digital transformation has changed the way we live and work and will continue driving social and economic change and redefine the nature of work. The authors present a clear explanation of how the traditional sequence of processes are being transformed into one of interconnected information flows and advanced capabilities, aka the digital supply network. Further, they present a very strong case for why every company must adapt or be left behind. The book is an essential guide and road map to creating a successful, fully integrated DSN that aligns with a company's business strategy. I highly recommend *Digital Supply Networks* for anyone wanting to gain insights and a competitive advantage through new technologies and processes.

—JIM ULLUM, Managing Partner, Sourcing International

"During this period of acute transformation and disruption—or waves of progress and supply chain evolution—understanding the logistics and supply chain market landscape is more crucial than ever for leaders and logisticians. Sinha, Bernardes, Calderon, and Wuest share insight into how to spot the nodes, networks, and innovations that have the best chance of succeeding and some of the pitfalls we must avoid to achieve true laminar logistics."

—MICHAEL J. STOLARCZYK, Senior Vice President, CakeBoxx Technologies

"This is a uniquely insightful and practical perspective on the opportunities and complexities of the digital supply network. The current pandemic, along with the resulting economic chaos will have a profound impact on the global supply chain, highlighting the demand for supply chain resiliency and driving the restructuring of our supply networks. This journey will demand the depth and breadth of DSN insight demonstrated in this book."

—JOHN DYCK, Chief Executive Officer, Clean Energy Smart Manufacturing Innovation Institute (CESMII)

"*Digital Supply Networks* is an excellent source to understand both the components and overarching framework for the digital transformation of the extended enterprise. With COVID-19 driving the future of resilient supply chain design and execution, this book provides practical guidance."

—STEPHAN BILLER, PhD, Vice President, Watson IoT and Chief Innovation Officer, IBM

"Navigating digital disruption is a key issue for those who handle supply chains. This book offers a comprehensive description of all relevant aspects and advice on how to create an opportunity by implementing a digital supply network."

"*Digital Supply Networks* represent a critical next step in maturity for smart manufacturing, which builds upon the foundation digital capabilities that have been introduced within manufacturing operations over the last decade. The authors provide practical insights and guidance on both the business drivers as well as technology trends that will help enable success. This is a must-read for all companies embarking on this critical journey for their future."

DIGITAL SUPPLY NETWORKS

TRANSFORM YOUR SUPPLY CHAIN AND GAIN COMPETITIVE ADVANTAGE WITH DISRUPTIVE TECHNOLOGY AND REIMAGINED PROCESSES

AMIT SINHA | EDNILSON BERNARDES
RAFAEL CALDERON | THORSTEN WUEST

New York   Chicago   San Francisco   Athens   London   Madrid
Mexico City   Milan   New Delhi   Singapore   Sydney   Toronto

1 2 3 4 5 6 7 8 9   LCR   25 24 23 22 21 20

ISBN   978-1-260-45819-0
MHID   1-260-45819-9

e-ISBN   978-1-260-45820-6
e-MHID   1-260-45820-2

Library of Congress Cataloging-in-Publication Data

Names: Sinha, Amit, 1980- author. | Bernardes, Ednilson, author. | Calderon, Rafael, author.
Title: Digital supply networks : transform your supply chain and gain competitive advantage with disruptive technology and reimagined processes / Amit Sinha, Ednilson Bernardes, Rafael Calderon, and Thorsten Wuest.
Description: New York : McGraw-Hill, 2020. | Includes bibliographical references and index.
Identifiers: LCCN 2020012185 (print) | LCCN 2020012186 (ebook) | ISBN 9781260458190 (hardcover) | ISBN 9781260458206 (ebook)
Subjects: LCSH: Business logistics—Information technology. | Inventory control—Data processing.
Classification: LCC HD38.5 .S5643 2020 (print) | LCC HD38.5 (ebook) | DDC 658.70285—dc23
LC record available at https://lccn.loc.gov/2020012185
LC ebook record available at https://lccn.loc.gov/2020012186

CONTENTS

FOREWORD

With more than two decades of professional experience leading supply chain transformations, I have witnessed the transformation of the supply chain itself from a business support function to the center of an organization's strategy. For the prosperity achieved in the past 25 years, along with the higher standard of living across the globe, supply chain management (SCM) has played a crucial role by optimizing efficiency, enhancing productivity, and reducing waste. It would not be an overstatement to say that the supply chain has shaped the world we live in.

The technological progress that happened over the past three decades allowed organizations to create a connected supply chain of business activities, enabling end-to-end planning and execution of processes and workflows. However, through recent technological and process advancements, the basic idea of supply chain management is outdated. Adoption of advanced technologies consisting of sensors, machine learning, artificial intelligence, blockchain, and robotics have facilitated end-to-end visibility, control, and automated decision making. In this new way of working, a traditional chain will be replaced by the always-on, always-connected, transparent, dynamic networks. We can call this a "digital supply network," or DSN.

As the global cofounder of Digital Supply Networks, at Deloitte, I have helped many organizations achieve tremendous value through the adoption of DSN-enabling processes. This book is intended to provide comprehensive knowledge about the DSN processes and associated technologies as well as an adoption playbook. I got the opportunity to share my thoughts and help the author team by reviewing the content and providing feedback. I am delighted by the content quality and coverage of this book. I must congratulate the author team—Amit Sinha, Ednilson Bernardes, Rafael Calderon, and Thorsten Wuest—for putting together this comprehensive text on DSN.

At present, we certainly find ourselves in an intricately complicated time, one that has been disrupted in the blink of an eye by an unforeseen virus. As of this writing, COVID-19 has brought societies to a halt, placing many leading economies into self-imposed "comas" to stunt the spread of the coronavirus and avoid overwhelming healthcare systems. Economies are currently going through the painful task of re-opening, balancing the potential for more fatalities with the need to restart activities to avoid further economic catastrophe. And let us not forget the tremendous toll this virus is having on the human workforce that participates in the many industries that feed the economy.

The current pandemic has shed a glaring light on the vulnerabilities of traditional supply chains across industries—from healthcare to retail, industrial manufacturing to pharmaceutical. Raw materials and components stopped shipping. Supplies were unable to reach their destinations due to canceled air flights and trucking capacity. What started in a few distinct geographies quickly blossomed into a domino-effect of supply disruptions, grinding production to a halt across regions and sectors. If there ever was a watchword for the current environment, it would be *resilience*.

Resilience can mean many things, but at its core, it defines the ability of an organization or organism, to recover from a shock to the system, rapidly adapting and adjusting to the new circumstances. Many companies have been on the road toward building resilience in their supply chains for several years, preceding this current massive shock. They have added digital technologies like forecasting and even artificial intelligence to help connect activities across the chain, bringing demand and supply more closely in sync through technologies and processes that enable greater visibility and planning. However, despite these efforts, the vast majority of supply chains are still falling far short of the end state of resilience, in many ways.

Now, more than ever, it is apparent that building resilience into the supply chain is a business imperative—along with the need to replace the "chain" and its linear approach with a "network" that reflects the fluid nature of the business that all companies experience. Those companies that fail to do so will likely not survive this current crisis.

The current wave of digital transformation is changing the business rules across the world. I believe that the most crucial part of digital transformation or any business transformation is the consumer and the solutions businesses provide to its customers. In addition, I visualize DSN playing a vital role in providing safety, quality, value, and innovation to all stakeholders. The intelligence possibilities for machines through artificial intelligence allows business teams to run an intelligently automated enterprise through total visibility and fact-based decision making. The dynamic decision making in this intricately connected world needs to consider multiple factors to achieve the required adaptability, responsiveness, and resilience.

With the industry and institution collaboration achieved for this book, it is relevant to executives, managers, consultants, students, and academics. The progress from SCM to DSN is well articulated along with the traditional SCM processes and reimagined DSN processes. I recommend this book for executives who want to understand the basic concepts of advance technologies like data analytics, machine learning, artificial intelligence, robotics, and blockchain. The text elucidates the basics of these technologies, managerial applications, and how to harness the power of those technologies. The real-world examples shared throughout the chapters that define the digital supply network, introduce the technologies that power it, and describe its measurable business impact are inspirational for companies of all sizes and types. I was able to share my ideas for the DSN playbook, which has been captured well through further research and the expertise of the author team.

We are seeing positive examples of digital supply networks in operation today that are helping companies respond to the current crisis and demonstrate the agility that is critical for survival. I am hopeful that the current crisis we are experiencing will serve as the wake-up call for business leaders to lift the covers off their supply chains and build a sustainable strategy for creating a digital supply network that will engender the resilience every company needs to not only survive but *thrive*.

I invite you to a tremendous learning journey on digital transformation and digital supply networks through the wisdom shared in this book!

Adam Mussomeli
Principal, Supply Chain & Network Operations Leader
Deloitte Consulting LLP

ACKNOWLEDGMENTS

Amit Sinha

I'm first and foremost thankful to my brilliant coauthor team comprising of Ednilson, Rafa, and Thorsten. Working with this amazing team is a fun experience without a dull moment. Gratitude is due to our wonderful publisher, McGraw-Hill, with special thanks to our editors Donya Dickerson, Noah Schwartzberg, and Steve Straus.

I'm thankful to many of my brilliant colleagues at Deloitte, who have helped us by sharing their thoughts. The most crucial support has been from Adam Mussomeli, Supply Chain Network Operations (SCNO) leader at Deloitte Consulting. From the initial ideation phase to the text review and suggestions, Adam's vision and his support have been crucial throughout the development journey of this book. Special thanks to the Deloitte team of Doug Gish, Peter Capozucca, Jason Bergstrom, Samir Uppal, Rachel Goydan, Erica Volini, Barb Renner, Eric Kaese, Tom Wilson, Hussain Mooraj, Vadhi Narasimhamurti, and Mark Walsh for sharing their insights with us.

I'm thankful to my friends, Ranjeet Wadatkar, Mrugank Desai, Tommaso Nardi, and Vivian Nieves, for their help with text and image development. The review work from Heather Ashton, and Brenna Sniderman and image development by Ron Bardelli have helped us to enhance the quality and impact of the text. Ideas from Laura McGoff, Breanne Wagner, and Janet Chang have been instrumental in the marketing communication of the book.

In the end, sincere thanks to my friends, parents, family, my wife, Surabhi, and kids—Ivan and Anaya—for their love, and encouragement.

Ednilson Bernardes

I am grateful to Amit, Rafa, and Thorsten, with whom I had the pleasure to work with and learn from during this fascinating voyage. I want to thank our publisher McGraw-Hill and its team for embracing and supporting our project throughout the entire publication journey, particularly Donya Dickerson, Noah Schwartzberg, and Steve Straus. Thank you to Adam Mussomeli for the visionary and inspiring insights. A thank you to all the supply chain executives and professionals I interacted with over the years and who contributed thoughts and ideas for the project. A special thank you to the supply chain executives serving in the WVU Supply Chain Advisory Council, with whom I have had the distinct pleasure of working and learning. I am grateful to West Virginia University and the Global Supply Chain Management Incubator at the Chambers College for providing fertile ground and support for thoughtful interactions and discovery. I am also very thankful to Sophie Wang for her insights and assistance in developing many of the graphics for the book.

Every journey starts with the first steps, and the current journey would not have been possible without the ones taken many years ago. I want to thank Jaime Fensterseifer for getting me started and Roger Schroeder, Kingshuk Sinha, and Rachna Shah for providing me with the opportunity and the foundations to proceed. A thank you to many friends and research colleagues for insightful and inspiring professional and personal conversations over the years, especially Paul Skilton, Stan Fawcett, and Mark Nigrini, among others.

Nobody has been more important to me in the pursuit of my projects than the members of my family. My mother, Maria Conceição, especially, is the ultimate lifelong model of support, strength, long-term vision, positive attitude, and perseverance.

Rafael Calderon

I would like to thank my coauthor team of Ednilson, Amit, and Thorsten for a wonderful journey together in this endeavor. It has been a true adventure and enriching experience. Amit, you were the motor behind this project and because of your energy and focus we are here. Very thankful to our publisher, McGraw-Hill, and special thanks to our editors Donya Dickerson, Noah Schwartzberg, and Steve Straus.

I would also like to extend my deepest gratitude to colleagues at Deloitte, who have helped us by sharing their ideas, reviewing manuscripts, and providing the inspiration we needed to get through this effort. Ranjeet Wadatkar, Mrugank Desai, Alejandra MacFarland, Manuel Peralta, and Imran Dalwani for their support; Brenna Sniderman and Heather Ashton for helping us review the content; Deloitte Development LLP, Deloitte Insights, and Deloitte University Press for helping us with ideas and inspiration for this book; and to Doug Gish, Mark Walsh, Adam Mussomeli, Jason Bergstrom, Brenna Sniderman, Peter Capozucca, Samir Uppal, Barb Renner, Eric Kaese, Tom Wilson, Hussain Mooraj, Rachael Goydan, and Erica Volini for their support.

Most of all thank you to my beautiful wife, Alessandra, and our kids, Rafael, Elena, Luca, Giuliano, and Apollonia, for supporting me in all my adventures and projects!

Thorsten Wuest

It was a pleasure to work with my coauthors Amit, Rafa, and Ed. The development and writing process of this book was intense but with these exceptional partners it was an opportunity to grow and learn! The continuous support of our publisher McGraw-Hill—shout out to Donya, Noah, and Steve who were always willing to help and answer questions—was highly appreciated!

I'd like to thank all my incredible students of our Smart Manufacturing Lab at WVU. Specifically, Makenzie Keepers, Muztoba Khan, Jonas Kohls, Dr. Juergen Lenz, Karan Menon, Dr. Sameer Mittal, and Patrick Schmid contributed directly or indirectly through their research. Without their inquiry and dedication this project would not have been possible. The continuous support of leadership and colleagues at WVU, Statler College, and the IMSE department, as well as generous alumni like Wayne and Kathy Richards was instrumental for the success of this book project.

Furthermore, I would like to thank my brilliant colleagues and collaborators around the world. The many fruitful discussions and inspiring projects provided the foundation for many insights presented in this book. While it is impossible to name everyone, I would like to give a special thanks to the following individuals (in alphabetical order): Drs. Farhad Ameri, Jim Davis, Ramy Harik, Christopher Irgens, Dimitris Kiritsis, Bruce Kramer, Gisela Lanza, Ang Liu, Torbjörn Netland, Rahul Rai, David Romero, Klaus-Dieter Thoben, and many, many more. The exchange and platform of IFIP WG 5.7 & 5.1, Society of Manufacturing Engineers (SME), CESMII, and the Institute of Industrial and Systems Engineers (IISE) provided a fun and productive environment as well as fertile ground for exploring new ideas, and exchanging best practices and lessons learned.

The biggest thank you, however, goes to my wonderful and supportive wife, Irene, and my amazing children, Dominic and Sofia. Their love, constant encouragement, and ability to make me smile despite looming deadlines allowed me to bring the best of me to this book.

DIGITAL TRANSFORMATION AND ITS IMPACT ON SUPPLY CHAIN MANAGEMENT

New breeds of disruptive technologies and the convergence of these technologies are transforming the world around us at an unprecedented pace. For a simple example from our daily lives, let us consider the smartphone, which has become an integral part of our modern lifestyle. These compact devices have more computing power than the mainframes that guided the first Apollo space mission in 1969. There is no doubt that technological innovation is accelerating at what many consider an exponential pace. The amount of disruption from digital technology over the past five years is more significant than that of the previous five decades. And, based on industry forecasts, this trend will only continue. The impact can be seen across industries, societies, countries, and continents. One only has to look at the global stock markets to see the effects of digital transformation. Companies that have been in business for a century are being surpassed or even driven out of business by new digital start-ups. Or if we focus on the 2020 COVID-19 pandemic, we notice that those organizations whose digital transformation was more mature before the outbreak found themselves at an advantage, as did those that quickly mobilized digital efforts at the onset of the crisis. While some of this change can be intimidating, there are endless commercial opportunities for digital transformation to improve operations, increase revenue, create new business models, and add unprecedented value to customers, stakeholders, and society.

One area that has been tremendously impacted by digitization and has continued to undergo a notable transformation with the emergence of new technologies is supply chain management (SCM). According to the Council of Supply Chain Management Professionals (CSCMP), SCM encompasses the planning and management of all activities involved in sourcing and procurement, conversion, and all logistics management activities. It also includes coordination and collaboration with channel partners, which can be suppliers, intermediaries, third-party service providers, and customers. CSCMP summarizes the SCM concept as the integration of supply and demand management within and across companies.[1] The recent wave of industrial and economic progress, enabled by new technologies, is challenging the assumptions, limitations, and mental models from traditional SCM. At the same time, it is unleashing tremendous opportunities to create value for the firm, customers, employees, and society. However, to unlock the potential for greater value creation, executives must reevaluate and transform existing processes and strategically combine new breeds of digital technologies to create novel capabilities. The best prospects for more value creation and unbeatable competitiveness will come from reimagining how to organize and run the value chain. Companies that enact new business models, enabled by migration from a traditional supply chain management mindset toward a digital supply network (DSN), will reap tremendous first-mover advantages and may raise unsurpassable benefits.

In this first chapter, we briefly describe the digital transformation and its importance for and impact on organizations. We also describe the primary waves of technological progress and industrial and economic leaps and juxtapose the recent developments in the supply chain within the latest waves. Finally, we introduce the concept of DSN and briefly contrast it to the prevailing managerial thought.

WHAT IS DIGITAL TRANSFORMATION, AND WHY SHOULD I CARE?

Digital transformation is the reimagining of end-to-end business processes to create value, enabled by disruptive digital technologies. Through digital transformation, organizations can provide customers with innovative products and services with the highest quality and the lowest cost. Smart optimization of resources can reach unprecedented effectiveness, and waste can be nearly eliminated from processes.

Digitization of the supply chain has been taking place for the past couple of decades through enterprise resource planning (ERP) system implementation, use of manufacturing robots, digital drawing, custom planning systems, and electronic data interchange (EDI). The current wave of digital transformation will bring entirely new organizational forms, more human-centric work and a more fulfilled workforce, unprecedented customer value, and the betterment of society. At the same time, it will also occasion notable disruption to the current world order, as it requires dramatically different skill sets, may drive many out of the workforce, and may exacerbate inequality. It will also drive and consolidate markets and industries and will render current business playbooks for success not only completely outdated but unable to compete with the new breed of digitally enabled organizations.

So, you may be asking, how exactly is digital transformation related to changing an organization and its SCM processes? Will supply chain processes and activities look the same as they do now, or will they be completely different with the emergence of disruptive technologies? Is the current managerial conceptualization of SCM still adequate, or is a new understanding required? What are the breakthrough technologies that are enabling the complete transformation of businesses? Who is my competitor in the digitally transformed world? How will digital transformation impact skills requirements, my own job, and work in general? How do I get started? What are the recommendations for success throughout the journey?

If you have thought about any of these questions, this book is for you. A lot of anxiety and uncertainty surround the current wave of technological developments. We acknowledge the blooming, buzzing confusion and address the pressing questions that are keeping business executives and supply chain professionals awake at night. We answer them through a comprehensive explanation of the process of digital transformation, the enabling technologies, the impact on traditional SCM processes, the effect on the workforce and the nature of work, and the approaches that can enable organizations to achieve the promised land while avoiding the pitfalls. Throughout our journey, we provide examples and use cases to inspire, motivate, and illustrate the evolution. We also present a practical, hands-on playbook that significantly reduces the initial barriers to engaging in digital transformation within your organization. For those of you who have not been preoccupied with the questions posed above, there is an even greater need to learn about and understand the changes brought forth by digital transformation that we discuss throughout this book—there is no turning back! More than previous waves, the unprepared will pay dearly.

But let us return to a fundamental question: Why should I care? Let us review the most critical reasons why digital transformation matters in a DSN context. In short, digital transformation is table stakes for engaging with customers, managing internal processes, and collaborating across the organization in this digital age.

Customer Expectation

Businesses exist to serve their customers and create value for their stakeholders. If a business cannot satisfy its customers' needs, it will not endure in a competitive global marketplace. Customer expectations are constantly changing, actually at an ever more rapid pace today; therefore, a successful business needs to constantly reinvent itself. Organizations such as Blockbuster, Kodak, Nokia mobile phone, and Xerox are examples of companies that failed to reinvent themselves in moments of transition. Considering that today's customers can order groceries for delivery through a smart device from their homes, remotely adjust their home's temperature, or see who is at the door while not at home, the threshold for engaging with them is higher than ever. Market leaders of the past will be forced to disrupt themselves or face extinction. On the other hand, organizations that are embracing and leveraging digital transformation to create customer value have been handsomely rewarded by the marketplace. In summary, the first reason that you should care is because your customers care, and there is no business without customers!

For example, here is how a shoe manufacturer is using digital capabilities to enhance customer value. With the company's app, a customer can snap pictures of her foot and provide information regarding her age, activity level, and other considerations. The shoe company uses this data to identify the most suitable product for the customer, and then deliver a customized pair to her doorstep through an agile supply network. The same app can track usage and tread wear, prompt the customer to confirm delivery of a replacement pair, and enable the recycling of the older shoes. This example illustrates the impact of digital transformation: customer satisfaction, increased revenue, and a better environment through an integrated network, from product design to product recycling.

Efficiency

As mentioned in the previous point, the ultimate goal of an organization is to deliver customer value and to create value for stakeholders. Organizations achieve these outcomes through operating processes; therefore, executives have always been concerned about the efficiency of these processes—how well they make use of inputs for the creation of value. It is not surprising, then, that the concepts of scale and scope have been important since the first significant wave of innovation back in the nineteenth century. Executives have pursued the benefits afforded by economies of scale and scope, both considered substantial drivers of efficiency and business operating performance. One big challenge in managing those concepts, though, has been the trade-off between scale and scope. Traditionally, to increase the economies of scale one has to decrease the scope or variability. Technology has been adopted to reduce this trade-off and optimize cost. However, another problem is the limit of the benefits from economies of scale, as they start to produce diminishing returns after a given point.

The digital age is radically changing how executives can approach those managerial concepts. New technologies allow organizations to scale up processes much faster than traditional ones and with a much higher scope because executives can connect them to other digitized operating processes and businesses.[2] The trade-off between scale and economy that has driven much of efficiency management becomes much less relevant, as return on scale can continue to climb to unprecedented levels. Digitally driven operating models and firms designed around a digital core can overwhelm traditional operating processes and organizations.[3] Digital transformation brings with it the potential for significant cost savings and efficiency enhancement. The digitally connected world, enabled by disruptive technologies, will further transform the cost structure of businesses and will harness greater efficiency and deliver profits for the winners. These gains in efficiency are another reason you should care; your current and emerging competitors are relentlessly pursuing them and will unforgivingly outpace you.

For example, an automotive component supplier produces ball bearings used in engine and drive assemblies. Statistical process control used for the past 20 years have helped the company enhance the quality and efficiency of the manufacturing process. In the current environment, out of thousands of items produced every hour, a sample number (approximately 30 units) is tested for quality. If one part fails, the entire lot is rejected. Even with a high success rate (e.g., 95 percent), the amount of waste is significant. Using a computer vision–enabled sensor on the assembly line, however, the manufacturing unit of the organization can now stop production the moment the first defective product passes through. Corrective action can be taken immediately, and waste and time lost go to near zero.

Revenue

Besides having a considerable impact on the profit of the organization through cost efficiency, adopting the current wave of digital technology has a substantial effect on revenue growth. Top-line growth can be driven by having more customers, more products, more services, or a combination of these, all enabled by higher throughput and superior customer value. Agile supply networks, capable of providing customized products and services, with the ability to reach a broader customer base, multiply the network's value and, as a result, magnify revenue. There are multiple real-world use cases in which organizations have augmented their income through digital tools and the creation of a "platform" effect in terms of scale. The easiest way to describe the platform impact is by looking at how successful Amazon has been in aggregating buyers to one location. It maximizes their collective value to attract volumes of sellers, which creates a virtuous cycle for buyers and sellers in the network.

An industrial components manufacturer that makes custom construction and mining equipment has created a digital marketplace to connect with customers and understand its customers' unique project requirements efficiently. This marketplace created new revenue streams through new products offered to current customers, as well as old and new product lines sold to new customers. Using sensor data linked to customers' in-field products, the company can help customers maintain optimum operating parameters, through alerts about tire pressure, engine temperature control, or a suggested oil change, to mention a few. This way, product usage is optimized throughout its lifecycle, enhancing customer value and making the replacement sale effortless.

Collaborative Network and Stakeholders' Expectation

It is essential to understand that digital transformation, if appropriately adopted, is a pan-business activity spread through the nerves and veins of an organization, not limited to a particular operation or business function. Organizations can harness collaboration, visibility, and efficiency to their fullest extent only if they follow a holistic approach, which today translates to being part of a bigger collaborative ecosystem. This collaborative network generates value in meaningful ways. In addition to serving the customer, such networks create positive impact for a business's stakeholders. The digital transformation adds value to employees (providing tools to be more productive and freeing employees from repetitive tasks), partners (using a connected ecosystem), and society (allowing optimum use of resources).

Consider a company that sells a data storage server brand. This company works through a group of collaborative partners. The partners manufacture memory drives, processors, switches, and so on and provide them to the brand owner company, which then performs assembly and serves customers directly. The value of digital transformation can be seen in the demand projections that are shared with partners through digital technologies, enabling the partners to respond with their supply planning to meet the demand. Having digital forecasts and planning shared across a collaborative network helps when one supplier faces a constraint. Other ecosystem partners can quickly solve this situation. For every organization to succeed or even to survive in this environment, digital maturity is a core requirement.

After understanding digital transformation and its importance for firms, let us review the impact it is creating on supply chain management.

DIGITAL TRANSFORMATION'S IMPACT ON ORGANIZATIONS AND SUPPLY CHAINS

While technologies have redefined industries for centuries, today it is the convergence of critical technologies, such as artificial intelligence, cloud, robotics, Internet of Things, additive manufacturing, and blockchain, that is enabling automation of business functions in ways that could only be dreamt of in the past. We will cover the key enabling technologies, their impact, and why they disrupt the traditional methods throughout different sections of this book. In the current digital age, organizations are expected to be always on and always connected with their customers. Let us take a look at three significant ways digital transformation is disrupting businesses: customer interaction, internal organizational processes including partner collaboration, and the roles of data and technology.

Customer Impact

The center stage of digital transformation is and should be customers and the value created for them. Customers need to have an excellent value-adding relationship as a connected partner in the digital age, instead of an "on and off" transactional interaction. Customer emotion plays a significant role in deciding whether a user becomes a vocal brand supporter, a one-time neutral buyer, or a dissatisfied customer. Digital technology enables organizations to transform the customer experience positively, automate processes, utilize unstructured data (tweets, email, etc.) surrounding a customer experience, and quickly take action to turn a frustrated supporter into a loyal patron for life.

Recently, a primary airline service provider had to cancel several flights due to bad weather. Instead of just following the traditional process of rescheduling passengers on flights based on their priority status, the airline used real-time analytics to gauge passenger emotions through social media posts. Using this insight, the airline pulled in staff from other geographies to respond to the service event, leveraging virtual customer service tools. It reached out to partner airlines to identify faster alternatives for the affected passengers. The intelligent optimization engine produced the best individual route schedule while taking care of the organization's as well as the partner's (a traditional competitor) resources. As a result of these behind-the-scenes efforts utilizing digital tools, the hundreds of retweeted messages from the passengers were about delight and thanks rather than frustration, creating many new brand loyalists. We will cover the "connected customer" in the digital age in greater detail in Chapter 11.

Process Impact

Digital transformation has rewritten the rules of the organization's processes of design, procurement, manufacturing, logistics, storage, transportation, and distribution. With machines' ability to sense, interpret, act, and improve, all the parameters in traditional supply chain management can be influenced in a highly positive manner, and with time the business can become a data-driven organization—an insight-driven organization whose foundation is data.

Sourcing in the digital environment is moving to predictive strategic sourcing and automated transactional procurement. Organizations can analyze massive procurement data to identify strategic suppliers, perform spend analysis, and effectively manage individual suppliers for value enhancement to the entire network. Blockchain is changing the way the contracts are handled by making them smart, automated contracts while reducing associated indirect costs. The digital procurement process is covered in Chapter 8, "Intelligent Supply."

For production operations and handling of the manufacturing assets in the organization, components of smart manufacturing are causing steep increases in manufacturing efficiency, lowering inventory costs, and speeding product movements. Additive manufacturing is enhancing product customization, and digital twin technology streamlines management and design of a manufacturing facility while improving agility and safety. An asset's availability can be highly increased using machine learning predictive algorithms. These areas are part of the digital supply network, illustrated in detail in Chapter 9, "Smart Manufacturing and Intelligent Asset Management." Additionally, the use of smart warehousing and smart transportation to automate the flow of materials and products is discussed in detail in Chapter 10, "Dynamic Fulfillment."

Data and Technology Impact

Data holds a key role in digital transformation, in ways never realized before. One cannot escape typical statements about data today, such as "data is the new oil to run the digital economy," "data is gold," or "data is the electricity of the twenty-first century." While these sound like hyperbole, given data's central role in digital transformation, they are not overstatements. Most digital innovations, from autonomous cars to robots that move boxes in warehouses to algorithmic models that predict consumer behavior, rely on massive amounts of data. This data is collected from multiple sources and analyzed with machine learning algorithms supported by high computational power machines to identify patterns and uncover insights that were previously impossible to identify and act upon.

In concert with the data that supports digital transformation are a myriad of supporting technologies, some of which have already been mentioned in this chapter. These technologies enable real-time insights, which drive real-time decisions that impact businesses at market speed. From artificial intelligence applications that use neural networks to perform complex machine learning to physical robots that can mimic sophisticated human moves to enable full automation on a production line, technology is a crucial underpinning of digital transformation.

The data and technology topics are captured in detail in Chapters 3 and 4 of this book. Recommended strategies to harness the impact of applying data and digital technology are covered in Chapter 13, our "DSN Transformation Playbook." Our goal is not to make you a data scientist through this coverage but to help you understand, appreciate, and use data and technology for digital transformation in your organization. Though the current transformation has a humongous impact on enterprises and society, there have been multiple transformations in the past, as illustrated in the next section.

WAVES OF INDUSTRIAL AND ECONOMIC CHANGE DRIVEN BY DISRUPTIVE TECHNOLOGICAL INNOVATION

In modern history, we have had four waves of profound technological change with socioeconomic and cultural components that impacted the way we live, work, and relate to one another. Figure 1.1 represents these waves of significant technological innovation and industrial leaps. It also highlights how leaders have been combining technology and innovations to create value in new and different ways—from "machines replacing muscles" to "machines replacing and augmenting human minds." Each wave represented a jump forward, bringing new developments not only in production systems but also in economic and social changes. The result was a broader distribution of wealth, political changes reflecting shifts in economic power, new state policies associated with the needs of an evolving society, social changes including a sprawling urban population and working-class movements, and cultural developments. Within the changes brought about by the latest wave, we now see the emergence of a new and disruptive way to organize and manage the chain and flow of supplies. To better understand the scope and the impact of the emerging model, let us briefly review some key features of past waves and subsequently situate the new model within the latest stage.

FIGURE 1.1   Waves of Technological and Economic Progress

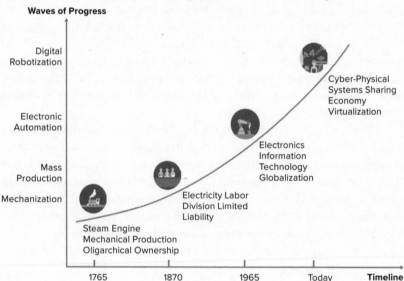

MECHANIZATION. The first wave extended from the end of the eighteenth century to the beginning of the nineteenth century and was primarily confined to Britain. During this period, water and steam power mechanized production. Coal and the steam engine propelled society forward, giving rise to railroads, forging, and the first factories and urban clusters. Mechanization displaced agriculture as the basis of the economic structure of society. Cities started getting established as manufacturing hubs with connections to other cities, suburbs, and rural areas. The labor force was mostly unskilled, cheap, and plentiful. The steam-powered printing press enabled mass education for the first time. Society experienced tremendous gains in productivity, while many artisan skills and instruments of the old economy were replaced.

MASS PRODUCTION. In the late nineteenth century, new organizational models based on mass production consolidated research and capital in large corporate structures. Science took roots in laboratories, and scientific principles guided the organization of factories. During this period, electricity and oil became prominent sources of energy, and large organizations enabled the emergence and advancement of various innovations, including the combustion engine, steel, chemical synthesis, and the automobile, airplane, telegraph, and telephone. This period created a middle class of skilled workers. Electrification advanced into cities and homes. Limited liability corporations reduced the risk to individuals engaged in entrepreneurial activities. Ownership of the means of production shifted from oligarchical to a broader distribution through the purchase of common stocks by individuals and institutions. Many European countries socialized primary sectors of the economy to meet the needs of a more sophisticated industrial society.

ELECTRONIC AUTOMATION. In the second half of the twentieth century, the transistor and microprocessor gave rise to the production of miniaturized components. Digital technologies replaced analog and mechanical devices. Advancements in space research, telecommunications, computer science, automatons, and robots led to a high level of industry automation and simple digitization. Other essential innovations from this period include the semiconductor, mainframe and personal computers, and the Internet. Nuclear energy appeared as a promising alternative to previous sources of energy. Lower labor cost in developing economies became a feasible alternative to mechanization, and easier access to other factors of production propelled companies to locate portions of their value chain where those factors were cheaper.[4] Electronics and information technology started to automate production and expand supply chains globally. It is within this stage that we situate the building blocks of the traditional supply chain management model we know today.

DIGITAL ROBOTIZATION. This new wave has been unfolding since the late twentieth century and is merging technologies that undo the distinction between the digital, physical, and biological spheres. Distinct from the previous waves, which involved mostly Western Europe and its branches, technologies are converging and evolving at an exponential speed, disrupting every industry across the world and profoundly transforming the production system and society at large. According to the World Economic Forum, these innovations define entirely new ways in which technology becomes embedded within societies and even human bodies.

Similar to previous waves of technological and industrial leaps, this one has the potential to improve the quality of life for populations around the world. Enabled by mobile devices with unprecedented processing power, storage capacity, and access to knowledge, we are achieving mass connectivity, which added to advances in AI ushers in unlimited prospects. Data is becoming a critical factor of production, and Internet-driven innovations, such as crowdfunding and peer-to-peer finance, are democratizing access to the economic system. Joint advancements in multidisciplinary bodies of knowledge are combining digital production technologies, such as computational design and additive manufacturing, with materials engineering and synthetic biology to pioneer a symbiosis between microorganisms, our bodies, the products we consume, and even the buildings we inhabit.[5] In the demand side of the economy, connectivity is increasing transparency, improving consumer engagement, and leading to entirely new patterns of consumer behavior.

Organization for Economic Cooperation and Development (OECD) projections suggest that the world will become about 10 times wealthier during this phase. As argued by Schwab, if it is shaped responsively and responsibly, the current wave "could catalyze a new cultural renaissance that will enable us to feel part of something much larger than ourselves—a true global civilization."[6] However, the current wave of technological progress also has its darker side: it can produce tremendous inequalities and disrupt the labor market in more profound ways than the previous phases.[7] It is within this broader context of transformation that we discuss the emergence of a new model for managing the flows of supply, one that can generate unprecedented value, open up new markets, enable entirely new ways of serving customers, and drive economic growth. Let us now juxtapose to this backdrop the recent evolution of supply chain management.

Recent Supply Chain Management Evolution

Modern supply chain management is the result of a progression blending technical, technological, and managerial improvements. This progression is marked by an increasing degree of integration of separate operations and tasks that began in the 1960s.[8] Figure 1.2 illustrates the sequence toward ever more encompassing arcs of integration.[9] Before the 1950s, the common term in the organizational lexicon was "logistics," and practitioners approached the function in the context of military activity, which encompassed the procurement, maintenance, and transportation of military facilities, equipment, and personnel.[10] In general, organizations did not yet recognize the importance of managing cost trade-offs and the benefits of getting the right goods to the right place at the right time. The typical firm organized the activities currently associated with supply chain management in a very fragmented form.

FIGURE 1.2   Recent Supply Chain Management Evolution

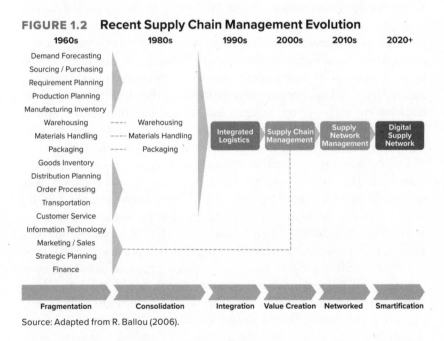

Source: Adapted from R. Ballou (2006).

During the 1960s, separate functional integrative efforts started taking place. On one side, the management attitude toward the role and importance of the physical distribution function began to undergo a momentous change.[11] Inspired by strong support from trade associations, the trade press, government, and the academic community, a new literature of management philosophy emerged, and forward-thinking firms began to approach the area from a more holistic perspective. Initially, the scope was limited to a firm's outbound movement of goods, but near the middle of the decade, the range was expanded to include physical supply.[12] Meanwhile, the purchasing profession, developing since the railroad era[13] and initially focused on the buying activity, also started to expand its scope to include functions associated with physical distribution, but from the inbound side of the firm perspective. The more mature operations and production activity remained conceptually separate from purchasing, and there was little coordination between them. While production and operations considered logistics activities as part of the product function, firms did not dedicate full attention to the total flow. Engineers designed material requirements planning (MRP I) to handle ordering and scheduling of dependent inventories.

The fragmentation and poor coordination of tasks caused functional conflicts and frequently led to sub optimization, inefficiencies, waste, and other managerial problems. The expansionistic efforts of the purchasing and business logistics professionals from opposing camps in the firm's distribution process led to an initial functional consolidation. During the 1970s and 1980s, the scope and influence of a system's approach to the area continued to evolve, and the tasks composing the distribution activity consolidated into materials management (more oriented toward the inbound movement of supply) and physical distribution (more oriented toward the outbound movement of goods). However, management still did not conceptualize all activities associated with the flow of materials as an integrated task; the focus was on coordination among the activities within each subfunction. On the production side, MRP systems expand to encompass more manufacturing processes, including financial estimates and demand and business planning. MRP became manufacturing resource planning (MRP II).

As the 1980s progressed, management began to focus on controlling and balancing material flow, which led to a tremendous reduction of inventory in the operations activity of many companies. However, this initiative was mostly confined to the four walls of the manufacturing organization: the inbound and outbound flow of materials followed a batching logic. In the 1990s, the initial efforts toward functional integration continued and led to a managerial focus on full internal integration. The activities associated with the flow of materials were conceptually organized under the umbrella of "integrated logistics." Organizations started implementing enterprise resource planning (ERP), which expanded MRP capabilities to include back-office functions such as accounting and human resources. These systems continued to evolve and integrate various functions into one complete system to streamline processes and information across the entire organization and eventually beyond. Toward the end of the wave of electronic automation (Figure 1.1), management started implementing modern information and communication technologies toward the flow of materials. Efforts regarding the control and balance of the flow of material began to be increasingly focused on the whole supply chain, beyond the boundaries of the organization. The most important benefits resulting from these efforts were better customer service, reduced inventory, and lower operating costs.

At the dawn of the twenty-first century, the continued use of advanced information and communication technologies enabled a more comprehensive integration. It was the rise of "supply chain management." The new technologies allowed the integration and coordination of not only the physical flows of materials but also the information and financial flows. Organizations started exploring new realms of production and distribution systems, and the activity expanded globally. Supply chain management became a complex sequence of activities aimed at creating and capturing value.

By then, managerial thought had fully recognized the importance of a systems-level or supply chain optimization. Organizations started investing increasingly more time and money attempting to predict and control their extended supplier systems. Supply management was recognized as strategic.[14] For practitioners, the strategic importance of integration is reflected in the popular Supply Chain Operations Reference (SCOR) model, which assumes all businesses include planning, sourcing, making, and delivering processes strategically linking suppliers and customers to manufacturers.[15] However, management soon realized that changes occurring at the tertiary supplier level (e.g., second and third tiers) are often beyond their managerial purview and control, so they struggled with the dynamic and complex nature of supply networks. Pioneering scholars advanced a conceptual model to more accurately reflect the underlying complexity and dynamism of the chain of supply, proposing it as a complex adaptive system.[16] This approach led to a stream of managerially impactful research throughout the 2010s, and the notion and insights are advancing with the rise of new ways to analyze data.[17]

Early in the digital robotization wave (Figure 1.1), we started witnessing the increasing automation of physical distribution and materials management. Digitization started taking advanced forms and providing tremendous value and competitiveness to pioneering companies. For instance, storage, materials handling, and packaging in distribution centers have made incredible inroads toward automation. However, prevailing managerial thought continues to conceptualize the overall activity very much from mostly linear logic. The plan, source, make, deliver, and return framework, which has successfully helped managers and industry during the rise of supply chain management, characterizes the current managerial thought. As the robotization wave continues to progress, though, innovations and disruptive technologies open up the possibility of genuinely managing the complex adaptive network of supply in entirely reimagined ways. Pioneering companies are pushing the envelope of the possible and achieving remarkable outcomes. We are witnessing the rise of the smart, always-on, always-connected, real-time, and dynamically adaptive digital supply network.[18]

So, how is the traditional SCM different from the DSN? We will describe this in broad strokes in the rest of this chapter, then in greater depth throughout the book, providing examples of what first movers are achieving and proofs of concept that hold tremendous promise and indicate possibilities. Before introducing the new and emerging model, let us briefly contrast SCM and DSN.

BASICS OF TRADITIONAL SUPPLY CHAIN MANAGEMENT

SCM refers to a broad range of activities related to product and service design, demand-supply planning, purchasing, supplier management, manufacturing, asset maintenance, material storage, transportation, and customer replenishment. The overarching goal, and the alignment principle unifying these activities, is to provide the highest customer service in the most efficient way possible. This idea is informally captured by the seven rights: getting the right product, to the right customer, at the right time, in the right condition, in the right quantity, at the right place, for the right cost.[19]

Let us take a closer look at a more formal and widely used way to think about supply chain processes as depicted in Figure 1.3. Initially, the process group contained the elements of "Plan," "Source," "Make," and "Deliver." These processes were later extended to contain "Design" at the start and "Return" at the end. Figure 1.3 also shows a simplified model of the supply chain entities and the critical supply chain flows. In general terms, products typically flow downstream from supplier to plant and then to customers, often through a network of intermediaries and distribution centers. The product return or recycling flows in the opposite direction, upstream. Usually, money flows upstream, while information flows in both directions.

FIGURE 1.3   SCM Processes and Flows

Supply Chain Management (SCM) Process

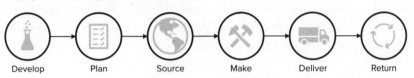

Develop   Plan   Source   Make   Deliver   Return

Supply Chain Management (SCM) Flow

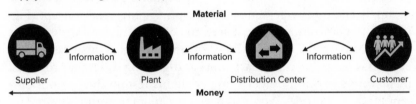

In general, sales or shipment history is used to statistically generate an initial demand forecast, subsequently finalized through a consensus process during sales and operations planning (S&OP) with collaboration from sales, marketing, supply chain, and finance teams. This process has proved quite useful in coping with uncertainty and reducing inventory levels and costs. The overall procedure follows various sequential steps and can be quite long and involved. The consensual forecast then trickles down to increasingly higher levels of detail, triggering a series of more specific planning activities and their execution, including the purchase of supplies, transportation, storage, movement, processing, and subsequently fulfillment. Each of these actions activates different entities across the supply chain, as information flows from node to node, often in stages, activating new decisions and actions. Customer involvement in product design is typically limited to market research based on sampling to understand requirements and trends. Communication with the customer until now has usually been aimed at influencing demand and, for the most part, involved a great deal of latency. The ultimate goal has been primarily to ascertain product availability when the customer places an order or walks into a store.

Every supply chain node has to deal with its uncertainties, hence requiring them to engage in a sequence of planning and execution.

Inventory is typically used to buffer uncertainty and prevent disruptions, stockouts, and lost sales. For a typical global organization, the customers can be in the thousands, suppliers in hundreds, and DCs and plants in dozens. Add to this the management of thousands of raw materials, semi-finished and finished goods, and other tens of thousands of maintenance products. Besides this, delays and amplification, added to the length of modern supply chains, compound the complexity and level of unpredictability and risks facing organizations and executives in managing the chain of supplies.

TYPICAL CHALLENGES OF SCM

Since the end of the automation wave (Figure 1.1), and with the rise of supply chain management as an accepted managerial concept (Figure 1.2), organizations have strived to connect the various processes associated with the physical flow within and across businesses. This effort has led to successful attempts at digitizing different processes, increasingly making modern supply chains responsible for our current modern lifestyles. For instance, one can go to a grocery store in, say, Morgantown, West Virginia, early on any given day and purchase a fresh mini pineapple produced thousands of miles away in South Africa, or grab an Australian ginger beer bottled in the United Kingdom, at an affordable price. However, despite the tremendous and successful strides in integration and earlier digitalization, traditional supply chain management is guided by a prevailing sequential and linear logic with many activities and planning occurring in stages, which challenges executives in many ways and limits the SCM potential.

In traditional supply chain management, planning is typically based on historical data and the assumption that the past is somewhat a suitable means to predict the future. Planning is performed ahead of time, and teams scramble when disruptions or unforeseen events take place. Collaboration takes place on a predefined basis that is somewhat challenging to change, and shifts in the marketplace require long and sometimes painful adaptations. Execution is mostly based on pre-optimization and scenario-based information. If unforeseen changes or opportunities occur, financial resources and time are required to modify the course. Even the more responsive supply chains are mostly reactive to shifts in demand. While it is universally accepted that speed is one of the most critical factors of a successful supply chain, the sequential nature of the activities and the quantity of somewhat weakly connected partners limit the potential for agility. Customers are mostly disconnected and have minimal involvement in the creation and delivery of the services or products.

While great strides have been made, many supply chain activities are still manually intensive and take place linearly and in somewhat siloed stages, from manually cleaning and adjusting data to lengthy and sequential actions and interactions throughout the planning and execution processes. Irrespective of the industry sector, the design of delivery processes is still protracted and surrounded by inefficiencies. While supplier involvement has become a critical staple in the innovation efforts of the modern organization,[20] the potential is still limited and affected by the sequential nature of activities. And even though integration efforts have progressed substantially since the inception of SCM as a systems framework, transparency is still siloed throughout the network, challenging and limiting organizations.

DSN—THE SMARTIFICATION OF TRADITIONAL SUPPLY CHAIN MANAGEMENT

Convergence of technologies, new technological developments, large amounts of data, and the widespread use of increasingly smaller, cheaper, and mobile devices in personal and organizational contexts all provide momentum for disruption and the potential for tremendous opportunities for organizing and managing supply chains. The emerging innovations can be used to create an overarching digital fabric across the end-to-end networks providing real-time visibility, automation, and control.

Since the end of the automation wave (Figure 1.1), and particularly during the recognition of the supply chain management concept in managerial thought (Figure 1.2), organizations and leaders have attempted to increasingly integrate the flow of materials. Enabled by modern information and communication technologies, these efforts have led to the initial digitization and automation of processes within and across corporate boundaries. Managerial decisions that could only be made over a few weeks in the past have become feasible within a few hours. Yet, while propelling the field forward and producing successful outcomes, this initial approach mostly leveraged the existing technology to automate and produce competitive advantage within the prevailing staged, siloed, and linear managerial view of the chain of supplies. Undoubtedly, the successful adoption and deployment of enabling digital technologies can produce benefits and value added. However, the real benefits and full potential will accrue to those organizations that leverage the ongoing technological developments to reimagine business models, products and services, and end-to-end value chains to generate maximum value for the customers, organizations, employees, partners, and societies.

Accordingly, DSN is the embodiment of a managerial thought focused on reimagining the organization and management of the flow of supplies, achieving an always-on, always-connected, real-time, adaptable, and smart digital network. The term "DSN" was initially coined by Deloitte and has gained currency in the managerial lexicon of the most innovative organizations. Figure 1.4 shows a simplified version of a DSN model; all parties belong to the same connected network. Product, money, and information flow seamlessly and in real time throughout the network. Customers are deeply connected and integrated within the network. Suppliers are also always connected and exchange information in real time. Network design is adaptive. The whole system functions as one entity to serve the customer, while maximizing the value for the entire network.

FIGURE 1.4   Representation of a Digital Supply Network

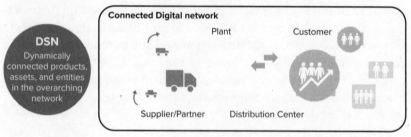

Advanced technologies like sensors and IoT (Internet of Things) provide sense-and-respond capabilities, and technologies such as blockchain provide trust, end-to-end visibility, safety, and control. But how does the traditional supply chain management approach differ from the emerging DSN? Let us brush some very broad comparative strokes here. We will delve into them in more depth throughout the book.

We can think of the DSN as the realm of the possible and of the reinvented. The inspirational but elusive Toyota Production System one-piece flow and zero inventory become not only feasible but possibly even outdated in some applications, with the possibility of replacing physical inventory with digital inventory. B2B and B2C customer service achieves unprecedented heights with the possibility of the customer placing orders on the go for consumption within hours and innovative on-demand business models with high levels of involvement. Organizations get to know customers in ways not previously possible. All enabled by truly dynamic and real-time collaboration between globally dispersed organizations. Transparency achieves its full potential, enabling more efficient processes and creating new customer value. The content of jobs becomes more fulfilling as technologies nearly eliminate the repetitive aspects of work. Planning shifts from a historical basis to a real-time adjustment, and execution shifts from a window-freezing approach toward a dynamic and adaptive affair. Besides, some managerial decisions can be made within seconds or autonomously. Not only can the network react faster to real-time events, but it can leverage data and analytics to operate under an anticipatory logic.

Figure 1.5 represents the DSN model, where all the processes are connected to each other in real time and information is always available and transparent across the network. We will expand the discussion of the transition from the prevailing supply chain management model toward the DSN, along with the characteristics, benefits, and structure of a DSN, in the next chapter.

FIGURE 1.5   DSN (Digital Supply Network) Capabilities

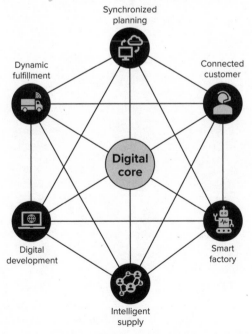

Synchronized planning

Dynamic fulfillment

Connected customer

Digital core

Digital development

Smart factory

Intelligent supply

SUMMARY

Digital transformation is impacting every aspect of our lives and has
been touted as the most critical strategic topic for organizations across
the globe. Digitization has the potential to create much more connected,
efficient, and transparent organizations and society. The supply chain
capabilities built by leveraging information and communication technologies, at the end of the previous innovation wave's progress, have
contributed notably to competitiveness and to raise our modern lifestyles.
However, the current wave of innovation is merging technologies that provide the opportunity to rethink and transform the flow of supplies in ways
not previously possible. DSN emerges within this context and is based on
an always-on, always-connected managerial mindset. The transformation journey is perilous and full of uncertainty, but the rewards are not only
worth the effort but will be required for survival.

DIGITAL SUPPLY NETWORK

In today's world, traditional supply chains are adapting to become increasingly flexible as technology drives the ability to make fact-based decisions, helping companies to stay abreast with the pulse of the changing business landscape. We stand on the cusp of a new interconnected supply chain model known as digital supply network (DSN). This DSN model empowers improved connectivity, greater visibility, resource optimization, and faster response time and assists companies in holistic decision making. As traditional linear supply chains collapse to form interconnected digital networks, companies are looking to leverage DSNs as a strategic advantage over their competitors. This chapter will help the reader understand the drivers behind the shift from linear supply chains toward the DSN of the future. Readers will also learn about the critical characteristics and components of DSN, the digital disrupters accelerating the transition to DSN, and the benefits of transforming to DSN.

COLLAPSE OF THE LINEAR SUPPLY CHAIN

Supply chain management (SCM) is an integral part of any business as it manages the flow of products or services meant to satisfy an end customer's needs. SCM does this by managing a five-step process of (1) obtaining raw materials, (2) manufacturing goods, (3) moving products closer to customers, (4) delivering the final product to the customer, and (5) servicing the product.[1] With the technologically advanced expectations of the modern-day consumer, the traditional supply chain approach of develop, plan, source, make, deliver, and support must transform to one of interconnected information flows and advanced capabilities (Figure 2.1). This interconnected model is enabled by new technology advancements and can act as a one-stop solution to serve today's dynamic business environment.

FIGURE 2.1   The Linear Supply Chain Model Evolving to a Digital Supply Network, DSN

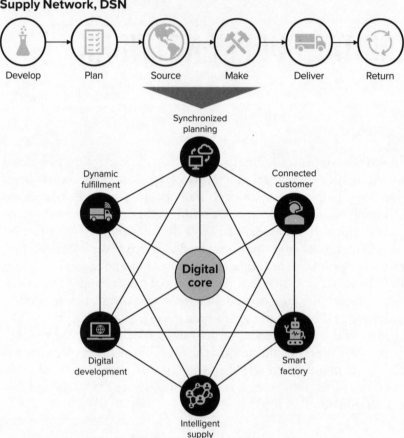

Figure 2.1 illustrates how each step within the traditional supply chain becomes an increasingly connected node within the DSN. The entire supply chain model then transforms into a more dynamic, integrated supply network. Ultimately, the DSN digital core uses input from its multiple nodes to self-strengthen, thereby accelerating production, distribution, and delivery to customers by providing real-time information to make informed decisions, anticipate risks, and provide better end-to-end visibility.

THE DSN MODEL

A digital supply network (DSN) can be broadly defined as an integrated set of digitally enabled supply chain capabilities powered by an interconnected flow of information, as displayed in Figure 2.2. At the center of a DSN is a digital core that simultaneously orchestrates six different supply chain capabilities.

FIGURE 2.2   The DSN Model

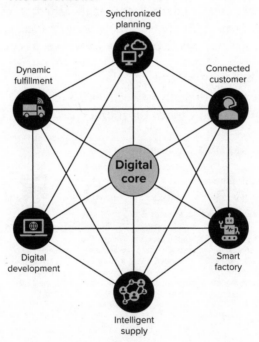

The data and information from all six supply network capabilities converge into the digital core to be stored, distributed, and analyzed. The DSN model, enabled by new and disruptive technologies, creates the following outcomes that differentiate DSN from the traditional linear supply chain:

1. **END-TO-END TRANSPARENCY** enabling visibility across the entire supply network

2. **HIGH LEVELS OF AGILITY** driving flexible and proactive response of supply network levers

3. **CONNECTED ENVIRONMENT** enhancing cross-functional collaboration across all partners and functions

4. **RESOURCE OPTIMIZATION** promoting a cohesive environment for humans and machines

5. **HOLISTIC DECISION MAKING** promoting optimal network efficiency, reduced cost, and increased revenue

These characteristics empower companies to fully leverage their supply networks and shrink the traditional barriers of resources, time, and space. This can lead to new levels of performance, improved operational efficiency and effectiveness, and new revenue opportunities.[2]

DSN Capabilities in an Enterprise

An enterprise that is digitally enabled with a mature DSN must have the six fundamental integrated capabilities presented in Figure 2.3.

FIGURE 2.3   Key DSN Capabilities

Digital Development	Synchronized Planning	Intelligent Supply	Smart Factory	Dynamic Fulfillment	Connected Customer
Optimize product lifecycle management with advanced digital tactics	Provide significant efficiencies through synchronization	Reduce costs through new advanced technologies, models, and capabilities	Unlock new efficiencies by a more connected, agile, and proactive factory	Boost customer service through new levels of speed and agility	Create seamless customer engagement from inspiration to service

Source: Deloitte Press, *DSN*

DIGITAL DEVELOPMENT. This capability leverages technology to conceptualize, design, and launch products into production, ensuring cross-functional collaboration through the product lifecycle and improving design efficiency to develop high-quality products. It reduces R&D expenses and product maintenance costs and increases manufacturing flexibility. Reduction in manual intervention results in fewer errors, delays, and inefficiencies, which helps the company respond quickly to changing customer requirements. Automation also promotes faster product launches while minimizing the environmental impact during development through process efficiency and digital technology.

SYNCHRONIZED PLANNING. This capability aligns strategic business objectives with financial goals and operational plans across various functions within the business. This helps to effectively anticipate customer demand and optimize inventory in the overall network. It utilizes cross-enterprise and big-data and customer perceptions to anticipate baseline customer demand. It helps in optimizing portfolios with product, service, and packaging road maps and in designing optimal supply networks, balancing the desired responsiveness levels with the lowest transportation, warehousing, and manufacturing costs. This capability allows companies to sense exceptions across the supply network to enable on-time demand fulfillment.

INTELLIGENT SUPPLY. This capability helps companies more effectively collaborate with strategic partners and improve the customer and supplier experiences by adopting advanced electronic platforms for requisitions and invoices. It also helps anticipate supply risks to proactively optimize end-to-end operations. Technologies such as machine learning and artificial intelligence (AI) can be used to predict cost fluctuations and select sourcing strategies to optimize costs.

SMART FACTORY. This capability uses a calculated balance of human intelligence and machine intelligence to drive improvements in business performance and worker safety based on production and demand data. Sensor data, image recognition, and collaborative robots can optimize overall production efficiency and provide safe and ergonomic work environments for employees. Smart factories also take a proactive approach to maintenance to optimize planned downtime and predict potential outages. It helps in making informed trade-off decisions to identify opportunities to improve performance standards and ensure compliance in real time, improving product quality.

DYNAMIC FULFILLMENT. This is an interconnected and cross-enterprise capability that enables companies to deliver the right product to the right customer at the right time, enhancing customer experience. It utilizes technologies such as IoT and robotics to provide visibility and flexibility across the supply chain, promoting cross-functional collaboration. It leverages cloud platforms to provide real-time visibility and improve responsiveness. Risk of product recalls due to counterfeit products is reduced as well, protecting brand reputation. It also helps enable intelligent customer order management, improving customer experience and reducing obsolescence costs. It can reduce start-up costs and increase risk resilience as well.

CONNECTED CUSTOMER. This capability allows companies to move from traditional transaction-based relationships to seamless customer engagement throughout the entire customer lifecycle. This results in better anticipation of customer needs, enriching the customer experience. It also enables faster resolution of issues and identification of customer consumption patterns. Capabilities like advanced analytics, machine learning, and artificial intelligence aid in effectively segmenting customers to provide relevant promotions. Utilizing dynamic fulfillment capabilities, companies can track and monitor physical products and ensure timely delivery of high-quality products to customers.[3]

Inside the Digital Core

The digital core that resides at the center of DSN integrates all the fundamental capabilities and ultimately drives the DSN. We will now learn about the key digital disciplines required for successful DSN and then focus on how the inside of a digital core looks and ways to enable the digital core.

Digital Disciplines

There are four key disciplines (Figure 2.4) that are indicative for successful DSNs. These disciplines are only achieved when all six DSN capabilities are interconnected and operate collectively as a network, orchestrated through a digital core.

SENSE. Instead of approaching the supply chain from a linear point of view, DSNs read the pulse of the network to identify and analyze linkages among all nodes. Historically, the main sensing activity in supply chain was demand. Today, sensing is a much broader discipline, covering critical aspects like supplier performance, customer sentiment, factory performance, and employee satisfaction.

COLLABORATE. Supply chains exist to facilitate trusted transactions between trading partners. While customers and suppliers have always collaborated, DSNs provide concurrent and transparent engagement across multiple nodes in the network. Emerging supply chain control tower technologies that use powerful chat-based problem-solving

FIGURE 2.4 **Digital Disciplines**

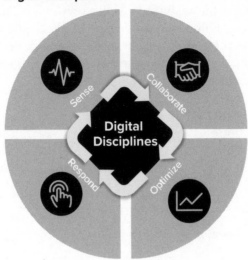

technologies to integrate multiple people, data forms, and communication methods provide one example of new collaboration capabilities.

OPTIMIZE. The purpose of collecting and analyzing the data provided by the DSN nodes is ultimately to optimize the supply network in both the short term and the long term. Previously, operations research departments were one step removed from operations, but now advanced optimization capabilities are embedded in the systems used daily by supply chain professionals as they perform day-to-day responsibilities.

RESPOND. After sensing a situation, collaborating with stakeholders, and deciding on the optimal solution, the enterprise must execute the plan. This means connecting the digital to the physical world. With the click of a button, supply network professionals can turn a plan into a series of orders, work instructions, or other actions that trigger operations on the physical product, software, or service.[4]

Enabling the Core Through the Digital Stack

To achieve the promise of DSN, a powerful suite of technologies must be implemented to enable new digital capabilities that address supply chain challenges. When charting the digital transformation path, leaders must maintain a clear understanding of the necessary core business capabilities and competencies and invest in the technical infrastructure that produces the analytical and decision-support mechanisms to support these capabilities and competencies. The digital stack provides a framework at the core to enable analytics-driven decision making that defines the digital era of supply networks. This stack is broken down into six capability layers (Figure 2.5).

FIGURE 2.5   Digital Stack

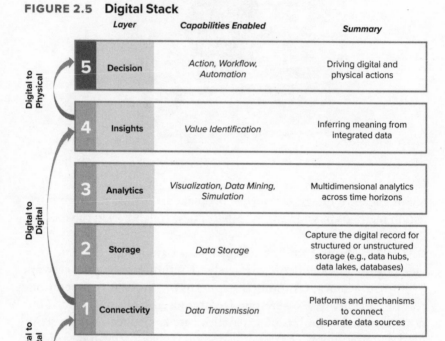

Source: Deloitte Press, *DSN*

At their core, all DSNs comprise these fundamental capability layers to lead the supply network from "device to decision." Figure 2.6 shows an example of a digital stack in action. At the base of this framework is data creation, which generates digital records of events in the supply chain with the help of physical devices (e.g., IoT sensors). Layer 1, Connectivity, is the technology that enables generated data from all nodes of the network to flow to a central repository (Layer 2, Storage). The data collected needs to be stored efficiently and securely and requires a single point of access for it to be effectively accessed and utilized (e.g., cloud). The technologies in these three layers are primarily responsible for generating, storing, and accessing data in a secure and efficient way. Security here is paramount. The 2020 COVID-19 pandemic highlighted the fragility of global chains. The next black swan event might be a cyber one.

FIGURE 2.6   Digital Stack in Action

Using this single point of connectivity provided by Layer 2, the data then moves into Layer 3, Analytics. This layer provides visualizations, advanced modeling, and real-time scenario simulations, arming supply network teams to make highly informed assessments and business decisions on a day-to-day basis. Additionally, the full network visibility enables proactive event management, predictive insights, and cross-functional collaboration, ultimately enabling asset efficiencies (labor scheduling, inventory diagnostics, plant utilization, equipment efficiency, etc.). Layer 4 moves into Insights, which takes the enterprise data one step further, to identify value for the business across the supply chain. This goes beyond day-to-day operations and reaches into insight generation, proactive sensing, predictive modeling, and artificial intelligence for a true pulse of the network. Finally, Layer 5 is the Decision, executing the transactions that bring the analysis from the digital world back to the physical. The actions in the Decision layer enable management support in a way that minimizes margin for error and increases overall efficiency of resources using advanced process management platforms such as robotic process automation.

The DSN digital stack gathers data from multiple systems, sources, and locations. Detailed examples of technology in each layer will be provided in the section "Technologies Enabling the Acceleration to DSN" later in this chapter. The DSN digital stack results in the ability to provide greater visibility and to surface actionable insights and drive value. The digital core then becomes a holistic integration point between all of the digital supply chain capabilities and provides a new way to orchestrate supply operations from the center of the network.

A Control Tower—Example of a Digital Core

A Control Tower, or command center, is an example of a digital core tool that allows executives to proactively manage their end-to-end supply networks in real time and achieve new efficiencies through connected visibility, proactive exception management, and predictive insights, using data collected by the digital core. This targeted approach offers a way to identify the outliers and apply the right triage of solutions to drive the maximum value without a large-scale technology implementation.

A Control Tower also allows supply chain executives to narrow their scope and focus on the few areas that are causing the majority of the issues, while the rest of the supply chain can continue functioning, business as usual. A Control Tower collects and analyzes multiple sources of data and provides teams with visibility, root cause identification, predictions and alerts, response agility, and performance management,[5] thereby shifting focus from reactionary management of day-to-day execution to a responsive planning for future action.

The concept of a Control Tower is broad, therefore it is important to lay out exactly what a Control Tower is. Figure 2.7 provides more context on the salient features of Control Tower solutions.

FIGURE 2.7   Salient Features of a Control Tower

Essential Elements of a Control Tower

Serves as an End-to-End Solution
Delivers real-time alerts, offers strategic insights, and enhances performance management

Stands Up New Enterprise Capabilities
Results in a new, better way of working, and often requires new processes and organizational structures

Breaks Traditional Functional Silos
Integrates disparate data sources, processes, and partners to deliver real-time connectivity, enhanced visibility, and prescriptive insights

Uses Advanced Analytics
Improves on a continuous basis via cognitive feedback loops and science-driven algorithms

Control Towers Are NOT . . .

Physical Rooms with Lots of Screens
Frequently, the question is asked: "Can I come visit your Control Tower?" A Control Tower does not have to be a physical location

Transportation Management Systems (TMS)
Although TMS systems can form an important source of data, a Control Tower can perfectly function without a TMS in place

Good-Looking Tableau Dashboards
While dashboards (from Tableau and other tools) can form a substantial part of a Control Tower solution, just connecting dashboards alone does not define a Control Tower in the right capacity

A Control Tower is scalable and adaptable. It can be a totally digital solution accessed through the computer or mobile devices, or it can have a physical mix with a separate area in the office with multiple screens to show the information in real time with the sensor-actuator integration to influence the processes and workflows from the Control Tower. It can be used to address many issues within the supply chain to deliver tangible benefits: increased revenue, better margins, asset efficiency, enhanced risk mitigation, and increased responsiveness. Additionally, developing a Control Tower can offer many indirect benefits that help improve the efficacy of a supply chain organization—helping organizations understand their data sources and shining a light on potential process improvements. Instead of just talking about digitalization or embarking on large-scale transformation, organizations can take action today by developing a Control Tower as the digital core for their DSN, harnessing the power of data to gain clear visibility and, in the process, driving real business results.

The Digital Twin Creates a Physical-to-Digital-to-Physical Loop

DSN introduces the notion of a digital representation of the physical reality of a supply network, which is referred to as the digital twin. A digital twin can be defined, primarily, as a digital replica that mirrors the characteristics, attributes, and behavior of a physical object or process, ultimately allowing a business to simulate actions in a digital world without having to conduct or invest in a physical action.[6]

To transition an enterprise into the digital age, traditional supply chains need to create a physical-to-digital-to-physical loop (Figure 2.8). This loop starts with the data generated by the digital twin and manages its evolution from the physical to the digital world, followed by the action that drives back to the physical world. This loop is broken down into three critical elements, which, when unified, are a source of continuous value creation in a digital enterprise.

FIGURE 2.8   The Physical-to-Digital-to-Physical Loop

1. Physical to Digital
Capture signals and data from the physical world to create a digital record

Physical   **Digital**

3. Digital to Physical
Deliver information in automated and more effective ways to generate actions and changes in the physical world

2. Digital to Digital
Exchange and enrich information using advanced analytics, artificial intelligence, and machine learning to drive meaningful insights

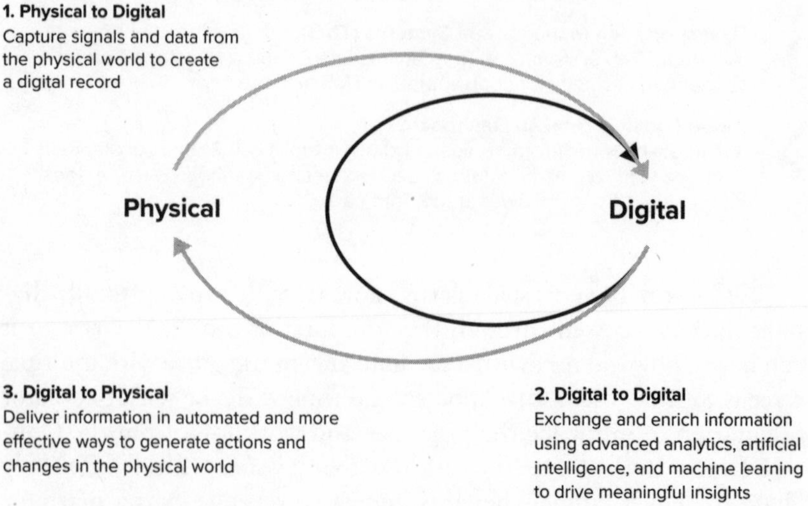

Source: Deloitte Press, *DSN*

PHYSICAL TO DIGITAL. At its core, this stage of the loop creates a digital record of the day-to-day supply chain operations. It digitally captures the basic transactions that occur at any enterprise: product development, sales, delivery, and any other function involved in the end-to-end supply chain process. Sensors, for example, measure critical inputs from the physical processes. They can monitor and collect data from various assets throughout the supply chain, products, and even the environmental or external conditions affecting operations. This data is then collected and aggregated into a data repository, processed to essentially create a "digital" fingerprint of the physical environment, and prepared for analytics.[7]

DIGITAL TO DIGITAL. The inner loop, digital to digital, is a rapidly changing space, disrupted in recent years by new, innovative software solutions that are now more accessible to companies than ever before. In this element, digital information records are enriched by new technology-enabled capabilities such as artificial intelligence, natural language processing, machine learning, and spatial analytics, resulting in improved information accessibility and meaningful insight.

DIGITAL TO PHYSICAL. The insights captured in the previous digital-to-digital loop inform opportunities for guided action in the physical world. With the power of automation technologies such as robotics, intelligent workflow automation, and machine control, physical actions can be triggered by digital directions to reach a desired outcome. As a result, teams can evolve away from passive dashboards and visualizations to active actions guided by business decisions. Going back to our manufacturing example, insights from the data analysis can pass through decoders and into the actuators on the asset, which are responsible for movement or for operating control mechanisms. This interaction completes the closed-loop connection between the physical world and the digital twin.[8]

Enabling the physical-digital-physical loop provides an enterprise with real-time access to data and intelligence. This shift fundamentally transforms the way business operates, creating new revenue streams, increasing agility, and developing digital capabilities.

TECHNOLOGIES ENABLING THE ACCELERATION TO DSN

There are seven primary enabling technologies that support the shift toward digital supply networks. They are illustrated in Figure 2.9.

FIGURE 2.9   Enabling Technologies

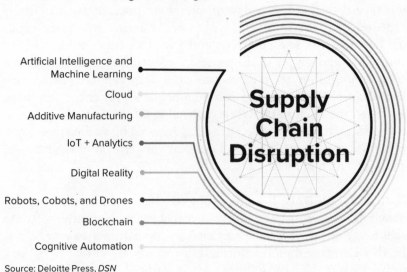

Artificial Intelligence and
Machine Learning

Cloud

Additive Manufacturing

IoT + Analytics

Digital Reality

Robots, Cobots, and Drones

Blockchain

Cognitive Automation

Supply Chain Disruption

Source: Deloitte Press, *DSN*

By leveraging the unique strengths and capabilities of each technology, the DSN can adapt faster to the dynamic infrastructure surrounding the digital core. The following sections explore each of these enabling technologies.

Artificial Intelligence

Artificial intelligence is about providing cognitive intelligence to the process and machines. This can use machine learning algorithms, which use pattern recognition algorithms to interpret data and translate it into real-time insights, thereby simplifying tactical planning and automating the decision-making process. For instance, machine learning can be adopted to improve sourcing insights and procure-to-pay process efficiency by studying historical and real-time data. This can be used to drive resource efficiencies through automation and improve process effectiveness. An AI system (Figure 2.10) combines and utilizes machine learning and other types of data analytics methods to achieve data intelligence capabilities.

Incremental steps toward AI and machine learning can be achieved by deploying robotic process automation (RPA) capabilities. Besides, by scaling RPA capabilities, there exists a potential to improve processes through machine learning for upstream and downstream enhancements impacted by bots, thus laying the foundation for a fully intelligent DSN.

FIGURE 2.10 Artificial Intelligence System

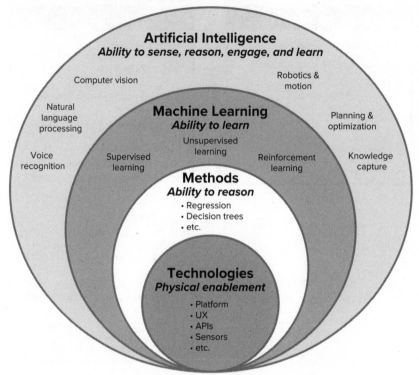

Cloud Computing Technology

Cloud computing technology is a network-based technology that allows access to a shared pool of configurable system resources and services that can be quickly provisioned with minimal effort.[9] In other words, cloud technologies use digital infrastructure to provide flexibility and increased speed in accessing online data.[10] The sheer volume of databases integrated throughout a DSN require an efficient means to aggregate and analyze information.

Figure 2.11 highlights key capabilities and benefits that cloud computing technology offers for a digital supply network to function most efficiently. With increasing complexity, it is necessary to have systems that can gather data from multiple nodes in real time and store it centrally. As planning becomes more dynamic, cloud technology enables quick and accurate decision making by providing real-time visibility into performance. It also offers a platform for ERP systems that enable seamless integration of the DSN.

FIGURE 2.11 **Capability and Potential Benefits of Cloud Technology**

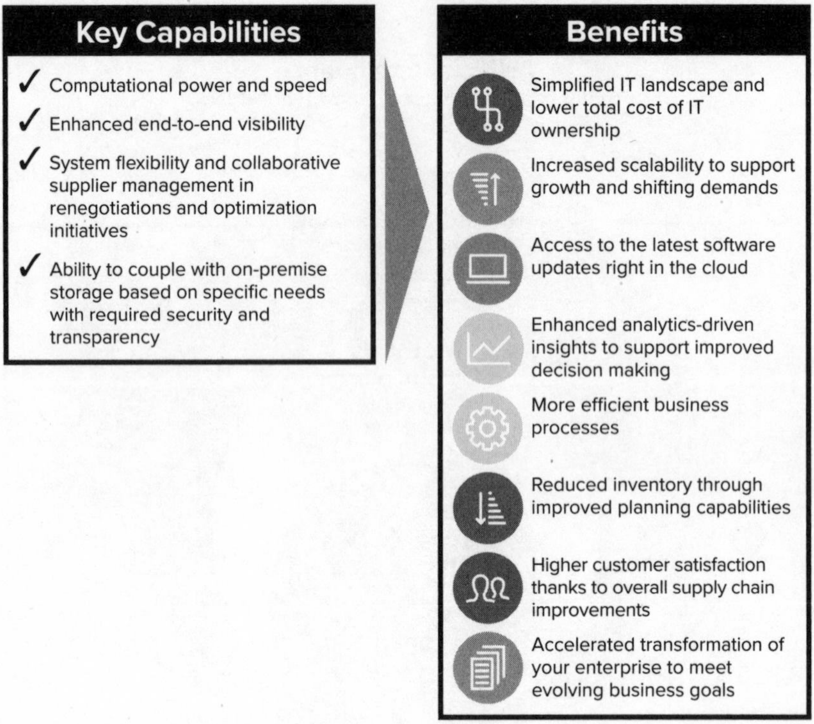

Key Capabilities	Benefits
✓ Computational power and speed	Simplified IT landscape and lower total cost of IT ownership
✓ Enhanced end-to-end visibility	Increased scalability to support growth and shifting demands
✓ System flexibility and collaborative supplier management in renegotiations and optimization initiatives	Access to the latest software updates right in the cloud
✓ Ability to couple with on-premise storage based on specific needs with required security and transparency	Enhanced analytics-driven insights to support improved decision making
	More efficient business processes
	Reduced inventory through improved planning capabilities
	Higher customer satisfaction thanks to overall supply chain improvements
	Accelerated transformation of your enterprise to meet evolving business goals

Additive Manufacturing (3D Printing)

Additive manufacturing, more commonly known as 3D printing, can physically replicate 3D objects originally created by computer designs.[11] This technology leverages digitization to unlock new sources of value in design, manufacturing, and supply chains. This model-based design greatly enhances manufacturing possibilities as digital threads of information can be shared with collaborators instantly and regardless of location. Furthermore, additive manufacturing boosts the first-time yield quality through virtual testing of designs prior to actual prototyping, reducing overall cost and increasing likelihood of prototype success.[12] By leveraging additive manufacturing techniques, companies can eliminate a rigid and inflexible manufacturing environment in their supply chains. Figure 2.12 further illustrates the impact of additive manufacturing on products and supply chains.

FIGURE 2.12   Impact of Additive Manufacturing

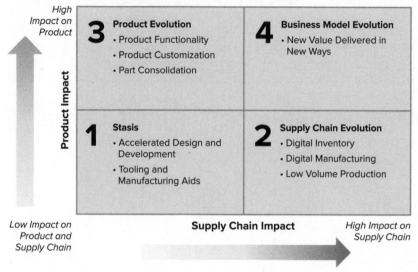

Impact on Products and Supply Chains

IoT and Analytics

IoT (Internet of Things) is a world of intelligent, connected devices that generate data that can be used by manufacturers and retailers to generate unique insights and transform their businesses.

As illustrated in Figure 2.13 (see next page), an end-to-end IoT solution consists of three main components: sensors, a data platform, and an analytics tool. Sensors capture data flowing into the data platform for storage in real time. The analytics tool pulls data from the platform, analyzes it, and derives insights. These insights are then used to perform "informed" actions in the physical world. This is the digital-to-physical loop of IoT. A robust IoT platform can help create an "always-on" supply chain with a physical-digital-physical closed loop.

Augmented and Virtual Reality

Augmented and virtual reality as an enabling technology is an amalgamation of augmented reality (AR), virtual reality (VR), 360-degree videos, and immersive technologies (Figure 2.14, see next page).[13] It works as a data source (from sensors, cameras, etc.) and creates a virtual environment built around the incoming data. Users can then interact with the new reality using a combination of gestures, vocal

FIGURE 2.13   IoT Framework

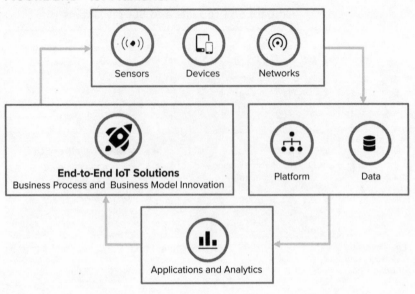

FIGURE 2.14   Digital Reality Types

Technology	Description
Augmented Reality	Overlays digitally created content into the user's real-world environment
Virtual Reality	Creates an entirely distinct environment that replaces the user's real-world environment
Mixed Reality	Blends digital content into the real world and creates an environment where both can coexist and react
360 Degrees	Provides a new perspective that allows the user to look in every direction
Immersive	Creates a multisensory digital experience and is delivered through any of these technologies

commands, and gazes at the digital experience.[14] While all these digital reality technologies play on the same theme, they each have distinct traits that make them unique to one another.

Robots, Cobots, and Drones

Figure 2.15 highlights the varied skills offered by robotic technology that can save companies substantial time and money. There are three

FIGURE 2.15   Skills and Benefits of Robots, Cobots, and Drones

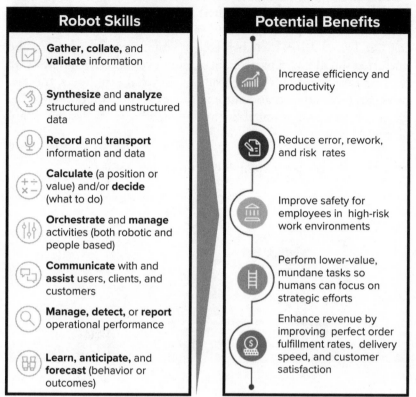

primary types of enabling robotic technology used in business today. The first, robots, are machines designed to perform a task, either autonomously or semi-autonomously[15] (e.g., the machines that seal bottles on an assembly line, also called "pick and place" robots). The second type are cobots. Cobots, or collaborative robots, physically interact with humans in a work environment.[16] For example, quality assurance machines that use advanced robotic technology in conjunction with human movement to quickly and efficiently go through quality inspection of parts on the assembly floor are cobots. Finally, the third type of robot, drones, are relatively new to the supply chain industry. Their concept has been made popular by the announcement of Amazon's Prime Air service. These unmanned aerial vehicles (UAVs) can operate under varying levels of autonomy.[17] The potential benefits of robotic technology are numerous as highlighted in Figure 2.15.

Blockchain

Blockchain is an open, distributed ledger that can record transactions between two parties efficiently and in a verifiable and permanent way (see Figure 2.16). It enables collaboration across competitive and untrusted supply chain participants to improve collective supply chain performance.[18] In fact, through smart blockchain contracts, transactions can be developed and automatically executed on decentralized systems creating an immutable, time-stamped, and everlasting means of record keeping.[19]

FIGURE 2.16   Blockchain-Enabled Connected Network

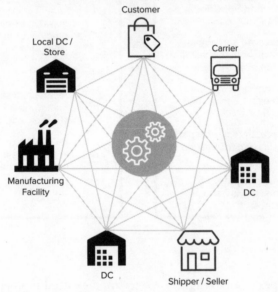

Blockchain will be the primary driver to convert a linear and siloed supply chain into an interconnected digital supply network. With the advent of sensors and IoT technologies, blockchain will act as a tissue that enables interconnections between various nodes of a supply network (Figure 2.17). Blockchain is primarily an asset-tracking mechanism, and since supply chains mainly focus on movement of goods, blockchain finds maximum use in asset management applications such as tracking, tracing, and discovery. This capability can be further utilized for broader applications involving real-time data visibility and data protection through secure sharing, helping organizations drive broader strategic goals by tying together various elements of supply chain, finance, human capital, and IT.

FIGURE 2.17   Blockchain as a Data Connecting Tissue

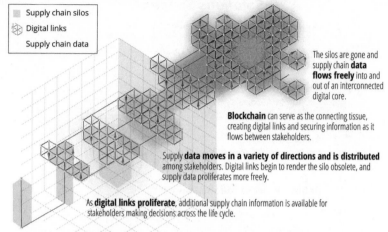

☐ Supply chain silos
⬡ Digital links
   Supply chain data

The silos are gone and supply chain **data flows freely** into and out of an interconnected digital core.

Blockchain can serve as the connecting tissue, creating digital links and securing information as it flows between stakeholders.

Supply **data moves in a variety of directions and is distributed** among stakeholders. Digital links begin to render the silo obsolete, and supply data proliferates more freely.

As **digital links proliferate**, additional supply chain information is available for stakeholders making decisions across the life cycle.

Supply chain data is **siloed**, and flows linearly from one silo to another.

Source: Deloitte analysis.

Cognitive Automation

Cognitive automation can be used to enable real-time data transfer from multiple sources to provide intelligent insights used to empower both people and machines. Simply defined, cognitive automation is based on bringing intelligence to information-intensive processes. It can deal with natural language, reasoning, and judgment to provide insights.[20] There is a spectrum of cognitive intelligence that spans from basic predictive intelligence, like the simple autofill, to stand-alone artificial intelligence. Figure 2.18 (see next page) breaks down this spectrum and provides details on the four main categories of cognitive automation: artificial intelligence, intelligent automation and analytics, autonomics, and robotic process automation.[21]

In summary, digital supply networks rely on the digital nodes of the system to create, contribute to, and strengthen the digital core of an organization. To reach peak DSN capabilities, data must seamlessly integrate a variety of networks (suppliers and distributors), stakeholders (sales and logistics), and formats (structured and unstructured) to produce actionable insights. Enabling technologies facilitate this exchange by establishing interconnected systems as opposed to singular applications or package technologies that remain siloed from each other. All of these technologies are covered in detail in dedicated chapters later in this book.

FIGURE 2.18 **Categories of Cognitive Automation**

Solutions Spectrum

Cognitive and Artificial Intelligence
• Decision making
• Interpretation of human language
• Dynamically self-adaptable

Intelligent Automation and Analytics
• Predictable quality
• Improved process control

Autonomics
• Improves nonroutine tasks that require true judgment calls
• Auto-adapts to new rules

Robotic Process Automation
• Used for rules-based, simple to complex processes
• Faster handling time
• Higher volumes
• Reduced errors and costs

BENEFITS AND CONSIDERATIONS OF DSN TRANSFORMATION

As the industry moves away from the traditional linear supply chain model, we see increased value and benefits from the DSN model. Several elemental advantages drive differentiated performance and value holistically across the organization.[22] The following section highlights some of the key advantages.

Benefits of DSN

Figure 2.19 highlights five key benefits of DSNs that allow improved decision making and knowledge exchange leading to differentiated value offerings and a strengthened competitive advantage.

1. **"ALWAYS-ON" AGILITY** represents the ability to flexibly respond, proactively operate, and exchange data in real time across the supply network.[23] Every node of the supply network is connected and relays information in real time. This is achieved, for example, by employing sensors or location-based services that continuously relay data, thereby eliminating any latency in the system. The "always-on" agility mindset is the realization of no more latency in responses even taking into account rapidly evolving network conditions.

FIGURE 2.19 Benefits of Digital Supply Networks (DSN)

"Always-On" Agility

Securely, DSNs pull together traditional data sets with new data sets that are, for example:

- Sensor-based
- Location-based
- "Right time" vs. "real time"

Outcome: Rapid, no-latency responses to changing network conditions and unforeseen situations

Connected Community

Real-time, seamless, multimodal communication and collaboration across the value network with:

- Suppliers
- Partners
- Customers

Outcome: Network-wide insights from centralized, standardized, synchronized data

Intelligent Optimization

A closed loop of learning is created by combining:

- Humans
- Machines
- Data-driven analytics
- Predictive insights
- Proactive action

Outcome: Optimized human-machine decision making for spot solutions

End-to-End Transparency

Use of sensors and location-based services provides:

- Material flow tracking
- Schedule synchronization
- Balance of supply and demand
- Financial benefits

Outcome: Improved visibility into critical aspects of the supply network

Holistic Decision Making

Based on contextually relevant information, functional silos are now transparent and deliver parallel visibility, such as:

- Performance optimization
- Financial objectives
- Trade-offs

Outcome: Better decision making for the network as a whole

2. **CONNECTED COMMUNITY** represents the ability to extend collaboration to suppliers and customers. This is the result of vast networks of suppliers, partners, customers, and others freely exchanging and sharing information directly, ultimately promoting "greater data synchronicity."[24] The vital value-add of this characteristic is the ability to utilize third-party data sets and integrate within the central system. Lastly, the connected community ability enhances cross-functional communication and collaboration among the various nodes that have traditionally operated in siloes.

3. **INTELLIGENT OPTIMIZATION** (also known as resource optimization) represents the ability to identify and utilize the right resource, human or machine, for optimal work. This ability promotes humans and machines to work together to deliver the desired outcome. Combined work effort of robotics and humans is the way the digital age is progressing as we push toward more efficient automated systems.

4. **END-TO-END TRANSPARENCY** represents the ability to gain complete visibility across the entire supply network. In order to stay ahead of the competition,[25] organizations need a basic understanding of critical system issues and to have the ability to identify the root cause(s) of those issues to offer insights and solutions. Organizations must then act quickly to control and contain the impact. Digital supply networks leverage sensors, new and existing data sets, and visualizations to track and create mapping structures for visibility into various supply network levers.

5. **HOLISTIC DECISION MAKING** represents the ability to continuously learn and make optimal network decisions. It involves having the transparency between functions for parallel visibility to drive better decision-making across the organization.[26] It is the combined effort needed to promote continuous learning and engage in strategic decision making. The ultimate benefit of DSN to drive value and increase performance cannot be accomplished without a high-level holistic approach to solving complex supply chain issues.

Considerations for Transforming to DSN

While much of the focus for DSN transformation is directed toward the advanced technologies and new capabilities that DSN enables, any such transformation will fail without encompassing how work changes through DSN. What does the DSN future of work look like? To answer this question, we will explore the impact DSNs have on talent, the organization, technology adoption, and the processes involved with this transformation. Figure 2.20 illustrates the stages in a path of evolution that an organization may follow as it incorporates smart technologies and categorizes the types of roles within the DSN.

FIGURE 2.20   Impact of DSN on Talent, Organization, and Technology

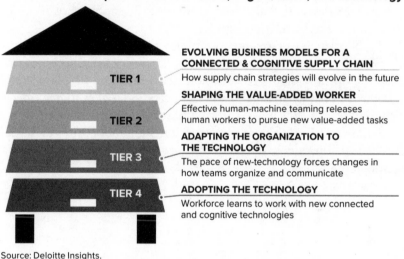

TIER 1

EVOLVING BUSINESS MODELS FOR A CONNECTED & COGNITIVE SUPPLY CHAIN
How supply chain strategies will evolve in the future

TIER 2

SHAPING THE VALUE-ADDED WORKER
Effective human-machine teaming releases human workers to pursue new value-added tasks

TIER 3

ADAPTING THE ORGANIZATION TO THE TECHNOLOGY
The pace of new-technology forces changes in how teams organize and communicate

TIER 4

ADOPTING THE TECHNOLOGY
Workforce learns to work with new connected and cognitive technologies

Source: Deloitte Insights.

Tier 4 involves the connectivity and the "always on" agile approach. This tier embraces new technologies and adapts to change. This requires flexibility and a behavioral shift to allow for technology integration into the current role requirements of skilled workers in their day-to-day roles.[27] For example, a mechanical maintenance employee must get used to using augmented reality to improve the maintenance process. A planner, on the other hand, must get used to incorporating AI to adopt better planning and forecasts.

With technology adoption underway, Tier 3 encompasses how an organization adapts to that technology. In many cases, roles may shift to a more holistic consideration of production processes, requiring workers to absorb how changes in one area, or node of the network, may impact performance in another.[28] For example, if a company plans on installing sensors on its physical inventory, then it must be ready to handle the huge collections of data, often stored in "data lakes," that will be created. These data lakes create new roles within the organization responsible for creating actionable insights from the data, roles such as data scientists, robot scientists, data engineers, and computing and analytical experts

In Tier 2, the future of work, we will likely see human and machine teams working alongside each other to accomplish a task that one cannot do alone without latency or limitations. For example, where a human may previously have had to handle certain process changes, a robot counterpart can fill in, enabling that human to execute other value-added activities to support the supply networks and sustain stakeholder relationships.[29]

DSNs can benefit any organization with a complex, difficult supply chain by converting it to a strategic, interconnected supply network enabling optimization, growth, increased value, and decreased risk. Ultimately, the way an organization operates and makes strategic decisions determines how it will thrive in the new digital landscape.

Chapter 13, "DSN Transformation Playbook," provides further details on talent, organization, process, technology, and data considerations.

SUMMARY

Today, we are at a pivotal point where traditional supply chains are transitioning to DSNs. This transition will help organizations unlock operational and financial efficiencies by leveraging the DSN's interconnected data flows and networks. Additionally, organizations have started using enabling technologies to optimize supply chain strategy and execution, expanding the realm of what is possible. DSNs have begun demonstrating and will continue to demonstrate more flexible and efficient operations, resulting in quicker decision making, greater cost savings, and increased revenue potential that tie with the organization's strategic business objectives.

BIG DATA AND DATA ANALYTICS

Data and data exchange are key factors of success for traditional supply chains. The more hierarchical structure of these traditional supply chains influences the way data is generated, exchanged, and analyzed, as well as the potential value-add of data for all stakeholders. In contrast, for digital supply networks (DSNs), stakeholders are working together at a more agile and collaborative level. This creates tremendous opportunities when it comes to capitalizing on the true value of data at the network level for all areas of business. However, the dynamics and complexity of such DSNs pose some distinct challenges when it comes to data, data exchange, and being able to derive insights from large amounts of shared data within the network.

In this chapter we discuss the importance of data as the lifeblood of digital transformation and DSNs. We highlight the impact of the increasing availability of large amounts of data (big data) on operations and business models, and we discuss the changing perception of the value of data in itself. We introduce the "five Vs" of big data and data management, highlighting specifically the impact of data quality and the data lifecycle. The increasing amount and associated value of data makes the topic of data security and authority important, especially in a DSN environment. We illustrate the key aspects of data security and authority before we touch upon selected technical developments, legislation, and infrastructure that enable this data revolution and provide us with unpreceded access to large quantities of data in a timely or even real-time manner. Interoperability, interfaces, and standards, as well as cloud platforms are some of the aspects we discuss in the last two sections of this chapter. These last sections serve as a transition to the next chapter, which will focus on machine learning, artificial intelligence (AI), and robotics applications that are the key to unlocking valuable insights for the organization or digital supply network.

IMPACT AND VALUE OF DATA

Data is currently at the peak of expectations in all areas of business. Today, we live in a time when data is available at unpreceded levels. At the same time, our ability to analyze these large amounts of data to derive insights is continuously maturing. However, data by itself is useless unless it can add value and make an impact for an organization or system. Table 3.1 illustrates selected DSN areas and tasks that directly or indirectly profit from the increasing amount of and access to data and the insights within it that can be unlocked through data analytics. While the table highlights key points, this is by no means comprehensive as new, innovative, and value-adding data-driven applications are emerging daily. Furthermore, these areas and tasks are collaborative efforts within DSN. Therefore, the impact of data increases significantly compared to using data only from individual organizations. Actually, in DSN many tasks cannot be successfully completed without access to and the ability to analyze relevant data.

Next, we explore how data is developing into a valuable resource in its own right and discuss the impact of data on an organization's or network's operations as well as the overall business model.

Data Accessibility and Acquisition

Digital supply networks are defined by their digital nature, connectivity, and the ability to electronically exchange and analyze data in real time. A key enabling factor of DSN is the ability to collect, process, communicate, and store data from a diverse set of sources. These data sources include but are not limited to information technology (IT) systems (e.g., ERP, CRM), sensors (e.g., temperature, GPS), operational technology (OT) systems (e.g., machine tools), publicly available data (e.g., social media, reviews), as well as financial (e.g., transaction data, stock market). These data sources can be located anywhere—within the organization, within the DSN, or externally, adding an extra layer of complexity to the system.

The type of data source is one key factor when it comes to accessibility. On the technical side, DSNs can be considered cyber-physical systems (CPS) or cyber-physical production systems (CPPS). In CPS,

TABLE 3.1   DSN areas and tasks with the highest impact and value of data (not comprehensive and in no specific order)

DSN areas with highest *impact* of data	DSN tasks with highest *value* of data
• Demand forecasting & procurement	• Operational efficiency (e.g., reduction of stockholding, reduced delivery times, digital kanban)
• Operations management	• Real-time demand prediction and forecasting based on large amounts of unstructured customer data (e.g., social media)
• Warehouse operations and logistics	• Lock-in of customers from the design to the end of life of a product by including them in the process digitally
• Transportation and route planning	• Automated adaptability of operations when faced with environmental disruptions
• Manufacturing and maintenance	• Prediction of bottlenecks in production and direct prescription of potential solutions
• Strategy and collaboration	• Develop and negotiate revenue and risk-sharing contracts/agreements within DSN
• Marketing, accounting, and other supporting functions	• Transparency and traceability of products, processes, and services

the physical world (machines, trucks, workers) and the virtual world (sensors, software, algorithms) are merging, creating a joint system. Sensors connect physical assets to the network, and through the Internet of Things (IoT) or the Industrial Internet of Things (IIoT), collect data and share that data via the Internet or cloud.

Another key factor is acquisition, and this involves a different layer of complexity. DSNs are collaborative networks, comprising various organizations and actors within the DSN that interact with various organizations and actors outside of the immediate DSN. While a DSN has an overall joint objective, the different actors within may have slightly different individual objectives that influence their ability and/or willingness to share data. Actors outside of the DSN are even more likely to have their own agendas and be rather restrictive in the sharing of data, especially as data is increasingly seen as a competitive asset. This can influence data accessibility as much as the technical infrastructure. In the following sections we dive deeper into the notion of the skyrocketing value of data, touch upon the nature of (big) data within DSN, and provide an overview of key policies and technical infrastructure components.

Data as a Valuable Resource in Its Own Right

Everybody agrees that (high-quality) data is a valuable resource for businesses, be it on the analyst, organization, or complex supply network level. However, today data is still predominantly connected to a certain business case, and its real or perceived value is tied to a distinct analytics goal, product, product family, or capital equipment, just to name a few. In the age of DSNs, we start to see the emergence of data being considered a valuable resource within its own right. While the value of data remains in the insights that can be derived from it, the direct relation to a certain clearly defined use case is not as obvious any longer.

Data itself, together with the ability to tap into the hidden truth within it (see Chapter 4, "Machine Learning, AI, and Robotics") enables disruptive innovation, including new business models or even entirely new industries. Data emerges as the lifeblood of industry disruption and provides organizations with the right strategy and abilities to develop a sustained competitive advantage.

Impact on Operations

Operations have always been driven by data. Logistics and supply chain management have been a fertile area for simulation, mathematical modeling, and operations research. It is broadly accepted that the better and more comprehensive the available data, the greater the potential for optimization. The technological advancements over the past decade provide unpreceded growth in the sheer amount, granularity, and timeliness of data relevant for operational efficiency optimization. Deeper integration of IT/OT systems, data exchange and flow, and data analytics allow DSN to be proactive instead of reactive, thus avoiding issues such as bullwhip effects or other coordination issues that are common problems within traditional supply chains. Overall, the impact of data on the operations of DSN cannot be overstated and is rather a necessity to manage the complexity and dynamics embodied within.

Impact on Business Models

In contrast to operations, which were always to some extent data-driven, data-driven business models are a newer development. One might argue that to successfully position an organization in the competitive marketplace requires an understanding of the market, and thus, the interpretation of some form of (market) data. This may be true. However, in this case when we talk about data-driven business models in a DSN context, our understanding of data-driven goes well beyond that traditional notion. In a DSN setting, the business model of each individual member organization as well as the DSN as a whole depends on data to begin with. Data sharing agreements are now commonplace within DSN, and data increasingly determines the share of revenue and risk for the different stakeholders. DSNs most likely have partners within the collaborative enterprise that focus on data analytics, and the results influence the activities and strategy of the DSN.

Generally, we see the emergence of new and innovative business models that are solely build on data. Nonownership business models such as pay-per-use or pay-per-outcome require a sophisticated technical infrastructure on one hand, but also an organizational setup with diverse stakeholders with different capabilities including designer, manufacturer, service providers, and operators to be successful. DSNs provide a possible vehicle to manage this complex collaborative setup. The benefits that emerge from such a data-driven business model are manifold, including lower overhead and operational cost, increasing customer loyalty and lock-in, improved product quality, continuous revenue, and detailed insights into real customer interaction with the product(s). Overall, the impact of data on future business models is tremendous and offers great rewards for DSNs that successfully innovate.

BIG DATA

In the previous section, we talked about data, its impact and value within DSNs. In this section, we examine what data looks like today and will look like in the future within emerging DSNs.

Five "Vs" of Big Data

Today, almost every organization is referring to its data management and analytics as "big data." However, the "big" in big data not only refers to "lots of data" but is defined by a number of dimensions that each present a distinct challenge for data management, infrastructure, and analytical tools and systems. The definition of big data has several variations. The most common and accepted one defines big data through the "five Vs" of volume, velocity, variety, veracity, and value (see Figure 3.1). Common variations of this popular definition include the three Vs, focusing on the three core dimensions (volume, velocity, and variety), and seven Vs, adding two additional dimensions (variability and visualization) (see Table 3.2).

FIGURE 3.1   Five Vs of Big Data: Volume, Velocity, Value, Veracity, and Variety

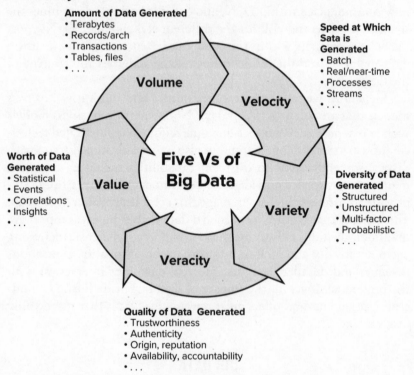

TABLE 3.2   Three Vs, five Vs, and seven Vs of big data

Three Vs	Five Vs	Seven Vs
• Volume	• Volume	• Volume
• Velocity	• Velocity	• Velocity
• Variety	• Variety	• Variety
	• Veracity	• Veracity
	• Value	• Value
		• Variability
		• Visualization

VOLUME. The dimension *volume* describes the sheer amount of data that is required to justify the term "big data." The volume that is associated with big data varies from industry to industry and use case to use case. Social media is often used as an extreme example of the large volume of data that is available for analytics. Hundreds of millions of messages, pictures, and videos are uploaded to social media sites daily and make up a massive amount of data that clearly meets the requirement of big data. In an industrial setting such as DSN, while the overall amount might be smaller, we experience an extreme growth rate when it comes to the amount of data with millions of connected devices within the IIoT continuously collecting data. Some processes create massive amounts of data within a single application. An example is laser welding, where the weld pool is controlled and optimized using high-resolution images, creating gigabytes of data for each part being manufactured.

VELOCITY. This dimension, on the other hand, refers to the speed at which new data is generated. Social media generates data at unbelievable speeds due to the large user base. Similarly, technological progress allows us to sample sensor data at much higher frequencies, and thus we are faced with new data coming in at extremely high rates. New communication protocols such as 5G and sensors reduce the latency further. Therefore both the growing number of data-producing sources and the speed at which each node is capable of producing new data contribute to the velocity of new data being generated.

VARIETY. The third core dimension of big data, *variety*, covers the diversity of kinds of data that make up big data. Image data, audio and video files, sensor data, standardized order data, location data, encrypted files, tweets, text files, and several more variations, including all thinkable combinations of these, pose a distinct challenge for data analytics and the processing of big data.

VERACITY. With the ever-increasing speed and volume of data being generated and the growing number of data-producing sources, the big data dimension *veracity* is emerging as a necessity. Veracity focuses on the quality of data and also the trustworthiness of the data source. In a big data environment, we cannot manually control all sources and certify the credibility of each node and data point. Increasingly, algorithms are tasked with plausibility checks and other advanced methods to ensure that the quality of the data fed into the analytical systems allows us to trust the insights derived from it. The old adage "garbage in, garbage out" stands true for big data analytics as well; however, managing the influx of data is presenting new challenges.

VALUE. This is a key dimension when it comes to big data and data analytics. Without providing value through decision support or otherwise useful and actionable insights from the data, the analytical effort and resources invested are hard to justify. In essence, "value" in this case refers to the ability to translate the wealth of big data into business. Value has to be understood broadly, as we only learn what constitutes good, data-driven business decisions within a DSN. New value propositions are emerging, and thus the value perspective of big DSN data is under constant development—and organizations and networks that are innovative and creative to turn big data insights into value will gain an edge in the competitive landscape.

Volume, velocity, variety, veracity, and value make up the five Vs of big data. Next we briefly introduce two additional Vs—which with the first five are sometimes referred to as the seven Vs—that are used in the big data context. In a DSN context, the two additional Vs, variability and visualization, are important aspects to consider when it comes to the data and data analytics strategy.

VARIABILITY. The dimension *variability* highlights a difficult problem for big data applications: the changing meaning and/or context of data over time. Variability is different from variety in that it does not refer to different variations of data, but rather data that changes in meaning over time. To make matters worse, this change of meaning and/or context is often not easy (or very hard) to predict. Variability presents a critical issue for data homogenization as well as for data analytics. Awareness about variability of data is crucial to manage the risk and trust put into the insights derived from big data analytics.

VISUALIZATION. This is the last key dimension of big data that we are going to discuss. It is grounded in the cognitive ability and individual preference of human stakeholders. Big data, as we learned, refers to large amounts of complex data that is, generally speaking, impossible for human minds to grasp without the assistance of advanced algorithms. However, to truly unlock value, the insights derived from the big data sets need to be communicated to human decision makers in a way that corresponds with their abilities, roles, and ideally preferences. For example, the machine operator will, in most cases, prefer a more detailed graphical representation of the results compared to the CEO's higher-level dashboard.

Structured and Unstructured Data

DSNs are natively located within a big data setting. Expanding on the core dimension of variety, it is important to better understand the differences of—and challenges presented by—structured, semi-structured, and unstructured data. Figure 3.2 provides a simplified visualization of the differences between structured, semi-structured, and unstructured data. The different shapes represent varying types of data (e.g., audio, picture, sensor readings). Table 3.3 (see next page) provides an overview of typical examples where the different types of data emerge within DSN operations.

While both structured and unstructured data can be generated by humans and automated systems alike, they present distinct differences with regard to searchability, required storage infrastructure, and ease of using data analytics and machine learning algorithms. Today, there are sophisticated and mature analytical tools available to discover insights from structured data, while the algorithms aimed at unstructured data are not as mature but rapidly developing. The latter present a huge opportunity as the value hidden in and expected from mining big data lakes made up of mostly unstructured data is tremendous. In a complex and dynamic system such as DSN, there is a large and growing portion of generated data that falls in the unstructured category. It is essential for all stakeholders to understand the implications of this in order to manage expectations and also develop innovative strategies to access the hidden insights within this often-untapped resource.

FIGURE 3.2 Schematic of Differences Between Structured, Semi-Structured, and Unstructured Data Sets

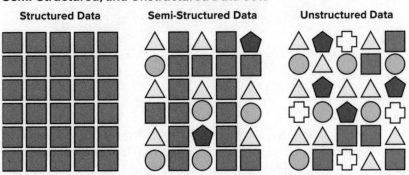

STRUCTURED DATA is typically stored in a relational database management system (RDBMS) that enables search queries using Structured Query Language (SQL). Structured data follows a predefined, often standardized data model that enables efficient search operations for both human operators and automated algorithms. In a DSN environment, several core data streams are considered structured data, such as demand forecasts, ERP transactions, and EDI invoices. Nevertheless, we increasingly have to deal with a more diverse set of data, and this change is expected to accelerate and continue.

SEMI-STRUCTURED DATA is a combination of structured data that does not follow standard data models associated with RDBMS or other standard schemas. However, it provides additional metadata in the form of semantic descriptors, tags, or keywords that enable search functionalities and other analytics.

UNSTRUCTURED DATA is essentially everything that does not fall under the umbrella of structured data described above. Unstructured data can typically not be stored in a classic RDBMS, but uses nonrelational databases such as "non SQL", sometimes called "not only SQL", (NoSQL). Unstructured data is not unstructured in the true meaning of the word as the data items do indeed have a certain (internal) structure. However, there is no common structure present that follows predefined and/or standardized data models or schemas.

TABLE 3.3 Examples of structured, semi-structured, and unstructured data

Structured data	Semi-structured data	Unstructured data
• ERP transactions*	• CRM data memos[+]	• Social media data[+]
• CRM transactions*	• Claims data*/[+]	• Image/video*[+]
• Phone numbers/logs*		• Audio[+]
• Zip codes*		• Emails/messages/
• Sales transactions*		tweets[+]
• EPCIS/RFID data*		• Satellite imagery*
		• Climate data*

* Typically machine generated
[+] Human generated

Whether a data set is considered structured, semi-structured, or unstructured has an impact on the perceived data quality; however, it does not necessarily impact the technical data quality. In the next section, we will explore what technical data quality means in a DSN context.

Data Quality

Data quality is a multidimensional concept that is defined relative to the stakeholder's analytical objectives. This goes hand in hand with technical requirements toward data quality put forth by data processing and analytics tools, applications, and services. Low data quality can result in major issues for organizations, ranging from operational to strategic errors. Once problems occur and can be traced back to data quality issues, it is often too late to address them effectively and efficiently. In order to avoid problems, data quality should be a continuous effort that starts as early as the design of the collection or acquisition, communication and storage, and data management processes, system, and infrastructure, as well as the data analytics tools and objectives.

As mentioned, data quality is a multidimensional concept that comprises technical as well as organization or contextual issues. Technical data quality issues include errors, missing values, corrupted files, completeness, and timeliness just to name a few. Conversely, organizational data quality issues include interpretability, representation, annotation, and relevance among several others.

Data Lifecycle

When it comes to data, the conversation is almost always driven by the question of how to access and collect more data to sharpen the analytics and derive more accurate predictions. The associated cost of this data is often neglected. This cost needs to be justified by the value the data actually provides. Today, many organizations and DSNs struggle with the question of when data can be deleted. With storage costs dropping in price, the solution many refer to is "don't delete any, we might need it in the future." This provides a short-term release from the pressure to find a better answer to this difficult question, but it is not a solution for the problem. Storing data that exceeds its useful life is expensive not only in the form of storage cost but also in potentially preventing efficient and effective data analytics. While the former is of course a nuisance and should be prevented, the latter is the truly costly issue that stems from avoiding addressing the question.

Unfortunately, there is no easy guideline on how to answer such a problem. Each case, organization, and DSN is different and so is the lifecycle of data. There is no one-size-fits-all solution to when data can be deleted (e.g., after two years, four months, seven days, and three hours). In the worst case, each data item has an individual expiration date that needs to be determined. Many companies move toward not deleting data completely but rather reducing the granularity of the data stored. As an example, after an individually determined time frame t_1, an organization transforms data with a hypothetical resolution of 50 data points per millisecond in an aggregated data set with a resolution of 6 data points per second. At a later point t_2, they aggregate further to one data point per hour, and so forth. This compromise enables the company to still retain and document its data picture, while reducing its hosting costs and processing efforts. Despite these intermediate solutions, the overall problem of when to safely delete data in a DSN is yet to be solved.

CYBERSECURITY, DATA GOVERNANCE, AND DATA AUTHORITY

Cybersecurity is crucial for every connected enterprise within DSN. In a nutshell, it encompasses all processes and practices that aim at preventing malicious attacks on computers, databases, servers, networks, and any other connected system or data source. With the rapid rise of IIoT and the associated growth of network-connected devices and systems, cybersecurity has risen to one of the top concerns of decision makers in DSN.

From a business perspective, aside from intentionally malicious attacks, questions regarding data ownership, governance, and authority need to be addressed within a DSN to function. Adding complexity, DSNs are often multinational constructs and therefore have to adhere to varying laws, policies, practices, and mindsets when it comes to data privacy and cybersecurity.

Ownership

In a DSN, each node of the network generates data—whether related to manufacturing, logistics, or accounting processes—and also consumes data for analysis, planning, or coordination. As we established previously, data is considered a competitive advantage, and the question of data ownership is not trivial in a DSN. Individual member organizations are often hesitant to share detailed data with others, at times for a good reason. Therefore, it is crucial for the success of the DSN as a whole to address this issue from the start and develop a transparent data ownership and sharing agreement among the members. New, innovative approaches associate a value (in dollars or a virtual data currency) to data that is shared to ensure accountability and reward for organizations willing to share data within the DSN.

One of these new initiatives addressing the ownership, data sovereignty, and data sharing across organizations is the International Data Spaces Association.*

Cybersecurity and Data Security

Cybersecurity is a broad, multidisciplinary field. It has a technical dimension (not within the scope of this book) as well as an organizational/business dimension. On the organizational/business side, cybersecurity can be further clustered in several subdimensions, of which we will briefly introduce two variants relevant for DSN. First, there are one-directional cybersecurity or data security threats, meaning that an attacker gains access to data and information (aka a data leak). We can differentiate further between access to individual documents and other information items, or the more severe direct access to databases, CAD files, and/or machine tools with real-time process data. Second, two-directional cybersecurity threats describe attacks where the intruder not only gains access to data and information but also is able to delete or manipulate data. Again, there are different levels, one where historical data is deleted, altered, or manipulated with malicious intentions, and a second level where the attacker can manipulate process parameters, CAD files of future products, and so on that can result not only in economic but also safety issues for operators and users.

Laws, Policies, and Regional Differences

We briefly covered the ownership as well as cybersecurity related issues when it comes to big data and data analytics in DSN. In this section, we touch upon a developing subject that every DSN needs to pay close attention to, especially when operating internationally: laws and policies, as well as differences in mindsets.

---

* www.internationaldataspaces.org. Their technology allows members to add a software readable contract to the data describing the terms and conditions of how the data can be used. The creator of the data keeps full ownership and can share the data for a defined purpose and/or at a defined price. Several major companies are supporting this including SAP, Siemens, Deloitte, Deutsche Telekom, thyssenkrupp, Audi, IBM, Volkswagon, and Google.

TABLE 3.4 Selected examples of data-related policies and laws in the United States, European Union, and China

United States	European Union (EU)	China
• *Export control*: Restrict and regulate sharing of technologies, data, etc., with foreign countries or nationals • *California Consumer Privacy Act (CCPA)*: Regulation on the use and transparency of the collection and use of consumers' private data • *Electronic Logging Devices (ELD) mandate*: Automatic tracking, management, and synchronization of vehicle information in the trucking industry	• *General Data Protection Regulation (GDPR)*: Requires consent of subject(s) for data processing, etc. • *US–EU Privacy Shield Framework (replaces US–EU Safe Harbor Agreement)*: Allows US companies to legally transfer and store personal data from EU to US	• *Data Protection Regulatory System* (currently in process): Intended to govern the collection and processing of personal data by private companies • *China Social Credit Score (in early stage)*: Collection and processing of personal data by government agencies to develop social credit scorecard of citizens

Virtually every country, sometimes even state and region, has different laws and policies in place. In lieu of a detailed discussion that would go beyond the scope of this book, we highlight selected examples of three major markets for DSN—the United States, European Union, and China, in Table 3.4. The concept of data sovereignty tries to bridge the differences and establish that data is subject to the laws and policies of the country or region where it was collected.

Besides the policies and laws of different regions, we recommend to also take into account the different mindsets that exist when it comes to data and data sharing. There are distinct differences between regions and countries. For example, the Scandinavian countries are very open and transparent, whereas Germany is very strict when it comes to data privacy. Awareness and transparency is crucial to avoid costly misunderstandings within the DSN that will affect its operations and collaboration.

INTEROPERABILITY

In digital supply networks, diverse stakeholders collaborate and exchange goods, data, and information. At the same time, the different organizations within a DSN use a variety of different software and hardware systems, tools, and services. It is neither practical nor economical to streamline the legacy systems in use by the different stakeholders. Therefore, interoperability plays an essential role in enabling effective and efficient data exchange within a DSN.

Interoperability describes exactly that—the ability of digital systems to interact, to exchange, process, and analyze data and information across platforms. Key aspects of interoperability include interfaces and standards. Interfaces enable two applications, systems, or networks to communicate. Standards define data models, schemas, and message formats, as well as other parameters that enable a system to interpret and process the data and information received from other systems. There are plenty of standards available, ranging from open standards, to industry-specific standards, to proprietary standards for specific purposes. Well-known examples of standards relevant to DSN include, but are not limited to, the following:

- **ISO 10303.** With the official title "Automation systems and integration—Product data representation and exchange," or STEP, ISO 10303 enables the exchange of CAD models across platforms.

- **MTCONNECT** is a relatively new standard that enables manufacturers to retrieve process data directly form the machine tool on the shop floor.

- **OPEN APPLICATIONS GROUP INTEGRATION SPECIFICATION (OAGIS)** provides a canonical business language for information integration by defining common content models and messages for effective communication between applications (A2A) and businesses (B2B).

- **ELECTRONIC PRODUCT CODE INFORMATION SERVICES (EPCIS)** is a global GS1 standard focused on creating and sharing events often connected to RFID technology (not a requirement).

- **ELECTRONIC DATA INTERCHANGE (EDI)** is probably the most frequented DSN data exchange technology today that enables the direct exchange of (business) data such as purchase orders or invoices between organizations.

BIG DATA AND DATA ANALYTICS INFRASTRUCTURE

Big data and data analytics within a DSN put forth challenging requirements in terms of enabling infrastructure. Add cybersecurity concerns, proprietary platforms, and interoperability to the equation, and we see why many organizations struggle with setting up the appropriate enabling technologies and infrastructure. The purpose of this section is to provide a basic overview of some key elements of a big data infrastructure from a hosting and business perspective. It is beyond the scope of this book to dig deep into the technical requirements, such as specific types of NoSQL databases and protocols.

The question of where the data should be stored or hosted, processed, and analyzed depends on many factors, including the business case, the location, the industry, and many more. From a DSN controls perspective the questions to be asked include whether we want to centrally control the system, enable decentralized control, or whether some form of hybrid control model suits the purpose best. In the following section, four key elements of a big data infrastructure in terms of data hosting and processing are briefly elaborated on: fog and edge, local, cloud, and hybrid (see Figure 3.3).

FIGURE 3.3   Key Elements of Big Data Infrastructure

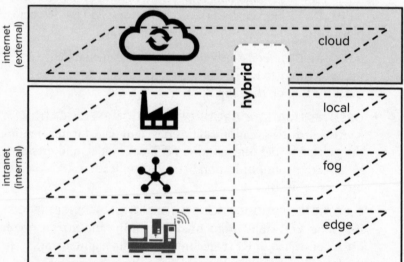

Fog and Edge

Fog and edge computing enable data processing and to some extent analytics closer to the original data source—for example, an IoT sensor system or connected machine tool. The terms "fog" and "edge" are often used interchangeably and the overall objective is similar, yet, they are sometimes differentiated. In fog computing, the intelligence and information processing is located at the local network architecture, while in edge computing the intelligence sits directly at or very close to the sensor, machine tool, or service generating the data. Historically, the cost, speed, and availability of data communication were the main reasons to opt for an edge architecture. In essence, "Fog computing bridges the gap between the cloud and end devices (e.g., IoT nodes) by enabling computing, storage, networking, and data management on network nodes within the close vicinity of IoT devices. Consequentially, computation, storage, networking, decision making, and data management not only occur in the cloud, but also occur along the IoT-to-Cloud path as data traverses to the cloud (preferably close to the IoT devices)."[1] On the other hand, "the edge is [technically] the immediate first hop from the IoT devices (not the IoT nodes themselves), such as the Wi-Fi access points or gateways."[2]

Today, there are a variety of reasons for enabling edge and/or fog computing capabilities within the big data infrastructure in a DSN. These include but are not limited to latency requirements, encryption, limited connectivity, speed, or reliability of data communication services. Furthermore, the progress in miniaturization, energy efficiency, and computing power further drives the fog/edge capabilities—for example, augmented reality systems with built-in real-time processing.

Local (Intranet)

Local storage and processing of data encompasses a broad field. It ranges from physical data storage on individual computer systems, DVDs/CDs, or hard drives, to local networks. For DSNs and big data purposes, the former is not applicable. Therefore, when referring to local computing, we focus on local networks, or an intranet infrastructure. Hosting, processing, and analyzing data locally was broadly used before the cloud infrastructure matured in recent years. It has the advantage of tighter control of the data and knowledge hidden within; however, many downsides exist compared to modern cloud-based infrastructures. In order to achieve similar scalability to a cloud platform, the costs of operating and maintaining the physical servers and software necessary on premises are hard to justify. Furthermore, in a DSN environment, the local setup does not enable the necessary data exchange enabling many of the services and operations in such a collaborative network. In some cases, where cybersecurity or other requirements dictate local hosting with the associated tight control, we see a move to hybrid systems combining the advantages of both local hosts and cloud-based scalability and access.

Cloud (Industrial Internet Platforms)

Cloud computing is broadly defined as services and applications remotely accessed and delivered via a network. Cloud services and applications include but are not limited to hosting services, data processing, and Software as a Service (SaaS). The network that enables access to and delivery of the cloud services and applications is the Internet. Cloud computing essentially decomposed the physical and virtual aspects of big data and data analytics and revolutionized how we interact with, scale, and perceive data in the twenty-first century. In a cloud-based environment, all data and services (e.g., software, analytics) can theoretically be accessed at all times via a web-based service. Cloud computing is often referred to as cloud or Industrial Internet (II)/IIoT platforms, offering a variety of built-in capabilities, standards/protocols, and interfaces. This reduces the initial investment and enables collaboration through joint access to data, services, and analytical insights, a crucial requirement for competitive, data-driven DSNs. Therefore, the cloud is a key component for most DSN big data analytics infrastructures.

Cloud computing and its enabling technological infrastructure have developed significantly, and thus, many initial critiques and issues are solved today. These include latency that prevented cloud services for certain shop floor applications and cybersecurity concerns. With the rapid growth of cloud-based services, other issues arise such as the significant associated energy consumption.

Hybrid Cloud

A hybrid architecture combines all or selected elements to address some specific requirements that cannot be tackled by an individual one alone. That can be challenging latency issues for real-time shop floor control that requires local processing, communication issues that require edge processing to reduce the amount of data transferred, or cybersecurity concerns that require selected data to be hosted on premises. Generally setting up a hybrid system is more complex than a purely cloud or local infrastructure. However, more and more of the leading service providers offer hybrid solutions with seamless integration out-of-box today.

SUMMARY

In summary, data is the lifeblood of modern DSNs. While the amount and availability of data is exponentially increasing, new challenges regarding data quality, authority, and also security emerge as differentiators of digital transformation success. It is crucial for companies to understand that high-quality data is the foundation for all other digital transformation initiatives that use AI and machine learning to develop insights.

MACHINE LEARNING, AI, AND ROBOTICS*

Today, "artificial intelligence" (AI), "machine learning" (ML), and "robotics" are terms that many of us hear on a daily basis. While previously AI was considered mostly science fiction, such as portrayed in the 1984 classic movie *The Terminator*, today we interact with and hear about AI and robotics applications in our homes (Amazon Alexa), at work (automated assistants), or in public spaces (public transport networks). Inevitably, AI, ML, and robotics have a strong impact on digital supply networks (DSNs) today, which will only grow in the future.

In this chapter, we will cover the impact of advanced AI and ML algorithms as well as robotics applications on today's and future DSNs. First we will provide an overview of AI, ML, and robotics. Then we will put these terms into context, explain the key terminologies, and provide insights on their application in DSNs. The first section focuses on the background and terminology of AI and ML, before we have a take a closer look at the different algorithms and the process of applying AI/ML to a DSN problem. The third section focusses on robotics and automation in DSNs. In the last section, we discuss several examples to visualize the applications, challenges, and potential benefits of their application in DSNs. We conclude the chapter with 5 + 1 rules for successful use of AI in DSNs.

---

* The authors would like to thank Dr. Juergen Lenz for his support and insights in developing this chapter.

Before we start to dive deeper in the topic, let's revisit what triggered this development. While AI, ML, and robotics are not a new topic, only in recent years do we see value-added applications across domains within our daily lives outside of dedicated, special solutions in the military, factories, or universities. Two key enablers are the increased connectivity along with the wealth of available data, and the progress made with regard to available computing performance. Two widely referenced laws, Metcalfe's law and Moore's law, exemplify the development (see Figure 4.1). Metcalfe's law describes the exponential effect of an increasing number of nodes in a communication network on the network's impact. Moore's law focusses on the high speed at which computing power increases by stating that the number of transistors on a dense integrated circuit doubles every 18 months.

FIGURE 4.1   Rapid Technological Development Benefits AI Solutions

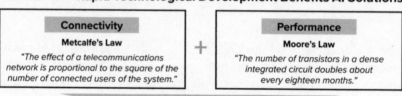

- All actors in a DSN are CP(P)S connected users
- Data transfer effective and efficient
- Execution of AI models computationally efficient (local or cloud)

Improved connectivity and performance benefit AI solutions

In the previous chapter we highlighted how the availability of data is key for any AI and ML solutions, and by extension robotics applications as well. Technological advances directly impact the cost of utilizing AI, ML, or robotics and thus lower the barrier of implementation and increase the competitiveness of applications in a DSN business context (see Figure 4.2). Furthermore, AI, ML, and robotics enable the establishment of platforms and thus solutions that are scalable across whole DSNs and beyond.

AI, ML, and robotics are all attempts to automate certain processes. In the case of robotics, these processes involve at least partly a physical component, such as a welding robot in an automated assembly line. For AI and ML, the automation is focused on a cognitive level. Therefore, we can distinguish AI and ML as cognitive

FIGURE 4.2   Improved Technological Basis for AI Applications

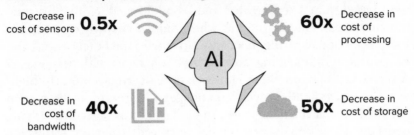

Source: Based on Taisch et al., 2018

automation, and robotics as physical automation. The purpose of these automation attempts is very important: generally we try to automate tasks that are repetitive, strenuous, and/or dangerous (see Table 4.1). Repetitive includes the need for extreme technical precision, such as placing fiber tape precisely in an automated fiber placement (AFP) process in composites manufacturing to avoid wrinkles and other problems. While for physical automation the descriptors are more clearly defined, in cognitive automation they are more indirectly associated. In both cases, the intention is to free up the human operator to do what humans do best: problem solving, creativity, and innovation.

TABLE 4.1   Examples for cognitive and physical automation tasks

	Cognitive Automation (AI & ML)	Physical Automation (Robotics)
Repetitive	Answer questions for an online retailer (e.g., chatbot with AI engine)	Place workpiece in milling center (e.g., articulated industrial robot)
Strenuous/difficult	Support human in multitasking (e.g., autocomplete/check math in documents)	Lifting/moving heavy workpieces (e.g., gantry robots)
Dangerous	Burnout due to mental overload (e.g., automating tasks like taking meeting notes)	Exploration of dangerous terrain after chemical spill (e.g., autonomous drone with sensors)

In most cases, the three descriptors (repetitive, strenuous, and dangerous) are not mutually exclusive. An example of a typical DSN application for such a multidimensional problem is self-driving trucks.

Consider an LTL (less than truckload) scenario where goods are to be transported from A to B, with A and B both located within busy metropolitan areas. Automating the whole route is challenging given the complexity of navigating in a dense city environment (close to A and B), loading and unloading, and the need to interact with personnel at A and B, just to name a few. However, once the truck enters the highway, the task at hand is much less complex with regard to automation potential, and at the same time can be classified as repetitive (driving hours upon hours on one street at defined speed), strenuous (driver has to be alert and concentrated for long periods of time), and potentially dangerous (accidents). Therefore, in this case, utilizing self-driving trucking capabilities for the highway portion of the route would solve multiple issues and address a pressing problem of the trucking industry at the same time: finding qualified drivers that are willing to spend most of their time away from home.

This example, while highlighting the three descriptors, also touches upon an important aspect when thinking about AI, ML, and robotics: the *degree of automation*. In most cases, implementing cognitive or physical automation is not a black-or-white issue, but there is an optimal degree of automation for the specific application and environment. This is essential to keep in mind when developing an AI or robotics strategy for your company or DSN.

ARTIFICIAL INTELLIGENCE AND MACHINE LEARNING

AI and ML are not new, despite the recent increase in media coverage. The first definition from the 1950s describing ML as the process of allowing computers (artificial systems) to solve problems without being specifically programmed to do so[1] is still valid today.[2] Since then, AI and ML have developed significantly and gone through several cycles of growth and decline, most notably the so-called AI winter from the end of the 1960s to the mid-1980s when AI was declared dead and funding almost completely ceased. Since then, especially with the emergence of neural networks, we have seen a continued growth in both AI algorithms and applications. Figure 4.3 illustrates the key developments in the AI field from the mid-twentieth century to today.

The terms AI and ML are often used interchangeably. However, there is a distinct difference that is key to manage expectations and understand how to add value through AI/ML in a DSN context. It basically comes down to the notion of *general AI versus specific AI.*

FIGURE 4.3   Historical Perspective on AI

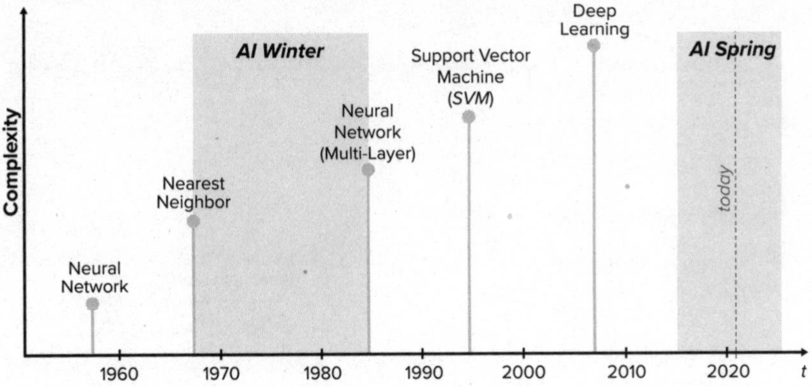

General AI refers to an automated system that is truly intelligent and able to adapt to different situation within a very broad scope. In its extreme form, it can develop new systems and thus evolve. Specific AI on the other hand is focused on a certain domain, process, or problem and applies ML algorithms to process data, learn, and derive insights without constant supervision. Figure 4.4 presents a comparison of the definitions of AI and machine learning, highlighting the key differences. In DSN and most industrial applications we focus mainly on specific AI and thus ML instead of a general AI.

FIGURE 4.4   Artificial Intelligence (AI) vs. Machine Learning (ML)

Artificial Intelligence	Machine Learning
AI means that machines can perform tasks in ways that are "intelligent."	Machine learning is technically a branch of AI, but it's more specific than the overall concept.
These machines aren't just programmed to do a single, repetitive motion—they can do more by adapting to different situations.	Machine learning is based on the idea that we can *build machines to process data and learn on their own, without our constant supervision.*

VS.

Source: Mills, 2018

Technically, ML is a subfield of AI that is based on statistics, mathematics, and visualization. Within ML we use a variety of different algorithms to derive insights from big data. Figure 4.5 depicts the relationships between AI, machine learning, and data analytics as well as different specific algorithms in a graphical model.

FIGURE 4.5   Relationship Between Key AI Terminology

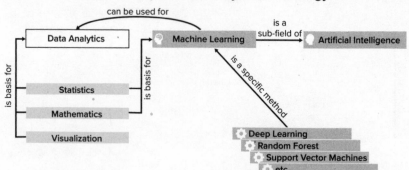

Let's take the example of one of the most hyped ML algorithms today, deep learning, to illustrate the hierarchy of terminology with an association (Figure 4.6). Imagining AI as a human, we can imagine AI being the head, ML the brain, and the specific ML algorithm, in this case deep learning, the neurons in the brain utilized to process the data and providing actionable insights.

FIGURE 4.6   Hierarchy of AI, ML, and Specific Algorithm (Deep Learning)

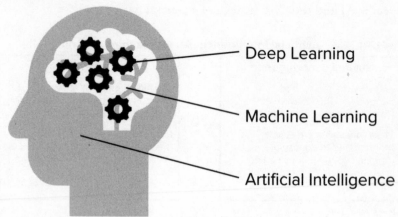

The overall objective of AI and ML is to discover patterns in big data and provide a prediction of future behavior of a system or process based on the identified, often complex patterns. These predictions can target a variety of different issues, including detecting problems or process inefficiencies, market trends, customer behaviors, environmental impacts, financial indicators, or quality issues. AI and ML are the foundation for many new concepts such as predictive maintenance (see Chapter 9), DSN planning (see Chapter 6), and dynamic fulfillment (see Chapter 10) just to name a few. The ability to analyze large data sets, identify hidden patterns, and derive meaningful, actionable insights from the predictions are a powerful tool that has applications in virtually every aspect of business within a DSN.

AI AND MACHINE LEARNING ALGORITHMS

The objective of this section is to provide readers with a basic foundation and understanding of AI and ML to enable informed decisions relevant for their DSN strategy. We do not aim to present a dive deep into the different algorithms and the process of applying ML itself. To do so, we first have a look at the different classes of ML algorithms before covering the principal process of applying ML. Machine learning algorithms can be clustered in three principle classes:

- **UNSUPERVISED LEARNING.** No label available.

- **SUPERVISED LEARNING.** Label available.

- **REINFORCEMENT LEARNING.** Feedback provided.

Unsupervised ML distinguishes itself from supervised ML in that it is used to analyze data that is not labeled. Labeled in this context means there is no evaluation of the examples available to provide insights to the ML algorithm. In ML terms, there is no teacher to add context and insights that can be utilized by the algorithm through the training data. Unsupervised ML tries to identify clusters in big data and thus provide actionable insights. *Supervised ML*, on the other hand, is built on the premise that the correct label (aka insight) is provided by an expert teacher. A common example is a quality label associated with a certain product instance to augment its parameters, state, and process data. *Reinforcement ML* algorithms do not rely on labeled data; instead they rely on feedback on actions taken through cumulative rewards. Therefore, compared to supervised ML, less feedback is given, since not the proper action (label), but only an evaluation of the chosen action is given by an expert teacher. Figure 4.7 illustrates a selection of different ML algorithms and their association with supervised or unsupervised principles. We can observe that several algorithms can be used in both an unsupervised and supervised fashion depending on the application case and data available.

In DSN we have applications for both supervised and unsupervised algorithms. When we dive deeper, certain DSN subdomains are inclined more toward either supervised or unsupervised algorithms—mainly dependent on the nature of the problem and the data picture available. For example, in manufacturing, most applications fall within the supervised ML algorithm realm, while in customer segmentation, we see mostly unsupervised methods in play. Therefore, we focus mainly on the process and applications of supervised ML in the remainder of this section. In Figure 4.7 an overview of selected, non-comprehensive ML algorithms is presented. We can observe that most algorithms in this schematic can be applied to both supervised and unsupervised ML problems. Similarly, reinforcement learning can utilize several of the depicted algorithms.

FIGURE 4.7   Overview of Supervised and Unsupervised ML Algorithms

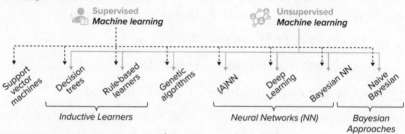

Source: Wuest et al., 2016

Another way we can structure ML algorithms is by the type of prediction we want to achieve. In general we can distinguish between classification and regression as well as clustering. *Classification* attempts to predict the class of a specific example in a discrete way. For example, associating a part with the class "acceptable" or "scrap" falls in this category. *Regression* on the other hand predicts a certain numerical value as an output. A prime example is the stock price of a company at a certain time. *Clustering* is similar to classification with the key difference that it is applied in an unsupervised fashion. Clustering algorithms find patterns in data and group similar examples. This is used to segment customers based in selected features to apply directed marketing tools.

The process of applying ML algorithms starts with an appropriate data set. Different algorithms have variating requirements toward the data set itself. This includes but is not limited to the size of the data set (big data), data quality, and the balance of examples (see Chapter 3). Covering all aspects of how the nature of the available data set informs the choice of a suitable ML algorithm is beyond the scope of this section. However, common issues that impact the choice of an appropriate ML algorithm within DSN are (1) the balance of the data set in terms of labels and (2) the ratio of examples and features.

In a nutshell, most ML algorithms perform better when the data set provides a balanced distribution of the different labels (e.g., good quality vs. bad quality labels). In a common application area within a DSN, the manufacturing shop floor, we often fail to provide a balance of labels for a simple reason that we try to minimize scrap or quality problems. Therefore, the resulting data sets emerging from a manufacturing setting regularly display a significant overrepresentation of "good" quality label with only very few "not good"/"bad" labels. This is in itself not problematic and actually desirable as we do not wish to produce large quantities of low-quality parts. However, it presents a problem for many ML algorithms in terms of the training data set. In a scenario where we have a data set with 99 "good" examples and 1 "not good," the algorithm can easily achieve a 99 percent accuracy by classifying all parts as "good"—and 99 percent accuracy is considered excellent in most cases. However, the resulting prediction would be totally useless in providing valuable, actionable insights to improve our process. Another issue is the discrepancy of examples (e.g., products/parts produced) and features (e.g., process parameters, quality measures). Both of these issues can be addressed and mediated during the preprocessing stage (see Figure 4.8).

FIGURE 4.8   Generalized Machine Learning Application Process

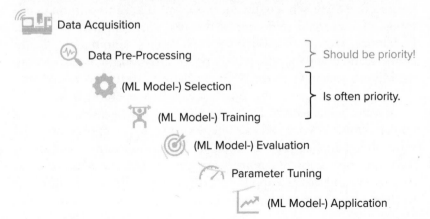

We want to make it very clear that the *available data and the pre-processing stage are crucial* to a value-added application of AI/ML in DSN. Many ML experts agree that data preprocessing is the most important step in the process of applying ML. A good data set with well-defined features with a basic algorithm often yields better outcomes than a low-quality data set without careful preprocessing and the use of a sophisticated algorithm.

The *basic machine learning application process* (see Figure 4.8) starts with the data set and the preprocessing of that data set. In a next step, a suitable ML algorithm is chosen based on the data set, the application objective, and other constraints such as computational resources and expertise available. Once the ML algorithm is chosen, we use a training data set to train the ML model. The training data is often created by splitting the available data set into 70 percent/20 percent/ 10 percent sections, with the training data set portion being the largest with about 70 percent of the data available. The remaining data is split into an evaluation data set (20 percent) that is used to optimize parameters, and a 10 percent test data set to test the model's performance. However, in practice we often see a split with a training set of about 80 percent of the data and a test set of about 20 percent. Training, evaluating, and tuning the ML model is a continuous process that includes several loops before the ML model is ready for deployment.

ROBOTICS AND AUTOMATION IN DSN

When we think of robotics, most of us either think of industrial automation solutions, such as automated moving assembly lines in the automotive or semiconductor industry, or advanced (humanoid) robots such as the Terminator or the viral videos posted by Boston Dynamics. However, self-driving cars, drones, automated vacuum cleaners, and many shop-floor systems are also robots. For this section, we will use one of Merriam-Webster's definitions for *robot*: "a device that automatically performs complicated, often repetitive tasks."

Given the breadth of DSN and the diversity of tasks and stakeholders DSNs encompass, we encounter various opportunities for value-added applications of automated systems and robotics. Similar to the application of cognitive automation (AI and ML), physical automation and robotics applications differ depending on the different levels of abstraction (see Figure 4.9).

FIGURE 4.9 **Different Levels of AI, ML, and Robotics Applications in DSN**

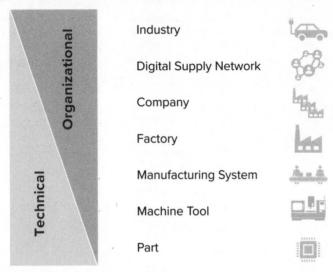

On the lower abstraction levels, on the manufacturing shop floors, in warehouses, and in logistics centers, we tend to see more robotic systems today. Nevertheless, the shape and form of the robots in use varies significantly. They range from automated systems that encompass whole rooms, such as welding robots used on the assembly line of car body production, to smaller collaborative robots supporting the operator in loading individual machining centers.

When thinking of robotics and automation in a DSN, it is advisable to first think about the task that might benefit from being automated. Again, prime value-adding application areas for automation and robotics have certain characteristics in common: tasks are repetitive, strenuous, and/or dangerous. Setting up and programming a robotic system is not trivial and requires expertise. Therefore, introducing robotics to automate certain tasks needs to be carefully planned and critically assessed. In DSN, there are selected areas that tend to benefit more from automation than others. Figure 4.10 depicts a selection of areas where robotics are most likely to add value to the operations. Logistics is a whole big area in itself, and significant progress is made in that space daily. The list is not comprehensive, and with the rapid progress in the robotics space, new applications emerge regularly.

FIGURE 4.10 General Application Areas for Robotic Systems in DSN

HANDLING OPERATIONS	PROCESS OPERATIONS	MISCELLANEOUS
Loading/Unloading e.g., place part in milling center	Finishing operations e.g., deburring, polishing	Measuring operations e.g., laser measuring, touch probe
Sorting e.g., place part from box on conveyer	Welding operations e.g., spot welding, laser welding	Cleaning operations e.g., compressed air, water, brush
Assembly e.g., assembly of different parts	Surface treatment e.g., painting, coating	Logistics (big area) e.g., AGVs
etc.	Cutting operations e.g., sawing, plasma cutting	etc.
	Additive manufacturing operations e.g., automated fiber placement (AFP)	
	etc.	

For truly autonomous robotics applications, a field where AI and robotics heavily intersect, applications in the DSN space are still rare. However, individual noteworthy applications just recently emerged, such as autonomous drones for surveillance for energy efficiency and/or leak monitoring. The next area where autonomous robotic systems will make a large impact on DSN is logistics, including warehousing and transportation. Autonomous trucks, "dark" warehouse systems (fully autonomous with no human present), and last mile delivery systems (e.g., via drones) are on the horizon and will be transformative for DSN.

However, when planning robotics applications today, a key aspect that we need to consider is the optimal degree of automation. Automation, if done right, tends to reduce the direct cost per part; however, with higher degrees of automation, the indirect cost increases significantly (see Figure 4.11). This increase in indirect cost can be associated with expensive maintenance, control, and programming of the robotic systems. In essence, the management of the introduced complexity (via the robotic system) consumes much of the savings in direct cost. Therefore, there is an optimal degree of automation for a part and/or production line that delivers the best performance. It is crucial for DSN to (1) be aware of this phenomenon and (2) not always assume that "more is better" when it comes to automation. In many cases, a semiautomated production outperforms a fully automated system— for example, when dealing with small batch sizes. *The goal of every DSN must be to achieve an as flexible, high-quality, and cost-effective production as possible.*

FIGURE 4.11 Optimal Degree of Automation (Degree of Automation vs. Cost per Part)

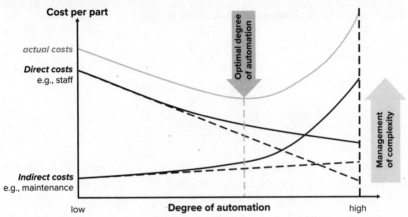

In many cases the degree of automation and the cost of implementation is not a linear development. There is a sharp increase in cost at a certain degree of automation that must be carefully assessed to see if value provided justifies this increase. An example where such a rapid surge of cost regularly occurs is automating the operations of a machine tool such as a five-axis milling center. In this case we can differentiate five degrees of automation (see Table 4.2). The first degree of automation in this case describes the operator manually loading, ejecting, and moving the part as well as having no push notification from the machine tool. Degree 5 is the other extreme where the machine loading, ejecting, and part transport is all fully automated and the machine is providing push notifications to the operator. In this case, we can observe a steep increase in cost after degree 3, when moving toward implementing an automated loading robot. The complexity of the task requires precision and task-specific programming that drives cost. Prior to that task, equipping the machine tool with a notification capability (degree 2) and automating the ejection of the part (degree 3) does not come with such a price tag, as the tasks are comparably less complex to achieve. However, they already provide real value for the operations. Justifying automation beyond such "low-hanging fruits" within a DSN is not trivial, however necessary it might become to remain competitive on the marketplace.

TABLE 4.2   Sharp Increase in Cost at a Certain Degree of Automation (Example of Automation Options for a Milling Center)

Degree of automation	Automated part loading	Machine tool with notification	Automated part ejection	Automated part transfer
1	x	x	x	x
2	x	✓	x	x
3	x	✓	✓	x
Sharp increase in cost at this point				
4	✓	✓	✓	x
5	✓	✓	✓	✓

The degrees of automation and the critical points where a sharp increase in cost may occur are individual to the application and cannot easily be generalized. Questions to be asked by DSN stakeholders faced with this problem should focus on applications that might need little precision and/or item-level adjustment. In case of ejecting a part versus loading a part, the costly difference is that in ejecting, the location, geometry, and orientation of the part in the milling system is precisely defined and readily available from the milling operation itself. Loading, on the other hand, requires locating, orienting, and precisely placing the part in the system—e.g., grabbing the part from a loose collection in a bin. This requires a vision-based system and high felicity in terms of the robotic tool.

APPLICATIONS, CHALLENGES, AND POTENTIAL BENEFITS OF AI, ML, AND ROBOTICS IN DSN

In this section, we will briefly look into numbers and applications associated with AI, ML, and robotics in DSN, as well as emerging challenges and benefits.

AI, ML, and Robotics in DSN in Numbers

There are many numbers and predictions floating around when it comes to the impact AI, ML, and robotics will have on the future of

DSN. These include predictions that advances in AI, ML, and robotics will replace 800 million jobs by 2030.[3] The report estimates a potential to automate roughly 50 percent of all current work activities by adapting already demonstrated technologies. At the same time, this does not mean that these jobs are "lost," but that the nature of work will transform with the maturity of these technologies. If history is any indication, the introduction of new technologies has not reduced the overall number of jobs, but initiated a shift. The 2019 World Manufacturing Forum report highlights the changing skills that are required to compete on the future job market driven by AI, ML, and robotics.[4]

When we look at the predictions for the impact of AI, ML, and robotics on DSN and the associated numbers we see that the expectations are substantial. Predictions include a reduction of scrap rates by 30 percent, of annual maintenance cost by 10 percent, of inspection cost by 25 percent, reduction in lost sales by 65 percent, of annual downtime by 20 percent, of supply chain forecasting errors by 50 percent, of supply chain administration associated costs by 25 to 40 percent, as well as possible inventory reduction of 20 to 50 percent based on advances in AI, ML, and robotics.[5] Other predictions include a 25 percent improvement of inventory turnover[6] and at least 50 percent improved prediction of performance degradation across multiple manufacturing scenarios.[7]

AI, ML, and Robotics Applications in DSN

The expectations within DSN for AI, ML, and robotics to make a transformational impact are huge. Every area of any DSN has at least some possible application where AI, ML, and robotics are currently being considered, and most likely already tested. However, there are some applications that lend themselves to be a more natural fit (see characteristics of suitable applications cases discussed before). In this section, we provide a list of selected areas where AI, ML, and robotics will have an impact and that might present a good start when your DSN is considering AI, ML, and robotics implementations. While DSNs are complex and cover a broad scope, we tried to provide a diverse list of application examples and areas to inspire innovation. Again, AI, ML, and robotics are strongly intertwined and not distinguishable black or white in most cases. Therefore, the following three collections are mainly to provide some form of structure to the reader.

First, we will look into AI and ML application in a more traditional supply chain setting:

- Data-driven supply chain planning
- Route optimization and delivery planning using real-time data (e.g., traffic information)
- Optimizing warehouse management (e.g., machine learning based forecasting of optimal stock level)
- Decentralized control of packages and other items that plan their own route, adapting to the environment
- Data-driven scheduling and prioritization of orders in distributed DSN

The following AI and ML applications are growing within the extended DSN domain:

- Automated procurement algorithms that crawl the market and negotiate automatically
- Data-driven demand forecasting (e.g., machine learning powered prediction of fashion trends based on unstructured social media data using natural language processing)
- Automated risk monitoring and/or supplier qualification, monitoring, and selection
- Increased product quality during production using data-driven optimization
- Zero downtime based on data-driven predictive or preventive maintenance algorithms
- Real-time tracking of orders by customers and other DSN stakeholders

Last we cover some typical physical automation applications within DSN:

- Autonomous trucking (driving) for distribution
- More inclusive workplaces with cobots supporting workers (including but not limited to workers with disabilities and an aging workforce)
- Competitive manufacturing operations located close to end customers enabled by lower labor cost using robotics on the shop floor

Challenges for AI, ML, and Robotics in DSN

AI, ML, and robotics have come a long way and are already providing value to leading companies around the globe daily. However, there are several challenges that companies need to be aware of when contemplating the introduction of these technologies in their DSNs.

One major factor is data itself. On the one hand, consider the previously discussed "Vs" (see Chapter 3), but specifically data quality and data sharing. Data quality has a tremendous impact on the potential value of AI, ML, and also robotics applications within a DSN. Even when only a fraction of the available data is of low quality, that can impact the prediction accuracy and in the end the overall usefulness of the AI/ML solution. The other key aspect, data sharing, is essential within a DSN where several stakeholders are working together, both on the technical and business sides.

A more AI- and ML-specific issue is the often black box nature of many AI/ML predictions. Similar to manufacturing, in a DSN the stakeholders aspire to understand why certain decisions are made. Often a simple "the algorithm said so" is not good enough—most certainly not in cases resulting in serious injuries or financial repercussions. This problem is heavily researched, among others by DARPA's XAI (explainable AI) initiative and several efforts to merge physics-based modeling with data-driven approaches. This is crucial for the social acceptance of AI, ML, and robotics and for trust to be placed in their outputs.

Still being comparably novel technologies, there are many technical issues that need to be addressed for them to become broadly adopted and accepted. These include but are not limited to distributed computing, hosting of services and data, real-time analysis in the cloud, latency, connectivity in remote areas, and use in "dirty" (abrasive, metal heavy, etc.) spaces.

The last challenge that we want to present is liability of AI, ML, and robotics in DSN. Partly connected to the black box nature of many of the algorithms, the question is still unsolved who is responsible if something goes astray. What happens when the forecasting algorithm's prediction is wrong and the warehouse system runs out of stock, halting production? Or when an autonomous truck has an accident and harms humans based on a decision of the AI algorithm? These are questions that cannot be overstated and that need to be addressed carefully, bringing technologists, policy makers, lawyers, and other stakeholders together.

Benefits of AI, ML, and Robotics in DSN

After covering the challenges that have yet to be overcome, we will now briefly discuss the benefits AI, ML, and robotics offer for modern DSN—and there are plenty! There are many obvious ones, mainly around reducing the efforts and resources needed to do certain things (automating). Many of the applications mentioned earlier in this chapter can be grounded in such initiatives. These are more obvious, and we will not focus much on them but rather on the more forward-thinking and not yet fully developed ones to inspire the creativity of our readers.

Globally, the many developed and developing economies are faced with an aging population. The baby boomers are close to retirement, and with that, companies are struggling to find qualified workers with the required skill set. At the same time, many older workers would like to continue to be productive members of society—and AI, ML, and robotics can be an enabler to facilitate this. Cobots and AI-based augmented systems can provide the tools for older workers to safely and productively continue working in an industrial setting. Both features, safety and productivity, are key dimensions where AI, ML, and robotics are impactful and value adding to various areas within a DSN.

On a global level, the pressure to reduce the energy footprint and a more mindful use of resources while providing highly efficient industrial production to a growing population is a challenge that AI, ML, and robotics can be integral in addressing. It is almost impossible to predict and optimize the energy footprint of a global DSN without AI/ML, given the complexity and dynamics involved. In this case, AI and ML are the only viable option to address this pressing challenge of our planet.

SUMMARY

Summarizing, there are several exciting benefits associated with AI, ML, and robotics in a DSN environment. The technologies are mature and continue to develop at a rapid pace. However, adopting AI, ML, and robotics does not come easy. Therefore, we have put together 5 + 1 rules that interested decision makers in DSN need to respect (see Figure 4.12).

FIGURE 4.12   5 + 1 Rules for Successful Use of AI in DSN

1. *Learn to walk* **before you run!**

2. **AI application must be** *business/value based!*

3. **AI vision, models, and prototypes are easy,** *AI solutions "on scale" are tough!*

4. **Start with specific,** *data-driven machine learning* **solutions in a DSN!**

5. **Don't do everything yourself!**

Most important:
AI is no silver bullet!

END-TO-END TRANSPARENCY AND TRUST THROUGH BLOCKCHAIN

Blockchain technology is evolving into a potential launching pad for digital transformation in general and the digital supply network (DSN) in particular. In this chapter, we discuss what blockchain technology is, how it works, and evolving designs. We examine how it can potentially add greater visibility, flexibility, and efficiency across the entire supply chain by optimizing business transactions and trading relationships, and how it can enable DSNs. We start with an illustrative proof-of-concept application.

BLOCKCHAIN APPLICATION IN AN EMERGENT DIGITAL SUPPLY NETWORK

Blockchain has the potential to relieve many supply chain pain points and enable the ongoing transition from linear supply chains to connected digital supply networks, as we discussed earlier. This evolution from linear and relatively siloed processes into dynamic and interconnected nodes will generate tremendous competitive advantages, enabled by a set of broad and diverse technologies. There has been an extensive discussion about the potential applications of blockchain technology in various contexts. One of the successful and widely publicized experiments of usage is in the agro-supply chain to trace provenance—we provide one such example in Chapter 10. The more promising use cases though are those that enable entirely new business models, such as fractional ownership in the automotive industry[1] or transformed network processes in the aerospace industry, such as part replacement digitalization illustrated in Figure 5.1.

FIGURE 5.1 Blockchain-Enabled Aerospace DSN

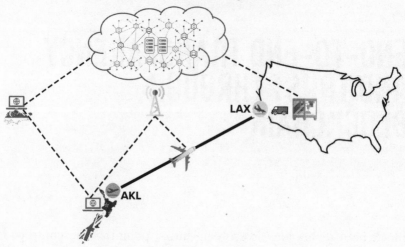

Aerospace suppliers and OEMs have started exploring blockchain potential to transform their very complex and highly regulated supply chains. Organizations in this industry must keep track of tens of thousands of different parts throughout the product lifecycle. For instance, reports of fatal accidents revealing that some airlines were not keeping track of the history of each individual component within an engine illustrate the challenges of such a mandate. The parts of an aircraft are produced and sold under a heavily regulated market. The sales require certification from authorities such as the Federal Aviation Administration and other agencies in a process that can be quite long.

In a recent successful proof-of-concept trial, an aircraft component maker tested a combination of blockchain and 3D printing to speed up the replacement of defective aircraft parts to a few hours from several weeks.[2] In the test, illustrated in Figure 5.1, a major airline ordered a replacement part for a long-range commercial aircraft en route from Auckland to Los Angeles using the component maker's blockchain system. Midair, the aircrew notified the maintenance crew on the ground in Auckland that they needed a replacement part, or they would lose a premier seat on the return leg. One of the airline maintenance teams in New Zealand ordered a digital file containing the part design from a Singapore-based engineering company that provides airline repair service. The blockchain system validated the order, and the digital data was immediately sent to an approved printer in Los Angeles, downloaded, 3D printed, and sent to the airport. By the time the aircraft landed, the part was ready to be installed on-site without the aircraft losing any uptime or revenue due to an unavailable premium seat.

The entire transaction, from purchase to installation, was logged into the blockchain system, which can provide an immutable and auditable digital thread proving hardware, software, and documentation authenticity and certification. In this proof of concept, the blockchain system allows an engineering partner to release its intellectual property in a controlled fashion. The supplier can 3D print only the number of parts it requires on demand. As this experiment evolves, blockchain can not only share a digital ledger of transactions and trusted manufacturers but also host information on the material used for aircraft parts, such as specific plastics or metals, so that the order can be routed to an appropriate 3D printer. Besides, it may be possible for the partners to eventually codify the agreement into a smart contract within an evolving DSN environment.

In this trial, shifting from a linear to a digital supply network, product design goes on a blockchain and parts are produced on demand from a digital blueprint, as opposed to mass-produced and shipped from distant locations. Instead of a linear and sequential path from manufacturer to airport, the order took place through a global network of companies under a developing DSN. Blockchain ascertains that the data file is not corrupt, the part meets all regulatory requirements, and the touchpoints are traceable and auditable. Besides, the traditional supply chain costs with packaging, shipping, warehousing, inventory management, and customs are nearly eliminated in this proof of concept. Now, let us delve into the anatomy and characteristics of the technology.

ANATOMY OF THE BLOCKCHAIN TECHNOLOGY

The most essential component of blockchain technology is the transaction, an online exchange of any digital asset. A digital asset is anything that exists in binary format with the right of use, such as photos, records, documents, files containing text, and so on. Here we should note that blockchain technology focuses on the transfer of value, while previous technologies have focused on faster and more secure exchange of information. Another fundamental component is the block, a set of transactions from a specific period that is distributed to all nodes in the network. We can think of each block as a page in a ledger or record book. Each block is time-stamped, placed in chronological order, and linked to the block before it using cryptographic algorithms, forming a chain. The chain becomes the chronological sequence of blocks containing all past verified transactions and eliminates the possibility of tampering.

> Blockchain technology focuses on the exchange of value, while previous technologies have focused on faster and more secure transfer of information. It functions as an asset-exchange mechanism.

Distributed Computing

The blockchain is a decentralized, distributed ledger of different types of transactions operating on a peer-to-peer (P2P) architecture. A set of computer systems using the network (the "peers," which we call nodes) simultaneously constitute its foundation by providing a portion of computing resources, such as processing power, to other members of the network in a P2P architecture. This configuration is in contrast to traditional client-server architecture as there is no central point of storage. Instead, all network participants continuously record and exchange information.

Cryptographic Security

An essential feature of blockchain technology is the use of cryptographic hash functions. A hash function is simply a mathematical algorithm that converts input data of arbitrary size (e.g., files, text, or image) into unique compressed output data of a fixed size (known as a "hash" or "digest").[3] A cryptographic hash is usually displayed as a hexadecimal number, and we can think of it as a file's digital fingerprint. Figure 5.2 illustrates a generic chain of blocks. We see that each block contains the hash digest of the previous block's header and this feature chains the blocks together.

Consensus Validation

Somewhat similar to a matryoshka doll (Russian nesting doll), where the set starts with the innermost doll and then has subsequent outer layer dolls that encompass the previous ones, any blockchain network

FIGURE 5.2   Chain of Blocks

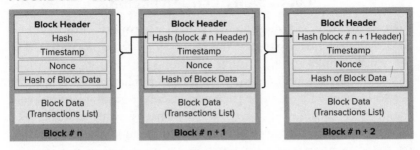

has a preconfigured, published "genesis block" to which we add all the new blocks according to the given network consensus mechanism. Anyone joining the blockchain network agrees on the initial state of the system, and each block created subsequently to the genesis block must be validated. This process allows users to agree on the current state of the blockchain independently.

Another aspect of agreeing on the state of the blockchain network is resolving conflicting data. At times, due to the distributed nature of the network and latency, a blockchain can fork unintentionally into two different chains, such that some systems in the network fall behind on or have alternative information, creating a temporary conflict.[4] Generally, most consensus protocols solve this issue by waiting until the publication of the next block and using that chain as the official blockchain—in simple terms, the longest chain wins. Figure 5.3 illustrates this situation, depicting an unintentional fork where two nodes create a different candidate version of block 3 at the same time. Inevitably, one chain will receive new blocks faster and will become the official chain, while any transactions present on the forked or orphaned block returns to the pending transaction pool.[5] We must note here that each node in the network maintains those pending transactions locally as there is no central server in the distributed architecture.

FIGURE 5.3   Blockchain Fork and Ledger in Conflict

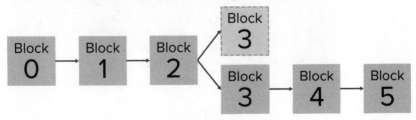

BLOCKCHAIN NETWORK DESIGNS

We can distinguish emerging blockchain network designs based on the level of data transparency and processing privileges conferred to the general public and intrinsic trust among participants. In terms of data transparency, on one side we have full public and decentralized networks secured by a game theoretic incentive mechanism to avoid fraudulent behavior, while on the other we have private networks with more tightly controlled access permission and maintenance operations restricted to a few users. The basic level of trust among participants and the mechanism through which each of these network designs ascertains trust differ. Public blockchains assume random users that could include bad actors, so there is lower intrinsic trust among members and a cryptographic protocol is used to coordinate transactions and avoid wrongdoing. Private blockchains assume prescreened or known participants, so there is higher inherent trust among members and a less computationally demanding consensus protocol.

Concerning data processing privileges, we have permissioned blockchain networks, which set some form of restriction on transaction processing, and, in contrast, we have permissionless networks, which allow anyone to process transactions so long as they satisfy some

FIGURE 5.4 Blockchain Designs

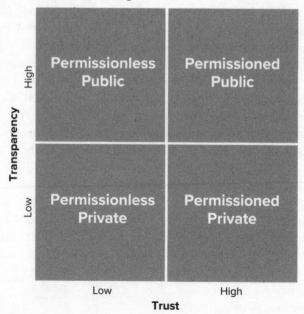

criteria not centrally controlled. These networks differ on the level of access to transaction data and operations each participant has. Putting those two dimensions together (inherent trust among participants and transaction visibility) yields the two-by-two matrix in Figure 5.4, which maps possible blockchain network designs against the two main aspects of data transparency and manipulation.

REPRESENTATIVE SUPPLY CHAIN CHALLENGES AND BLOCKCHAIN CAPABILITIES

Let us now take a look at some typical issues in traditional supply chains and how blockchain technology can potentially play a role in addressing them. First, we should keep in mind that, in a conventional supply chain, information usually flows in a linear sequence: develop, plan, source, make, deliver, support.[6] Activity in each step of this linear chain depends significantly on the activity in the previous step. Besides, the operational and decision-making actions in each linear stride are, for the most part, tidily siloed. This linear and insular modus operandi disseminates and frequently amplifies inefficiencies and disruptions from one stage to the subsequent steps.

Provenance, Traceability, and Compliance

Transparency has become an ever more challenging issue in supply chains. For instance, Walmart carries about 50,000 products across 6,000 stores and deals with thousands of suppliers across the globe.[7] Such complexity makes it almost impossible, even for a major multinational corporation, to keep track of each and every transaction record. This lack of transparency drives up costs and increases various forms of risks. Blockchain technology can potentially solve these issues by facilitating record keeping and provenance tracking. All the transactions about the flow of a product, from its origin to the present location, becomes available through blockchain. The ability to trace a product accurately can facilitate the detection of fraud across the various stages of the chain, improve product safety, and increase forecast accuracy and collaborative planning.

For many items, such as aeronautical products, precious stones, and food, proof of authenticity and origin has grown increasingly important. Blockchain-enabled DSN can play an essential role in addressing these supply chain challenges, as it can provide assurance that data has not been tampered with as it flows through the chain. This is because blockchain ascertains data visibility to all participants authorized to access it, minimizes the possibility of one single entity altering the data, and time-stamps the transactions.

An illustration of the impact of these issues and the potential of the technology is the E. coli outbreak at Chipotle Mexican Grill outlets in 2015, which left customers ill, led to shutdowns, tarnished the restaurant chain's reputation, and ultimately dropped the share price by 42 percent. This event illustrates the continuous problem of lack of transparency and accountability across complex traditional supply chains, in which focal companies depend on multiple suppliers to deliver parts and ingredients.[8] The critical issue here is that organizations rarely have visibility beyond their immediate suppliers. The use of blockchain in a DSN to transfer title and record activity logs would enable knowledge of the complete history of the product, so we could use details from the initial cases to rapidly and precisely identify the outbreak's origin. Unable to monitor its suppliers in real time, Chipotle could neither prevent the contamination nor contain it in a targeted fashion after its discovery.

Cost and Efficiency

Hundreds of hands may touch a given product moving through a supply chain. International trade entails a multitude of actors and continues to rely extensively on manual processes and paper. For instance, in 2014, Maersk followed the journey of a refrigerated container filled with avocados flowing from Kenya to the Netherlands. The company discovered that the shipment involved around 30 actors and more than 100 people interacting over 200 times.[9] The 34-day journey included 10 days waiting for documents to be processed. A substantial portion of shipment expenses pertains to documentation. Besides the cost of sending paperwork from one location to the next, there is often the risk of missing or damaged paperwork, and of errors or discrepancies. Blockchain-enabled DSN can make possible the digitization of international trade transactions, enabling real-time tracking, the acceleration of administrative processes, and elimination of intermediaries, duplication, and physical documentation, reducing costs.

Customers and suppliers rely on intermediaries to process payments in international trade. Blockchain-enabled DSN can provide faster and more efficient processing with fewer intermediaries. It can also allow accurate record keeping, which reduces the risk of losing products or critical documents, as was the case in the journey of the container filled with avocados that Maersk studied. In the shipping industry, blockchain can enable paperless processes, which would improve efficiency while making it easier for all the actors involved in the transaction to access the necessary data. Buyers and sellers of cargo, banks, shipowners, port authorities, and customs agents can interact with each other, store and exchange information, complete transactions, and securely exchange payments without the endless paperwork used by current processes.

Visibility and Flexibility

Another supply chain challenge and increasingly strategic necessity is visibility across procurement, manufacturing, transportation, and distribution networks. Efforts toward the integration of upstream and downstream supply chain processes derive from the simple insight that they are connected and interdependent.[10] However, while we have achieved the ability to streamline many supply chain transactions in real time, updates typically take place within silos. More frequently than not, many organizations continue to record events after they have taken place, and the ability of every involved actor to learn simultaneously about a supply chain event in real time remains an elusive goal.

Visibility becomes an even more significant challenge in a complex multicompany, multitier global supply chain scenario. Deficiencies in transactional data become more readily evident as the number of organizations involved in a given chain process grows. While earlier technologies, such as electronic data interchange, have streamlined the exchange of data between supply chain dyads for standardized high-volume transactions, they become far less efficient as their use extends to multiparty operations. A more significant number of participants increases the need for speed, the risk of data being lost along the way, and the risk of data coming out of sync as it flows from node to node along a traditional linear supply chain.

Blockchain-enabled DSN can provide higher visibility, increase the accuracy of transactions, and reduce the execution time found on synced information from multiple participants on a network. For instance, supply management professionals can quickly update the quantity, attributes, and location of transactions with vendors and suppliers and share with other participants involved, such as manufacturers and shippers, via a blockchain network. This blockchain-enabled update would allow the manufacturer to receive an alert about the shipment far in advance of it reaching the destination. The manufacturer could update the warehouse schedule, and the shipper could plan the pickup and delivery in advance of shipment execution guided by the updates from the manufacturer. The supply chain professionals could receive information about impending delays or difficulties in real time and take proactive corrective action.

The following summarizes core blockchain capabilities that can remedy the supply chain inefficiencies discussed above[11] as linear supply chains shift toward DSN:

- **AUDITABILITY.** Blockchain provides an audit trail of data, creating a permanent means of record keeping along a supply chain and enabling the capability to monitor events and metadata associated with a product.

- **IMMUTABILITY.** Blockchain transactions are time-stamped and tamperproof, providing a single source of data integrity and enabling the capability to provide evidence that standards and regulatory conditions are satisfied.

- **DISINTERMEDIATION.** Blockchain enables peer-to-peer interactions that can be trusted based on the digital signatures, allowing the capability to communicate, reduce risk, and create trust among involved parties.

BLOCKCHAIN'S ROLE IN THE EMERGING DIGITAL SUPPLY NETWORK

We can conceive of traditional linear supply chains in general as complex and globally dispersed ecosystems, connected by fragmented information technologies and characterized by the absence of trust among parties with misaligned interests. Excellence in the supply chain, however, involves close collaboration among stakeholders to ascertain a smooth flow of physical goods, information, and financial transactions. For years, companies have invested in integrating supply chains for better coordination. In fact, integration has become something of a mantra for supply chain professionals, academics, and consultants alike, although some circumstances might occasionally call for different levels of integration.[12] Independent of the levels of integration, a critical point is that modern supply chains are complex, involving several stakeholders, often with conflicting interests and priorities, and incorporate different systems to manage the various flows throughout the globe. In other words, traditional supply chains present inefficiencies, little traceability, and interoperability problems.

At the most basic level, we can see traditional supply chains as an extended process of value-added transactions among stakeholders with supporting systems often fragmented. Each node within a network has its own ledger, and it can take several days to synchronize them. This latency is because information typically moves in a step-by-step sequential manner, from development to delivery to support.

As we transition from the linear and somewhat siloed supply chain processes that we currently observe across industries into the digital supply network, characterized by a set of dynamic and interconnected nodes,[13] it becomes central for us to understand the role and strategic implications of blockchain technology better. Let us start by reflecting on the nature of blockchain as an innovation. Disruptive innovation is change that, at the outset, initially presents a different package of performance attributes from the ones mainstream customers value, but that over time brings improvement at such a rapid rate that the new technology can later overtake traditional business models and invade established markets.[14]

Blockchain, however, has been regarded as a "foundational" and not "disruptive" technology. A foundational technology has the potential to create a new basis for economic and social systems, but the process of adoption is gradual and steady rather than sudden.[15] So, what do we know about technology adoption and the transformation process typical of other foundational technology? The insightful framework that Iansiti and Lakhani (2017) developed to describe how a foundational technology and its particular business case evolve can prove managerially insightful here. They suggest that technology development takes place typically in four phases, each defined by the novelty of the applications, the degree to which an application is new to the world, and the complexity of the coordination efforts needed to make them workable—the number and diversity of parties that have to work together to produce value with the technology.

Their framework maps innovations against these contextual dimensions, dividing them into quadrants, each of which represents a stage of technology development. We can apprehend the levels of collaboration and regulatory and legislative efforts and the infrastructure required by mapping a given blockchain innovation to the framework. Bitcoin, for instance, falls into the "single use" quadrant, where low-novelty and low-coordination applications create better, less costly, and highly focused solutions.[16] Let us focus on the "transformation" quadrant, where completely novel applications can change the very nature of business if successful, such as smart contracts.

Applications that fall under the transformation quadrant require the coordination of transactions among many parties and gaining institutional agreement on standards and processes. The strength of transformative applications materializes when they enable a new business model in which the logic of value creation and capture differ from existing approaches. We see not only blockchain applications that will allow the digital supply network, such as smart contracts, but also DSNs themselves falling into the transformation quadrant. As argued by Iansiti and Lakhani (2017), transformative applications will be the most powerful when tied to new business models, such as digital supply networks, in which the logic of value creation and capture departs from existing approaches (see the example from the aerospace industry later in the chapter).

So, what is the role of blockchain in this above context? It can function as an enabler of the digital supply network and the connecting tissue that will hold it together as we move through the evolutionary stages. Figure 5.5 illustrates the concept of blockchain sitting on top of several independent systems across different participants in a supply chain.[17] A blockchain layer can integrate the insular systems and data of traditional linear environments and subsequently extend to additional participants and network nodes.

FIGURE 5.5   Blockchain Layer on Top of the Supply Network

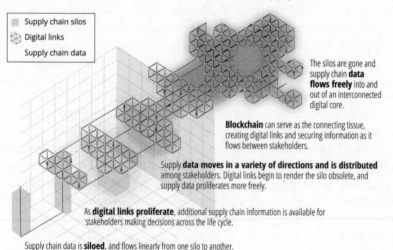

Source: Deloitte analysis.

As blockchain applications evolve from single-use toward the transformation stage, siloed transaction processes should become gradually distributed, as blockchain capabilities (disintermediation, immutability, and auditability) enable the unification of the current linear supply chain systems and data through sharing of commonly relevant information[18] in a DSN environment. These features can create a business context where the various network nodes involved have a shared account of the state of an asset, physical or not,[19] reducing the delay of information flows and friction between processes.

> Blockchain technology creates value in the transition to the digital supply network by enabling the creation and connection of links between nodes, such that siloed systems and data become distributed.

In terms of blockchain, assets include not only information that describes the state of a physical item but may consist of also those assets that never assume a physical state (native digital assets), such as an invoice number. For instance, a company's purchasing organization may record billing information for service as an invoice number, while the accounts payable area may generate and store a wire transfer number and the logistics area receiving the service may create an internal case number.[20] In this case, the asset is not the service the purchasing organization contracted, but the unique descriptive information about the internal business processes involved in the procurement and receipt of the service. As such, the ID number itself is the asset and not the service procured.

SMART CONTRACTS

To greatly simplify our discussion, we can see a vending machine as the simplest form of a smart contract. The rules of a transaction between two parties (vendor and customer) are programmed into the vending machine. When we select a product by pressing a number related to that product and insert the required coins, the device acts as a smart contract, checking whether we entered enough money, and if so, the machine is programmed to dispense the corresponding product and change if warranted. If we do not insert sufficient money, or if the machine has run out of product, the device will return what we added. It is easy to see that automatic vending machines decreased transaction costs substantially by making human vendors obsolete and also expanded service, offering 24/7 availability instead of limited opening hours of a kiosk. This comparison captures, in a nutshell, the general idea behind smart contracts. However, it is essential to highlight that while non-blockchain smart contracts can exist, they present the same potential problems as centralized databases: there is a single point of failure and they are not tamper resistant.[21]

Smart contracts fall in the transformation stage of the evolution of foundation technologies. Blockchain-based smart contracts are a collection of self-executing code that automatically implements the terms of an agreement between parties using cryptographically signed transactions on the blockchain—see Figure 5.6 for a pictorial description. Smart contracts extend and leverage blockchain technology from merely keeping a record of transaction entries to automatically implementing terms of multiparty agreements in a DSN. They constitute a transformative evolution of blockchain applications, streamlining processes that are currently dispersed across multiple databases and enterprise resource planning systems. As such, parties can agree upon terms and trust that code will execute them automatically, with reduced risk of error or manipulation. Thus, smart contract applications provide capabilities that are critical building blocks for the transformation toward the digital supply network.

FIGURE 5.6   General Description of a Smart Contract Transaction

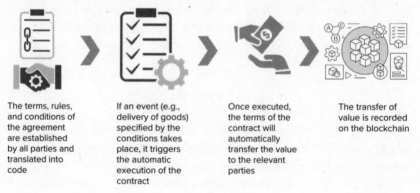

The terms, rules, and conditions of the agreement are established by all parties and translated into code

If an event (e.g., delivery of goods) specified by the conditions takes place, it triggers the automatic execution of the contract

Once executed, the terms of the contract will automatically transfer the value to the relevant parties

The transfer of value is recorded on the blockchain

We can implement a smart contract to work in isolation or set it to be dependent and work along with any number of other smart contracts, such that the successful execution of one smart contract can trigger the start of the next one. A whole DSN can potentially run entirely on smart contracts. For instance, Maersk and IBM established a joint venture through blockchain technology by introducing an entire shipment system based on the blockchain network. More than 100 companies have joined in, streamlining the industry through freight forwarding and trade finance with a focus on end-to-end services and blockchain as a means to transfer value. Now it is essential to clarify that smart contracts are not smart; there is no cognitive or artificial intelligence component under the hood, but instead, the automatic execution of a predefined task when certain conditions are met.[22] They are not contracts in the legal sense either.

About Blockchain Challenges

The deployment of blockchain in the DSN is not without challenges, just as any new and developing technology. First and foremost, we have seen a lot of hype about the potential of the technology, which for emerging technologies often can succumb to the hype cycle, "passing through the peak of inflated expectations and landing in the trough of disillusionment."[23] Another challenge is the poor understanding about security issues involving blockchain. As business transactions typically contain sensitive commercial information, data protection and privacy are critical consideration factors. Interoperability is another challenge, as companies may be using outdated systems to record information. Access can become painful if system sensors and data pools are not compatible. The quality of the data is also a critical factor, as poor quality entered into the chain will result in inaccurate data assumptions in subsequent chains. The widespread adoption needed to enable the digital supply network is another critical challenge that needs to be overcome as well.

SUMMARY

Blockchain technology uses well-established cryptographic principles and serves as a repository for information about transactions, which is recorded and shared through a decentralized peer-to-peer network. Within this network, all participants maintain a copy of the digital ledger and validate new entries to the chain through the use of a consensus protocol. There are four emerging blockchain network designs based on the level of data transparency and processing privileges conferred to the general public and intrinsic trust among participants. This technology focuses on the exchange of value, while previous ones have focused on faster and more secure transfer of information.

Blockchain creates value in the transition to the digital supply network by enabling the creation and connection of links between nodes, such that siloed systems and data become distributed. To summarize the discussion in this chapter and drive the main point home, as a foundational technology, blockchain use cases should prove more valuable when combined with other critical technological developments (the Internet of Things, robotics, smart devices, 3D printing, etc.) to enable the transformation or creation of new business models, such as the digital supply network we discuss in this book.

For instance, we may be able to embed smart devices securely to a physical product to autonomously record and transmit data about item condition over blockchain to ensure product integrity. We may be able to combine IoT and blockchain to enable smart contracts, such that a connected pallet automatically transmits confirmation and the time of delivery as well as the condition of the goods to the blockchain network. The network can automatically verify the delivery, confirm whether the agreed condition was satisfied, and release correct payments to the appropriate parties.

SYNCHRONIZED PLANNING

Digital technologies are increasingly being adopted by entities across the ecosystem (consumers, customers, companies, suppliers, and other providers), effectively creating an interconnected and dynamic value network. This interconnectedness presents a great opportunity to more dynamically and effectively plan the need and consumption of capital and goods. With increased interconnectedness comes the ability to create a synchronized plan that is then translated across the enterprise and used by all functions to run and execute scenarios. This plan can then be extended across entities in the value chain, effectively leading to a world where you can synchronize the complete ecosystem. This state is what we refer to as "synchronized planning."

Synchronized planning describes a state in which "constant flows of data throughout the supply network enable organizations to accurately and dynamically plan real supply against real demand. In an interconnected Digital Supply Network, data filters across other nodes, enabling suppliers, logistics, and fulfillment to plan more accurately and take all necessary actions to provide the right resources at the right time and the right place. These actions are enabled by the convergence of human and computer where the human brain is 'augmented' by machine learning (ML) and artificial intelligence (AI). The result is a highly flexible, dynamic, efficient, predictive and proactive planning capability that enables entities to course correct in real time"[1] Ultimately, the vision of synchronized planning is to integrate strategic business objectives with financial, commercial, operational, and tactical plans into a single dynamic plan for the ecosystem.

In a synchronized planning state, sales and operations planning (S&OP) and integrated business planning (IBP) are effectively transformed into a series of automated and machine learning assisted collaborations that accelerate the ability of the enterprise to solve for demand/supply imbalance. This effectively is a world where organizations can operate without the need to wait for a weekly or monthly cycle but instead achieve a synchronized state where planning and execution happen concurrently.

TRADITIONAL S&OP AND SUPPLY CHAIN PLANNING

Since its inception in the 1980s, sales and operations planning (S&OP) has been evolving to enable the enterprise to achieve a synchronized view of the business across all functions. Through this monthly management process, the leadership team is empowered to continually improve key supply chain drivers through structured collaboration between sales, marketing, planning, production, inventory management, procurement, and new product introduction. The natural evolution of this process led to a more sophisticated version of S&OP known as integrated business planning (IBP). IBP's focus has been to strengthen the financial integration and reconciliation of plans, as well as increase the responsiveness of the supply chain using improved visualization reports and what-if scenario analyses. Synchronized planning takes it a step further and enables a transformation of the IBP process into an automated, cognitive-enabled series of interactions that help the enterprise become more agile in its decision making. This transformation significantly accelerates the cycle time and effectiveness of the IBP process while reducing its complexity due to enriched real-time ecosystem inputs, enhanced analytics, workflow automation, and the ability to simulate end-to-end scenarios using a digital replica of the value chain.

The S&OP Plan and Time Horizon of Traditional SCM

The traditional S&OP cycle encompasses four key steps: demand review, supply review, operating review, and executive review (Figure 6.1). This process typically runs monthly and focuses on a 12-to-18-month horizon. The demand review process focuses on understanding demand signals, creating a managed demand forecast, and reaching consensus, while in the supply review, the focus is on identifying demand/supply gaps and capacity issues and recommending scenarios to mitigate those issues. In the operating review, the objective is to

FIGURE 6.1 Traditional S&OP/IBP Cycle

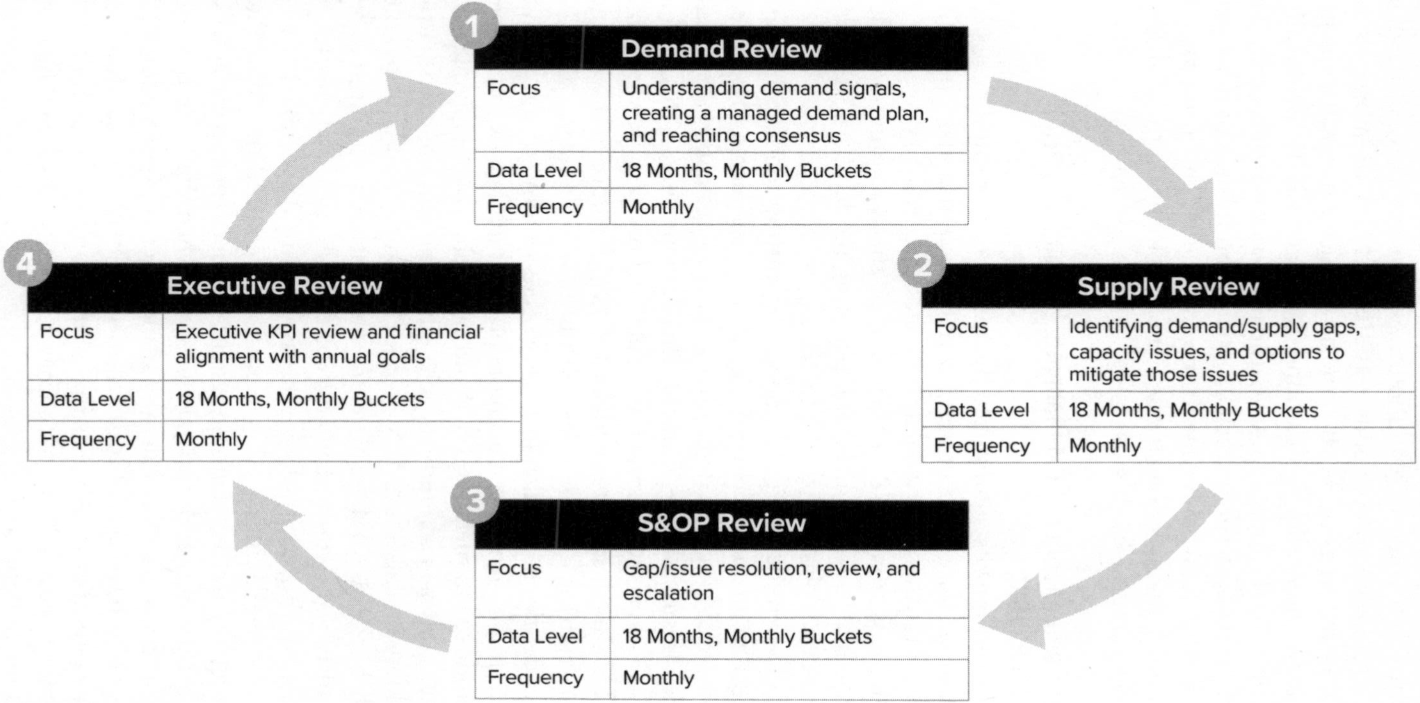

1 Demand Review

Focus	Understanding demand signals, creating a managed demand plan, and reaching consensus
Data Level	18 Months, Monthly Buckets
Frequency	Monthly

2 Supply Review

Focus	Identifying demand/supply gaps, capacity issues, and options to mitigate those issues
Data Level	18 Months, Monthly Buckets
Frequency	Monthly

3 S&OP Review

Focus	Gap/issue resolution, review, and escalation
Data Level	18 Months, Monthly Buckets
Frequency	Monthly

4 Executive Review

Focus	Executive KPI review and financial alignment with annual goals
Data Level	18 Months, Monthly Buckets
Frequency	Monthly

Source: Deloitte Press

perform risk/issue/gap resolution to achieve consensus of the demand and supply plan and the understanding of financial impacts of supply gap closure scenarios. Finally, in the executive review, the focus is to enable executive alignment around financial goals, KPIs, and aligning on where the business is headed. The IBP process builds on the S&OP by strengthening the financial participation in each of these steps by conducting financial reconciliation in parallel, providing more focus to product lifecycle management and augmenting the ability of the business to run what-if scenarios to achieve consensus.

Other Components of SCM Planning: Demand, Supply, and Scheduling

The evolution to synchronized planning is the natural next step in a continuous improvement journey that has traditionally been limited by data transparency, availability, and synchronicity over the years. These limitations have in turn shaped the way processes, metrics, governance, and organizational planning models have functioned in supply chain planning for a long time.

Let's consider a typical nonretail planning model. The planning process begins with demand planning, where demand planners use commercial inputs to determine what is the unconstrained demand needed to support the business. This demand plan is then compared to the planned, actual, and projected inventory targets, which consider the lead time it takes to produce and get inventory to those locations. These "netting" results in a distribution requirements plan (DRP), which defines how much inventory needs to move to the distribution nodes and by when, and a supply plan, which is how much needs to be produced to meet the DRP and by when. This supply plan is then broken down in a rough capacity plan (monthly buckets), a master production schedule (MPS) (weekly buckets), and a finite schedule (daily buckets). All these plans are interdependent and need to be synchronized—however, they are typically not, primarily because until now, planning technology and supporting data lacked the transparency, availability, and synchronicity required to support it. The existing logic in the planning systems assumes that activities will happen per the master data parameters, and when that's not the case, the planning system is unable to see and react to these changes. These limitations have slowly been diminishing over the past decade, with advances in demand forecasting, shaping and shifting, multi-echelon inventory optimization, and supply planning and scheduling synchronization, to name a few.

THE NEED FOR SYNCHRONIZED PLANNING

As the economy becomes more globalized and the world more digitized, there has been an increase in both the number and level of sophisticated consumers. Mobile devices have become powerful enablers of information that have made consumers nimble and able to put products against each other. The need to understand consumer taste as a function of geography, time, and context and then synchronize all aspects of supply to that demand pattern is paramount. Regardless of industry, consumer preferences and sentiments are increasingly shifting toward more personalized products and services. Moreover, most customers expect these goods and services to be delivered at a significantly faster pace and at a competitive price point. This has resulted in highly complicated SKU portfolios with longer tails and a shift to a "unit of one" construct. As SKU portfolios become more complex and customers' customization increases, enterprises must significantly improve their ability to sense demand and plan across multiple channels.

With the advancements in digital computing and data processing, enterprises are now able to begin the journey toward a synchronized planning state. In this state, companies can elevate their S&OP/IBP to a new level supporting the same objectives that have been at the core of this integrated planning process. Using techniques like artificial intelligence, machine learning, and robotic and cognitive process automation, enterprises can optimize outcomes at the most granular level, automate the decision workflow, and enable a real-time end-to-end ecosystem collaboration. Together with the use of a real-time digital replica of the supply chain, enterprises are also able to simulate scenarios across all dimensions (financial, physical, operational) and optimize their overall strategies.

In a synchronized planning state, the supply chains using machine learning can identify the patterns that create failure. This is turn provides the ability for the supply chain to self-correct and "self-heal." This is the true augmentation of the supply chain planning function.

FOUNDATIONAL CAPABILITIES OF SYNCHRONIZED PLANNING

The journey to synchronized planning will vary depending on the current state capability and desired state maturity that an organization aspires for. The move toward synchronized planning is a journey with increasingly gradual stages of sophistication.

In a synchronized planning state, there is a leap in thinking with the introduction of a single data model to enable end-to-end scenario modeling as well as artificial intelligence and other cognitive techniques that enable the adjustment of fixed parameters. This combination is truly powerful and can enable the supply chain planning function to aspire to be in a single state of synchronicity. To enable this state, several foundational elements must be in place.

Shift from Sequential to Concurrently Collaborative Environment

The traditional mindset in supply chain is linear planning around a weekly, monthly, or quarterly cadence. This primarily stems from the fact that historically decision making took time as information had to be gathered, reconciled, and compared and scenarios analyzed to achieve an optimal decision. The concept of concurrent planning involves shifting from that linear mindset to an iterative cadence where issues are solved in "near real time" as they appear. This has now become possible with the advancements in technology, data storage, and memory processing that exist today. In a concurrent planning scenario, a network planner continually monitors supply chain performance and collaborates across the extended supply chain network, allowing for near real-time adjustments to the supply chain plan to improve profitability. Concurrent planning leverages a common data model to achieve real-time or near real-time information exchange and closely integrates demand and supply planning functions to improve response times. Planners inform and synchronize strategic decisions across time horizons and quickly integrate into tactical and operational plans.

The concurrent planning model also challenges the traditional construct of siloed jobs—for example network planners who can look across the complete value chain instead of the traditional separate planners in demand, supply, materials, and so on. These network planners can perform cross-functional planning activities, hence reducing the need for supply chain functions to operate vertically in silos. This is a transformational concept with important implications to the traditional planning function talent model.

Model Synchronized Processes with a Real-Time Digital Replica and Artificial Intelligence

A real-time digital replica of the value chain is a virtual representation of the physical supply chain. This creates a virtual model of process steps across the enterprise using historical records and then applies predictive and prescriptive analytics to determine the impact of strategic or tactical changes. It offers the capability to replicate the physical world and model small and large changes to derive real-time bottom-up cost insights and gain predictive insights on the financial impact of decisions emulating the planning ecosystem. The implications for the supply chain to learn and self-improve are tremendous. By combining the supply network digital replica with machine learning and artificial intelligence, organizations can train the supply chain to try different ways to optimize itself, to learn from the real world and recommend improvements to the user. This foundational element completely changes the way we operate in a synchronized planning world.

The synchronized planning state is enabled by bots that replicate human actions and judgment by leveraging cognitive and machine learning technologies on top of existing current assets and applications. AI drives resource efficiencies due to automation and improves process effectiveness as it learns from many outcomes.

As an example, a large beverage company has created a digital value chain enabled by a cognitive control tower with seven visibility layers and an AI-enabled algorithm to prevent stock-outs. The digital value chain uses real-time information to simulate and learn from the physical value chain and help the planner make better decisions on what to do.

SUPPLY NETWORK DESIGN FOR DSN AND SYNCHRONIZED PLANNING

Traditionally, organizations updated their network strategies at major events or changes in their network. As the world becomes more dynamic and interconnected, the question is whether organizations need to increase not only the frequency but also the scope of their network design and optimization. In a synchronized planning state, the objective is to enable network rebalancing dynamically by enabling an always-on, always adapting network model that constantly senses and predicts what will happen with the network.

The first piece of this puzzle is the strategy. The way we set strategy today in supply chain doesn't really change in a synchronized planning state—what changes is the ability to modify that strategy real time. An example of this would be setting an inventory location with safety stock buffers based on historical deviations at a point in time. In a synchronized planning state, the objective is to use cognitive technologies and demand sensing to make recommendations and adjustments to the safety stocks as well as to dynamically rebalance the network including recommendations on storage and physical location.

END-TO-END PLANNING MODEL

Synchronized planning enables the management of the end-to-end supply chain as a single ecosystem. As seen on Figure 6.2, the extended supply chain includes internal functions along with the extended actors: customers, consumers, suppliers, and contract manufacturers. By taking a holistic approach to planning, organizations can unlock a new level of performance in the supply chain that is enabled by three building blocks: collaborative demand sensing, internal synchronization, and collaborative supply planning.

COLLABORATIVE DEMAND SENSING. The objective of this building block in the synchronized planning state is to establish a baseline demand for product or services using data science methods that "sense" various factors such as historical data, customer perceptions, and environmental factors. This baseline demand is augmented by correcting judgments that continuously learn from past planner decisions. Once a baseline demand level is built, AI can be applied to the data sets to learn, predict, and understand how to best model demand patterns.

INTERNAL SYNCHRONIZATION. In this building block, we enable the capability to integrate financial, strategic, and operational plans seamlessly, aligning all functions in the organization to the common goal that affects an organization's top and bottom line. This synchronization leverages the single data layer that underpins the synchronized planning model and constantly senses signals from all ecosystem players and drivers connected to it. In this cycle, humans and computers are operating to dynamically reroute and move product across the supply chain. Ultimately, the objective is to find the most economically optimum production and inventory levels through concurrent planning of all constrained resources: capacity planning, inventory positioning, and labor planning.

COLLABORATIVE SUPPLY PLANNING. In this building block, the objective is to integrate suppliers, contract manufacturers, and other entities that supply product to the company. If these entities are modeled

FIGURE 6.2 End-to-End Supply Chain Planning Model

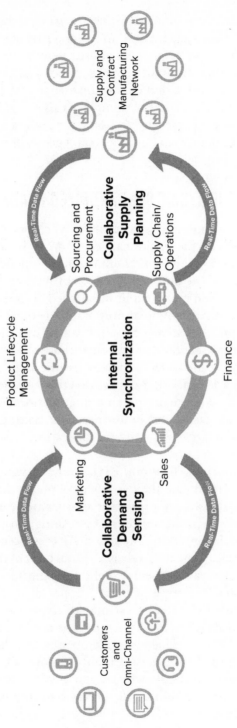

Source: Deloitte

as company-owned resources and information exchanges are set up properly, they effectively become an integral part of the synchronized planning cycle. This creates opportunities to link demand and supply, effectively enabling full visibility of supplier capacity and availability as well as the correlation of consumer signals to their aggregated effect on the supplier base. An example of this would be a global juice company using consumer insights on taste profiles to determine the optimal type of oranges to buy in a certain geography and time.

BENEFITS OF SYNCHRONIZED PLANNING

One of the most important benefits of the synchronized planning state is that it transforms the traditional S&OP cycle. Today, organizations plan their business outlook via multiple plans (financial, operational, sales, commercial) at different levels and functions thereby driving suboptimal decision making and misaligned objectives across stakeholders. In a synchronized planning state, the organization achieves the ability to integrate strategic goals, financial objectives, and tactical operational plans seamlessly and concurrently. This is accomplished by the near real-time collaboration across the value chain, enabling reduction in cycle times through information symmetry and latency alignment. The value chain can thus align performance plans cross-functionally for faster and better decision making and improved enterprise value, revenue growth, operating margin, and asset efficiency.

The other major benefit of the synchronized state is the ability to automatically coordinate the movement of goods through the value chain and make corrections as potential issues are detected. Critical to this is the ability to predict outcomes by creating and evaluating a variety of scenarios before taking any action. All these scenarios can be run in a digital replica that effectively is a virtual copy of the supply chain. Scenarios act as a way for users to replicate changes in business to find the most appropriate response across supply, demand, and product. After simulating these responses and evaluating the impact, scenarios can be graded against a scorecard to ensure the scenario aligns with a company's KPIs and objectives. Companies can then dynamically replan and assess the impacts of their decisions. Over time, supply chain managers can decide which decisions they want to automate based on known probabilities of success resulting in increased efficiency and accuracy.

The digital replica of the value chain combined with the use of machine learning and artificial intelligence provide a very powerful platform for the enterprise. This platform enables the near real-time financial analysis of changes to the plan and financial impact driven by controllable and uncontrollable factors. Additionally, it reduces product development cycle times by enabling the prediction of total delivered cost while SKUs are in development. More important, it enables the enterprise to determine total cost implications driven from SKU complexity expansion, raw material supply harmonization, and omni-channel growth.

Another advantage is the ability to understand what orders are associated to what supply, hence enabling the planners to determine which customer orders might be impacted by changes in supply availability. Additionally, this allows reporting of all component supplies required to fill a given demand or supply order. Take a scenario where a production line goes down—most line outages are unplanned events and represent an exception from the agreed-upon operating plan. Upon detecting this capacity loss, a planner or a computer (or both) can be alerted and can check inventory levels, determine impacts, and trigger a few remedial actions such as moving to another production line or facility, redeploying raw materials or components, or arranging for expedited freight to ensure supply is uninterrupted. Another key consideration when making decisions about how to replan in the event of an outage is that the planner may choose not to run a lower-margin commodity item on the alternate production line, using the capacity instead to fill demand for the higher-margin or more strategic items. Similarly, decisions might be made around strategic customer/item combinations when a product is in short supply or in allocation mode.

ENABLING THE SYNCHRONIZED PLANNING STATE

Figure 6.3 depicts the typical state of a global, multi-matrixed organization. Multiple inputs into the system exist that are consumed by different functions across the organization. These inputs are ingested, and processes and initiatives are in place to execute upon them creating signals with other parts of the enterprise. These patterns can be structured, unstructured, organized, or ad hoc, so the combined effect is a disorganized system full of noise. This noise manifests itself in terms of email traffic, phone calls, conversations, and many different activities that are usually non-value adding, leading to a loss of productivity.

FIGURE 6.3 Typical State Multi-Matrix Organization

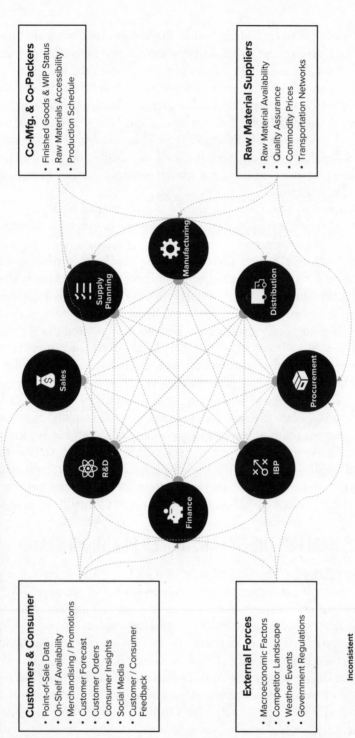

Co-Mfg. & Co-Packers
- Finished Goods & WIP Status
- Raw Materials Accessibility
- Production Schedule

Raw Material Suppliers
- Raw Material Availability
- Quality Assurance
- Commodity Prices
- Transportation Networks

Customers & Consumer
- Point-of-Sale Data
- On-Shelf Availability
- Merchandising / Promotions
- Customer Forecast
- Customer Orders
- Consumer Insights
- Social Media
- Customer / Consumer Feedback

External Forces
- Macroeconomic Factors
- Competitor Landscape
- Weather Events
- Government Regulations

Inconsistent
Information Flows

Source: Deloitte

Manufacturing

Supply Planning

Distribution

Sales

Procurement

R&D

IBP

Finance

Figure 6.4 (see next page) depicts the same entity in a synchronized planning state. In this state, signals are ingested and consumed by all actors that need them, but they are distributed in an organized way through the enterprise, triggering an effective and efficient set of interactions. This is possible via the combined effect of the following characteristics:

- **COGNITIVE DECISION SUPPORT LAYER.** A single and common cognitive digital data and decision support layer cuts across the end-to-end ecosystem connecting all the entities. Signals from all entities are ingested into this layer and are then shared across all entities based on predefined rules. The entities in the ecosystem can then interact and communicate, and all use the same version of the truth for planning and execution.

- **REAL-TIME RESPONSE TO DATA.** The ability to sense variation and signals from the ecosystem by using AI- and ML-enabled bots that can constantly sense and act on the variations. In some cases, these bots can interact with the master data in ERP and planning systems and make updates to the data based on observed patterns and events. This enables the supply chain to become "self-correcting" resulting in better execution.

- **AUTOMATED WORKFLOW.** Enabling an intelligent and automated workflow with a set of rules and ways of working that is continually being updated and directs humans to interact with each other. An example to demonstrate these characteristics would be the resolution of a potential demand/supply balance that can be corrected concurrently before it becomes a major issue.

- **CENTRALIZED "ENTERPRISE BRAIN."** A common "enterprise brain" that serves as the intelligence and insights center of the enterprise and houses a library of powerful algorithms to solve optimization problems across the value chain. What some companies are starting to realize is that you can use the same algorithms and math to solve both a demand and a supply problem. By having a central set of algorithms and math, organizations can apply analytics across the entire enterprise.

- **DIGITAL REPLICA.** A digital replica of the supply chain network that can be used to simulate any decision before committing it to the physical world. This is one of the most important aspects of a synchronized planning state and one that provides

FIGURE 6.4 Synchronized Planning State

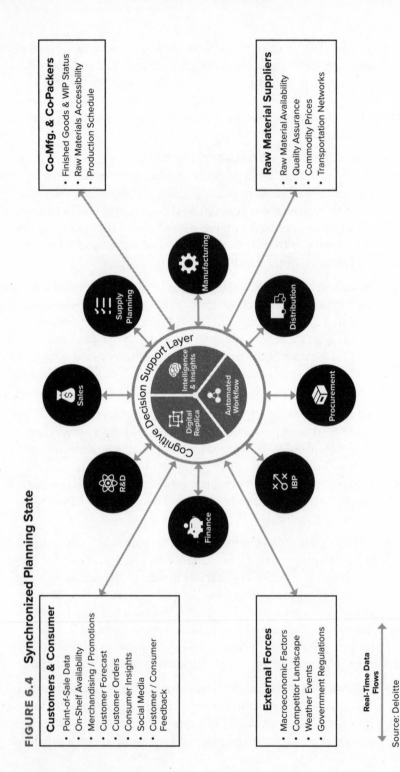

Co-Mfg. & Co-Packers
- Finished Goods & WIP Status
- Raw Materials Accessibility
- Production Schedule

Raw Material Suppliers
- Raw Material Availability
- Quality Assurance
- Commodity Prices
- Transportation Networks

Customers & Consumer
- Point-of-Sale Data
- On-Shelf Availability
- Merchandising / Promotions
- Customer Forecast
- Customer Orders
- Consumer Insights
- Social Media
- Customer / Consumer Feedback

External Forces
- Macroeconomic Factors
- Competitor Landscape
- Weather Events
- Government Regulations

Manufacturing

Supply Planning

Distribution

Sales

Procurement

R&D

IBP

Finance

Cognitive Decision Support Layer

Intelligence & Insights

Automated Workflow

Digital Replica

Real-Time Data Flows

Source: Deloitte

118

the most opportunity for disruption of the status quo. If we take the full enterprise and model it and we can understand impacts before any decision is made, then computer and analytics can be applied to any problem and tests can be run in the digital replica until the solution is perfected. Over time, the users can set certain decisions on automatic based on known probabilities of success.

SYNCHRONIZED PLANNING ORGANIZATIONAL CONSIDERATIONS

A move toward synchronized planning capabilities entails a shift in the responsibilities and required skill set of the planners—the required skills, tasks, and roles of those individuals—from a focus on one particular task to multitasking; from master of one task to jack of many tasks; from information gathering to root cause analysis and optimization; from a focus on individual functional KPIs to shared KPIs across the organization; and from reporting into the functional lead to a matrixed reporting. As with many smart technologies, many envision a day when AI and robots coexist with humans.

Supply chain planning has always been rooted in analytic insights and reaction. While the network planner of the future may need a different skill set than today, the core skills may not be fundamentally different. Roles will likely evolve to focus more on achieving strategic imperatives through analytical insights and proactive actions; routine and repetitive tasks may be taken over by robotic automation, cognitive analysis engines, or a combination of both. While technology contributes to advanced analytical processing and thinking in many supply chain planning functions, it will not replace any individual's essential human traits: communication, empathy, intuition, and the ability to contextualize, interpret, and question data. This could introduce new capabilities to the workforce as individuals offload repetitive tasks or become augmented with digital capabilities to handle complex tasks. Nevertheless, the humans and machines working closely together could require workers to learn new skills and new ways of operating.

Historically, planners used tools without understanding why the tools made a recommendation. They would rely on tribal knowledge and rules of thumb to make decisions. These decisions may have not been optimal; however, workers knew how they arrived at the decision. The potential gap for most companies is not that advanced algorithmic engines do not work; instead, it's a user adoption challenge of the new technologies and lack of understating on how the recommendations are generated. This inevitably creates challenges on embracing the so-called "black box" artificial intelligence—where the system not only makes recommendations but also executes most of the decisions. The planner's ability to understand why a specific recommendation was made becomes crucial.

Finally, a connected planning community offering end-to-end transparency empowers workers to collaborate with stakeholders throughout the supply network: suppliers, customers, and business partners in different channels and geographies.

Old vs. New Roles

In order to take full advantage of a synchronized planning state, organizations will also need to transform their workforce's roles, responsibilities, and mindsets focusing more on strategic initiatives.

Traditionally, companies have organized their teams into four primary roles within their demand and supply planning teams as described in Table 6.1, but these roles will change in a synchronized planning state, as shown in Table 6.2.

TABLE 6.1 Tradition roles of demand and supply planning teams

Demand Manager	Supply Manager	Master/ Transaction Data Lead	Logistics and Operations
• Demand planners • Forecast and modeling leads • Market research analyst	• Supply planners • Inventory planners • Category and allocation planners • Procurement analysts	• Business analysts • Master/trans-action data analysts	• Fulfillment planners • Production planners

TABLE 6.2 New roles in synchronized planning

Connected Planner	Data Lake Maintenance	Algorithm Maintenance	AI and ML
• Manages supply and demand	• Manages structured and unstruc-tured data to maintain data integrity	• Typically out-sourced or handled by SaaS providers	• Leads the development of the tool, over-all strategy, and data visualiza-tion tasks

Source: Deloitte

Technology Considerations

As companies assess the different technology platforms needed to support a journey to synchronized planning, here are some of the elements that need to be considered:

- **HEURISTIC VS. OPTIMIZATION PLANNING ENGINES.** The aim of optimization and heuristic solutions is the same—to provide the best possible solution for a given supply chain problem—but their outcomes are very different. Heuristics works well when the planner is looking for speed and a solution that is good enough, but not necessarily the best optimal solution that for example maximizes services at the lowest possible cost. Optimization is much more powerful but more complex to both understand, use, and interpret, and additionally it takes time and resources to build. Ultimately, the chosen method could be a combination of heuristics and optimization with a specific level of accuracy and "best overall solution" that an organization desires.

- **PRIORITIZED DEMAND AND SUPPLY PLANNING FUNCTIONAL REQUIREMENTS.** Some functional requirements are standard across vendors; however, others may require significant configuration, which may impact the implementation timeline. For some industries where the SKU portfolios are extensive and the supply network is complex and limited in capacity, solving for the supply complexities is paramount to overall speed and profit maximization. In other sectors, solving for demand complexity might be more important, and being able to address, analyze, and ingest a multitude of variables is paramount. For some industries both demand prioritization and supply complexity planning might be required. An organization should understand the complexity of these requirements for both demand and supply and then conduct a fit gap against solutions in the market versus the possibility of a customized in-house solution to address these requirements.

- **CLEARLY DEFINED AND ARTICULATED USE CASES.** Effective use cases are essential so vendors can prove their solution's capability to solve for company-specific business needs. Taking the necessary time to identify the desired state from a strategy and process standpoint and how a company needs to deliver value over time is essential. When an organization takes time to do this correctly, leaders can articulate extremely relevant use cases that truly tie to delivering value in the organization. These use cases can then be used to develop a dynamic transformative road map that enables value every reporting period, thereby keeping the momentum going with the organization's executive team.

Selecting the right technology (and possibly technology vendor) requires addressing some strategic points that can help narrow down the options to consider:

- Is the organization looking for an overlay solution to enhance end-to-end visibility with concurrent planning?

- Does the organization need to enhance functional excellence in specific demand, supply, and other advanced planning solution areas?

- Does the organization need to address "white spaces" in its planning capabilities through a micro-app strategy?

- Does the organization need to enhance its existing solutions with advanced analytics tools to address specific requirements?

- Does the organization want to augment its existing solutions with advanced analytics tools to address specific needs?

Addressing these questions can help a company both evaluate and assess the different needs for technology in the road map. There are multiple packages and solutions today that have natural strengths based on what their genesis was and can also be configured with relative ease. More important, the advances in computing and data processing as well as digital technologies have also enabled a democratization that can serve for companies to develop their own solutions. The days of multiyear developments are really in the past, and companies can now easily deliver value in quarter duration sprints. This greatly opens the possibility of options that exist from a technology enablement standpoint for companies transforming their planning capabilities.

SUMMARY

Synchronized planning is a destination that is already here. The ability of companies to target this state of maturity is very real from a process, people, technology, and data standpoint. The concept of augmenting human intelligence with computers is truly transformational and enables paradigms to be broken and new realities created. The key is having the stakeholder alignment necessary to drive the level of sophistication that is required. Ultimately, companies must determine what level of performance they want to achieve and when they want to achieve it. Organizations need to define an end state vision, take a thorough assessment of their current capabilities, and then assess what changes to their planning road map are required to achieve their destination in the timeline desired. Ultimately, organizations that understand where they want to go and take assertive investments to get there will be able to perform at a higher level while being synchronized—both internally and externally.

DIGITAL PRODUCT DEVELOPMENT

At the core of digital supply networks (DSNs) are always products and/or services that provide value to customers. With the advent of digital technologies in DSN, the way new products and/or services are developed and designed is changing as well. In this chapter we discuss how the digital transformation impacts the development of new products and services, with a special emphasis on the "digital" components of the new product and service development process itself. We will touch upon the opportunities of collaborative tools for the emerging digital design teams distributed around the globe, before introducing the concept of smart-connected products. The chapter concludes with an overview of the convergence of products and services to industrial product service systems and servitization driving companies in the direction of subscription and nonownership business models.

Only a few will object to the notion that the digital transformation has a tremendous impact on all aspects of how we do business in DSN. Digital product development is a new way of developing and managing products responsive to customer experience and transformed by smart real-time data, advanced technologies, and agile innovation.

Digital product development is interlinked with digital product lifecycle management (PLM), as the digital thread of data is the key enabler. The major transition in how we develop products and services in the world of DSN can be traced back to three interconnected elements: (1) collaborative tools enabling effective diverse and distributed design teams; (2) smart-connected products providing insights throughout the lifecycle; and (3) the convergence of products and associated services fueled by usage data and data analytics.

TRADITIONAL NEW PRODUCT DEVELOPMENT IN SCM

The new product design and development process is traditionally centered around the original equipment manufacturer (OEM) or leading organization in a supply chain setting. This process takes a significant amount of time, increasing the time to market. The reasons for the long lead time include the hierarchical collaboration and the disconnected nature of the process in these traditional supply chains. With time to market and the ability to rapidly understand and deliver on changing customer preferences becoming a critical capability for company and supply chains, this traditional product design and development process presents a liability.

The traditional approach is manifested in different design frameworks and organizational charts throughout various industries. A standard model that is prevalent in the supply chain space is the design chain operations reference model (DCOR). This model presents the design equivalent to the supply chain operations reference model (SCOR). The DCOR model depicts the design process in distinct process steps: plan design chain (P-DC); research (R); design (D); integrate (I); and amend (A). It has to be noted that the DCOR model's objective is not the design of a new product itself but rather the management of the design process across a collaborative supply chain. This has clear merits given the complexity of the task; however, the model's hierarchical structure is diametrical to the idea of adaptable, scalable, and agile DSN.

We argue that the future digitally transformed DSNs have different requirements, especially in terms of connectivity and time to market, that are not effectively facilitated by the traditional precut development process and models such as DCOR without critically assessing their suitability for the new DSN capabilities. Therefore, in the following section we present the new digital product development process with an emphasis on enabling technologies.

DIGITAL NEW PRODUCT AND SERVICES DEVELOPMENT PROCESS

When discussing digital product development in DSN, we are naturally inclined to think about the new product development (NPD) process. In recent years NPD includes services (NPSD) as well. Many different variations of the NPSD process are available, depicting four to eight different stages. Looking closer, however, most process models can be boiled down to three distinct phases: concept, design, and delivery (Figure 7.1). We will not discuss each granular aspect of the NPSD process in this chapter, but rather illustrate the impact of digital transformation on each stage to highlight the transformational changes across the board.

FIGURE 7.1 **Digital New Product (and Services) Development (NPSD)**

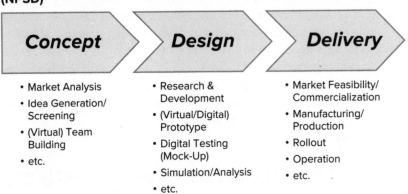

Concept
- Market Analysis
- Idea Generation/ Screening
- (Virtual) Team Building
- etc.

Design
- Research & Development
- (Virtual/Digital) Prototype
- Digital Testing (Mock-Up)
- Simulation/Analysis
- etc.

Delivery
- Market Feasibility/ Commercialization
- Manufacturing/ Production
- Rollout
- Operation
- etc.

CONCEPT. During the concept stage, we focus on understanding the market, market opportunity, stakeholders, and requirements. Furthermore, we look at how different concepts and ideas can be evaluated and ultimately selected, as well as team building and collaboration. All these aspects are impacted by digitalization and digital technologies. Access to large amounts of market and usage data fuels requirement elicitation, increases the accuracy and quality of requirements, and fosters a better understanding of the market and opportunity identification. Innovative concepts for product/service development and concept evaluation such as customer co-creation and living labs are only possible leveraging digital technologies on scale.

DESIGN. The design stage is more technical in nature and equally inclined to be disrupted by digital technologies. Data-driven automated design based on requirements and usage data, digital testing and simulation (mock-ups), digital/virtual prototyping, and complex data-driven and adaptive cost modeling are just some of the many aspects that change tremendously with the introduction of the IoT, AI, and social media, just to name a few. A side effect is the emphasis on the entrepreneurial mindset that applies to start-ups as well as traditional industries today.

DELIVERY. The final stage, delivery, includes all commercialization activities and also the production of products and delivery of services. With products and services more closely associated and bundled, the operation of the product becomes ever more important. NPSD stakeholders in the DSN have to adapt to the new reality and reflect the different requirements of truly satisfying customer needs versus the previous practice of handing over a product and forgetting about it. Access to data and drawing the right insights from it is crucial for these new business models to be sustainable. Digitally enabled concepts such as predictive maintenance are examples of necessary tools to make manufacturer-operated equipment a win-win for both the user and the manufacturer in the long run.

CAPABILITIES OF DIGITAL PRODUCT DEVELOPMENT IN DSN

The new digital product development process changes the way we connect to customers on a more individual basis and promises a significantly improved time to market. In addition to these advantages, there are eight distinct capabilities that are enabled by the digital transformation in DSNs. Figure 7.2 presents these eight crucial digital product development capabilities with a brief explanation. It has to be noted that these are partly case specific, and there are several others that emerge under certain circumstances. The selection in Figure 7.2 provides a mere overview of the most commonly accepted capabilities.

COLLABORATIVE TOOLS AND DIGITAL DESIGN TEAMS

Digital product development in DSN is a collaborative endeavor and in most cases involves various stakeholders that are distributed around the globe. This provides many upsides, including the ability to leverage different time zones so the development teams can work virtually 24/7, flexibility to include the best experts in the world, and inclusion of cultural insights, as well as cost benefits by leveraging low-wage locations. On the other side collaborative distributed teams add complexity that is difficult to manage, as well as potential for misunderstanding and conflict due to the lack of face-to-face interaction. Without effective digital tools such a collaboration is not possible.

FIGURE 7.2 The New Way of Working: Digital Product Development Capabilites

1 **Model-Based Product Definition**
Go beyond just 3D geometry of fit/form to modeling the context of the product, including:function, manufacturing, and performance

2 **Real-Time Collaboration**
Eliminate design hand-offs and reduce iterations by enabling the entire value chain to work together on a single, live instance of the latest product definition

3 **Rapid Design Optimization**
Design a better product in less time through rapid prototyping, virtual testing, and virtual/augmented reality evaluation of design iterations

4 **Design for Customer Experience**
Deliver a customer-focused product by leveraging sensing, virtual reality, and systems modeling to better capture, evaluate, and test requirements that deliver customer value

5 **Model-Based Manufacturing**
Prevent costly engineering churn and investment by simulating and validating manufacturing processes before the first units are produced

6 **Real-Time Product Intelligence**
Gather and process data from products "in the field" to gain insight on real-life operating environment and use cases for design feedback and proactive product improvement

7 **Design for Manufacturing Innovation**
Solve for the optimal/alternative geometry, materials, and production methods to improve product performance, reduce cost, and improve delivery times

8 **Connected Customer Experience**
Link physical products to their digital definition to deliver new services, predict support needs, and optimize current/future product performance

Source: Deloitte, 2017

On the *technical* side, the numerical chain and digital thread managed by comprehensive product lifecycle management (PLM) systems is the foundation for effective and efficient collaboration. PLM systems are available from various vendors such as Siemens Teamcenter, PTC Windchill, SAP PLM. PLM systems provide value to their users beyond the design phase itself. They include features for computer-aided manufacturing (CAM), computer-aided process planning (CAPP), and several more. The crucial distinction between a PLM system and traditional computer-aided design (CAD) solutions, however, is the fact that the former also includes tools for end-of-life (EOL) and middle-of-life (MOL) applications. For instance, the PLM system provides the basis for establishing an item-level digital twin of a physical product by creating a unique digital instance fed in real time with usage data of a particular system in operations.

Diminishing time-to-market is another factor where digital tools play a key role in the design process. Virtual testing and digital mockups reduce the need for physical prototypes. Hence, they reduce the amount of time needed to manufacture the physical prototypes and thus streamline the whole creation process significantly. The digital evaluation, verification, and test protocols are so sophisticated today that even highly controlled industries that require intensive certifications employ them on a large scale. On the other hand, comprehensive PLM solutions provide the necessary remote collaboration capabilities including version control and other support features enabling large virtual teams to effectively work together on complex projects.

On the *human* (communication) side, digital design teams that work collaboratively across distributed locations need to communicate effectively with each other. Digital technologies are the cornerstone that provides this communication on scale. Cloud platforms that enable exchange of data and collaborative creation of documents and video conferencing tools connecting virtually anybody in real time are only one aspect of this process. Virtual and augmented reality (VR/AR) as well as holograms are technologies that are currently introduced to make collaborative distance work even more effective. The ability to interact not only with fellow product/service designers but also with potential customers and focus groups in a virtual environment has huge potential to revolutionize the digital product development process further. These technologies make the theoretical concept of customer co-creation all of a sudden feasible and a valuable tool to create customized or even personalized products and services at scale.

DIGITAL SMART-CONNECTED PRODUCTS

Smart-connected products are physical products that have the ability to "sense" and interact with their environment and communicate wirelessly with other systems (including other smart-connected products).

Smart-Connected Products Terminology

Smart-connected products have recently gained significant attention with the rise of Industry 4.0 and smart manufacturing; however, the theoretical basic concept dates back to the turn of the century. Back then the term "intelligent product" was more common, yet the definition aligns with today's understanding almost 100 percent as "a physical and information based representation of an item . . . which possesses a unique identification, is capable of communicating effectively with its environment, can retain or store data about itself, deploys a language to display its features, production requirements, etc. and is capable of participating in or making decisions relevant to its own destiny."[1]

In DSN, smart-connected products lead to a new level of customer relations and innovative services. This development is expected to continue to grow and presents manufacturers with an opportunity to be a differentiator as well as a key factor to achieve sustained competitive advantage on the marketplace of the future. Smart-connected products enable manufacturers to continuously engage with their customers (users of their products) and gather valuable intelligence regarding the way their products are used in real life, differences in individual customers' behavior, and potential for value-adding services.

Dimensions, Challenges, and Barriers

Smart-connected products can be classified following certain dimensions. An established approach by Wong et al. distinguishes two levels of intelligence.[2] Level 1 describes an information-oriented smart-connected product that possesses a unique identification, is capable of communicating effectively with its environment, and can retain or store data about itself. This is basically the bare minimum to qualify as a smart-connected product. Level 2 builds on top of that and is more decision oriented. This level is characterized by deployment of a language to display features and capability to participate in decisions relevant for its own destiny.

Another classification model for smart-connected products by Meyer et al. distinguishes three dimensions: the level of intelligence, location of intelligence, and aggregation level of intelligence.[3] The level of intelligence can be split into three levels: information handling, problem notification, and decision making. The dimension location of intelligence distinguishes where the processing ability is located— on the object (product) itself or provided through the network (cloud/ edge). The last dimension, aggregation level of intelligence, distinguishes whether the sensing, data storage, and processing ability is available on the intelligent item itself or on an intelligent container. In most cases, smart-connected products during their middle-of-life or usage phase have their intelligence aggregated on the item itself— and only in a few cases on the container, such as a monitored container for a heart transplant. During the beginning-of-life (BOL) phase, on the other hand, the aggregation level of intelligence on the container is much more common as the product is still physically manipulated (i.e., manufactured), which may prevent the sensor system on the item from functioning properly.

We see a rapid increase of smart-connected products in recent years. However, there are still several open questions to be answered as well as certain barriers and challenges to be overcome. On the technical side, the connectivity and energy provision issues are still a challenge. In Table 7.1, we depict different barriers and challenges when it comes to the widespread adoption of smart-connected products. Challenges are issues that present difficulties within a company DSN, or technologies that need to be addressed to be successful, for example, complexity of a machine learning algorithm. Barriers, on the other hand, while they can be overcome, are connected to factors outside of the stakeholders' control, such as government policies. In the end, both challenges and barriers need to be carefully assessed for the unique circumstances of the digital transformation initiative. The data presented in Table 7.1 stems from a recent study with experts in the field.[4]

In the following section, we will touch upon digital enabling technologies that are essential for the creation of smart-connected products.

Digital Enabling Technologies

Many new digital technologies are introduced into the marketplace. Some are directly customer facing, such as social media platforms; others are more on the back end, such as new manufacturing technologies. New advanced manufacturing technologies such as additive manufacturing (AM) are digital in nature—a purely digital technology. Not

TABLE 7.1   Challenges and barriers of (pro-)active smart-connected products

Barrier	Challenge
Privacy concerns	Identification of clear benefits
IT security	Need for fundamental change
Government	Ownership of data
Laws for ownership of data	Underdeveloped key technologies
Lack of sharing behavior	Complexity of algorithms
High costs and fear for customer acceptance	Decision when product should be active
Fixed perception of a product	Designing the network so that information is consistent and reliable
Companies investing in "wrong technologies"	Information availability for individual stakeholders
	Heterogeneous systems with intelligent and nonintelligent products

Source: Wuest et al., 2018

only do they provide the designer with previously unheard-of freedom of design but also an unpreceded flexibility in terms of variants that can be produced economically. In essence, AM enables the manufacturing of personalized products ("batch-size 1") at a price point close to mass-produced large batch sizes.

The design freedom and flexibility paired with the ability to collect and analyze large amounts of user-specific usage data (big data) via smart-connected products is a powerful tool to develop and design products that fulfil the customer needs and requirements at a level that was not possible prior to the introduction of these digital technologies.[5]

In addition to the new level of personalization, digital technologies such as AM can create value for DSN on multiple dimensions. Taking, for example, the GE CT-7 mid-frame (Figure 7.3) through a complete redesign that fully utilized AM not only led to a significantly better product and product performance, but also reduced the previous assembly comprising roughly 300 individual parts and seven subassemblies to only one part/assembly. This has tremendous implications on the DSN in terms of complexity of materials management, stock levels, supply tiers, maintenance, and several more. Given the novelty of these digital technologies, we are only scratching the surface of capitalizing on their full potential.

FIGURE 7.3   GE CT-7 Engine Mid-Frame Redesign for AM

Original Mid-Frame Design
- ~300 parts
- 7 assemblies

Redesigned Mid-Frame Super Structure
- 1 part
- 1 assembly
- >10 lbm weight reduction

Source: GE Aviation

A second key technology enabler that will drive the digital product development of smart-connected products are *integrated sensor systems*. Sensing and communication are essential components of the IoT and also the basis for big data analytics and AI. Advances in sensor technologies allow us to utilize digital technology not only in the way we design and develop products but also in how the products are actually used and how we interact with them in our daily lives. AM for instance provides the capability to directly print electronics in the structure of a part, and 5G promises constant, reliable, and fast connectivity everywhere. Furthermore, advances in sensing materials will soon enable products to sense in a holistic way never seen before without the current limitations imposed by battery life and allocated space.[6] Closing the loop, the rapid increase in data stemming from more and more sensorized and connected products (smart products) provides more input to the digital design and development process.

Another effect of smart-connected products is the ability of manufacturers and other stakeholders to continuously monitor and manage their products while they are being actively used by their users. This enables a wealth of new opportunity in terms of new data-driven services, product-service bundles, and new business model innovations—many of which we will discuss in the next section of this chapter.

INDUSTRIAL PRODUCT SERVICE SYSTEMS AND SERVITIZATION

We already mentioned services throughout this chapter on digital product development multiple times. We argue that the new digital product development process in DSN cannot be seen separately from services. Digital technologies and embedded sensors demand the provision of advanced services, or services are already an integral part of the product itself. In this section, we will briefly distinguish what a digital product and a digital service is before arguing that the difference between them is becoming more and more blurry with the maturing of DSN and digital technologies. Last we will highlight the impact of this development on the business itself and the business models of stakeholders throughout the DSN.

Digital Products and Digital Services

Traditionally there was a clear distinction between products and services. Products had a physical presence and could be produced to stock—in essence the creation and consumption was separated. Cars, for example, including Ford's famous Model T, were products that were build, shipped to dealerships, and then stored until buyers decided to buy them. Traditional services, on the other side, are consumed while being created. A barber providing the service of a haircut is a prime example. The haircut cannot be created and stored until the customer decides to buy it. It has to be performed at the time of creation, with both the provider and customer involved.

Fast-forwarding to today, this traditional differentiation does not apply any longer. Cars, for example, are highly customized, and the physical product, the car, is embedded in various services. For example, when buying a new Mercedes the configurator allows for more than 1 trillion different variants—including customized colors for exterior paint and leather. In this case, it is impossible to build customized or personalized cars on stock. On the other side, services changed tremendously with the introduction of the Internet, software, and digital technologies. While an app on the app store is not a physical product, it may be said to be created before its consumption. However, it is characterized by a very different level of scalability from physical products. Any additional digital copy of a software service (aka program or application/"app") does not diminish quality nor add considerable cost for production. In this new environment it becomes increasingly difficult to classify sharply between sole products and services.

Product Service Systems

Product service systems (PSS) were first introduced in 1999 as "system of products, services, networks of players and supporting infrastructure that continuously strives to be competitive, satisfy customer needs and have a lower environmental impact than traditional business models."[7] Alternative terms describing in essence the same concept include "extended products," " product service bundles," " hybrid services," "integrated services," and in some cases "smart services." In the industrial B2B space, PSS are regularly referred to as industrial product service systems (IPSS).

Two more recent definitions showcase the evolution of PSS toward a more customer needs and value centric perspective:

[PSS are a] mix of tangible products and intangible services designed and combined so that they jointly are capable of *fulfilling final customer needs*.[8]

A PSS is an integrated product and service offering that delivers *value in use*. A PSS offers the opportunity to decouple economic success from material consumption and hence reduce the environmental impact of economic activity. The PSS logic is premised on utilizing the knowledge of the designer-manufacturer to both increase value as an output and decrease material and other costs as an input to a system.[9]

PSS are often perceived in a sustainability context—including all three dimensions: social, economic, and environmental. The PSS notion formulates a value proposition for manufactures to retain product ownership and responsibility for the product's (comprehensive or partial) functionality, operation, maintenance, upgrade, and disposal. This transfer of the responsibility to the manufacturer creates an incentive to develop and design the best possible products for the use case. This includes different dimensions including performance/operation (less energy consumption), functionality, maintenance (less downtime). A main promise of PSS is to create a win-win for provider and user as a more resource-efficient and effective solution with less environmental impact compared to conventional product-oriented solutions.[10] On the other hand, a solution composed of physical products and related services may be harder to replicate for a competitor, compared to solely product and process-based manufacturing.[11] Table 7.2 presents selected benefits and challenges of PSS in DSN.

TABLE 7.2 Benefits and challenges of PSS in DSN

Benefits	Challenges
Continuous revenue stream throughout lifecycle	Difficult to manage complexity
Better insight in how products/services are used in reality	Ecosystem required for comprehensive PSS (such as DSN)
Closer relationship with user/customer	Risk remains with provider (e.g., in a "power by the hour" scenario)
Deep product/service knowledge utilized beyond design/manufacturing	Technology not available (at competitive price)
Decoupling of material consumption from economic success (sustainability)	Users mindset (especially B2C) still focused on "ownership"
Personalization and customization	Design and development complexity increases significantly (e.g., reflection of lifecycle perspective, interfaces, technology integration)
Opportunity to lock in customer/lock out competition (by providing superior value)	Revenue sharing models among stakeholders providing PSS

PSS are always complex cyber-physical systems that require a variety of capabilities and resources that can only be provided by multiple stakeholders working closely together. It can be safely said that offering an effectively and efficiently sustainable PSS on the marketplace requires a DSN. The digital technologies are the lifeblood connecting the required capabilities through data, communication, and analytics.

Servitization and Nonownership Business Models

Servitization is an older concept, introduced by Vandermerwe and Rada in 1988,[12] that describes the phenomenon of manufacturing firms developing a value proposition by incorporating additional services[13] in order to attain a competitive edge in the market.[14] The previously discussed PSS can be understood as a special case of servitization.

The major difference of the two concepts is that servitization is mainly focused on the economic perspective. Servitization focuses on the economic opportunities of PSS for DSN stakeholders and how that can be translated in business model innovation. We can all agree that the business models need to evolve together with the advances of digital technologies to be successful on the global marketplace. Disruptive new PSS business models such as Uber or Airbnb established a new "gold rush" of scalable, platform-based PSS as part of the shareconomy.

For DSN, a focus is on identifying the most valuable business model and vehicle of providing value to their customer base. Popular options are nonownership business models such as pay-per- use and pay-per-outcome. Both describe the transition toward the provision of advanced services, yet with a major difference when it comes to risk involved and digital technologies required. There is no simple method to establish which business model variation should be adopted. The decision is a very individual one that is industry, customer base, and capability specific. And the result will have a major impact on the future business success of the DSN.

EXAMPLES OF DIGITAL PRODUCT DEVELOPMENT

In this final section of the chapter we will briefly look at two examples of products stemming from digital product development in DSN: personalized footwear and cyber-physical jet engines. Both products are available from different manufacturers and combine different technologies we discussed previously.

Footwear

Footwear is a prime example of digital product development in the consumer market (B2C) that combines several aspects: data-driven design, personalization, servitization, and advanced manufacturing technologies. Formal, high-end footwear is traditionally personalized when we look at handmade leather dress shoes. This traditional design and manufacturing process is almost the complete opposite of digital product development. It is characterized by artisan, high-priced, and low-tech manual labor. However, when we take a look at high-end sports shoes, the demand is similar: personalized products that are design based on unique requirements utilizing digital and advanced manufacturing technologies.

In this space, we can now observe new products, or better product service systems, entering the market where the whole design process is data-driven, highly automated, and based on a digital thread. In a nutshell, the customer's feet are digitally measured and analyzed using a dedicated sensor system, and then a personalized design is derived providing a unique shoe for the requirements of that one customer. Additionally, optical and design personalization (color, features, etc.) is enabled through a web interface for further customization. These one-of-a-kind shoes cannot be manufactured using traditional methods as the economies of scale cannot be achieved. Therefore, highly flexible advanced manufacturing technologies are applied to create the physical instance of the digital design—in this case additive manufacturing, a purely digital technology in itself. This enables the provision of a high-quality personalized product in a reasonable time frame at comparably low cost for a mass market.

Today, most available variations of personalized footwear do not include sensor systems and electronics to collect data throughout the life of the product. However, the next evolution of these products is envisioned to expand the data collected and analyzed to create the personalized experience from today's one-time measurements to a continuous stream of data from real measurements in everyday use situations. This will further improve the performance and uniqueness of the product—and create a positive lock-in for the customers/users as they profit from the long-term learning their footwear provider gathers over time to provide the best product.[15]

Jet Engines

Let's switch gears for our second example—jet engines. Modern jet engines are extremely complex systems that are packed with sensors and connected at all times, producing large amounts of data (big data). Jet engines are a prime example of servitization and product service systems. All major providers are switching toward a servitized business model, in essence not selling their systems anymore but providing "thrust" or "power by the hour." To sustainably enable such a transition, access to high-quality data at all times is crucial. The system provider is responsible for maintenance, uptime, and performance, as well as safety. Based on the smart-connected jet engine and its virtual counterpart, its digital twin, the manufacturer can predict future maintenance needs and performance improvements lowering the fuel consumption in various conditions. The access to thousands of active systems provides a large database that enables data-driven design and operation. On the digital product development (design) side, the data provides insights into possible design improvements and more specific requirements for next generation design. While on the operations side, the real-time data and its analysis across different systems enables advanced learning models that allow optimization of engine parameters for different situations (takeoff, cruise, high temp, low pressure, etc.) for different airplane times using the same engine, optimizing the performance, fuel economy, and so on.

SUMMARY

The digital product development process becomes faster, more con-nected, and more customer-centric in light of the digital transformation of DSN. While traditionally, the NDP process was managed (often centrally by the OEM), the new digital product development process needs to be technology-driven, scalable, and truly collaborative to take advantage of the real-time access to data to facilitate personalized design, new business models, and rapid time to market. Existing NPD models such as the DCOR model need to be critically assessed and adapted if possible (or alterna-tively replaced) to break with the hierarchical structure.

INTELLIGENT SUPPLY

Procurement functions in the digital age have matured to strategic importance, a notable improvement from their origins as a transactional support role. In this chapter, we will introduce the concepts of procurement as part of legacy supply chain management (SCM) and its transformation to intelligent supply in the digital supply network (DSN). We will discuss the capabilities, their associated technologies, and how intelligent supply positively impacts customer service, operational efficiency, revenue, cost, and user experience.

PROCUREMENT CONCEPTS BEFORE THE DIGITAL ERA

Purchasing as a business function has existed since the evolution of civilized society; almost every business, irrespective of size or type, must source materials from other entities. The Industrial Revolution began to streamline this with the creation of an ecosystem of organizations that formed a manufacturing network. The formalization of SCM concepts crystalized this process by making "source" an essential part.

The common terms for the processes related to sourcing are purchasing, procurement, and sourcing. Purchasing commonly refers to business transactions that procure materials and pay for them. Sourcing refers to more strategic activities of collaborating with the suppliers to find the right materials that support business goals. Procurement is the combined activities of purchasing and sourcing. The end-to-end activities are also classified as *procure to pay (P2P)*. The terms "source to pay (S2P)" and "source to settle (S2S)" are also used interchangeably with P2P.

Prior to the 1980s, purchasing was entirely transactional, and its main objective was to replenish products and services needed by the business at the lowest cost. Purchasing was disconnected from finance and manufacturing, which caused delays and production losses. From 1980 to 2000, enterprise resource planning (ERP) maturity and adoption allowed for an integrated transactional system, one that encompassed procurement, finance, and production. During this time, connections were made between cost-saving efforts of the purchasing team and profits due to savings on the bottom line of the organization's income statement. Purchasing suddenly demonstrated its business value.

Growing trade and globalization enhanced procurement activities and their business impact. As the world approached the twenty-first century, strategic sourcing became an essential part of the procurement function, though the goal remained cost minimization and risk optimization. In the early 2000s, with the rise of the Internet, procurement matured to "e-procurement" and terms like "eRFX" (eRFX is the term used for eRFI, eRFP, eRFQ, etc.), "eCatalogue," and "eAuction" blossomed. The "e" signifies electronic capabilities rather than manual. The digitization of procurement data began in early 2000, and many organizations are still on this journey.

Procurement activity begins with the decision to "produce" or "purchase." If the decision is to produce, the next step is to review the components required for production and ask the same question for each of them: produce or purchase. If the decision is to purchase, the next step is to follow the sourcing activities of identifying a supplier, negotiating a contract, releasing the purchase order and scheduling agreement, receiving the material, and honoring the payment. The sourcing process involves supplier management at different levels, ranging from a purely transactional relationship to partnership development. The strategic value of a supplier relationship is related to the vital importance of the procured goods. Figure 8.1 shows the categorization of the suppliers as tactical, leverage, critical, and strategic, while considering the risk and value of the relationship. As part of procurement there is a need to manage suppliers at different levels depending on their importance and complexity, enabling transactions that reflect the nature of each supplier relationship. One way supplier performance is monitored is through analyzing the supply quantity and date expected by the supply contract and represented by the performance parameter OTIF (on time in full).

FIGURE 8.1 **Supplier Categorization Based on the Risk and Value of the Procured Products and Services**

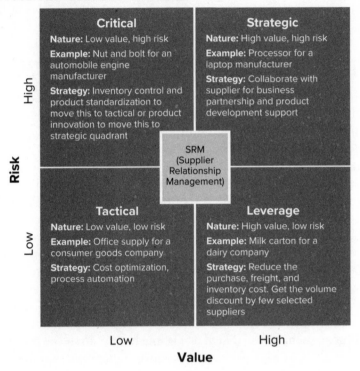

The supplier continuum can move from purchase order–based transactional relations to supply agreements, then to long-term contracts. As the supplier's strategic impact increases, the contract can evolve into an alliance, one that balances the value and risk of the relationship. For products or services that are identified as the highest strategic value for the business, analysts would recommend owning through acquisition or backward integration to make this in-house produced item.

In summary, prior to the digital era procurement activities were considered essential for business support and cost optimization, but have not been central to the organization's strategy. Even strategic sourcing in its traditional form is aimed at exploiting suppliers for cost minimization and risk mitigation. Innovation activities have remained confined to the boundaries of the organization, with minimal supplier involvement.

In the digital era, as the supply chain transforms toward the digital supply network, intelligent supply refers to much more than the digitization of the existing procurement functions. Let's delve into the details of intelligent supply as an essential part of the DSN.

INTELLIGENT SUPPLY: PROCUREMENT IN THE DIGITAL AGE

Intelligent supply refers to the next generation of the procurement function (purchasing and sourcing) with the benefits of value maximization, cost optimization, risk minimization, and business automation, harnessing the value of data, technologies, and transformed procurement processes. Traditional sourcing practices rely on a multitude of assumptions and are prone to unpredictability in both supplier performance and market conditions. Inefficiencies can occur at all levels of the supply chain. Intelligent supply overcomes these inefficiencies by enabling organizations to secure capacity with world-class suppliers at predictable costs; collaborate with strategic suppliers to accelerate innovation; transform the experience of internal customers through automated requisitions, contract management, and touchless invoicing; and monitor supply risks in real time to proactively optimize end-to-end operations.

Procurement in the digital age is much more than the traditional goals of OTIF order performance while squeezing supplier costs. Intelligent supply is the shift from administrative purchasing tasks to strategic, value-generating sourcing activities. Figure 8.2 represents the transformation of procurement business functions through intelligent supply. Data and technology transform strategic sourcing to predictive strategic sourcing; procurement transactions become procure-to-pay automation; a large innovation ecosystem exists instead of a confined innovation effort; a cost-focused approach becomes a lifecycle value with a total cost approach; and a damage control–based supplier management model becomes proactive supplier management aimed at optimizing operations.

Viewing suppliers as strategic partners is changing the way supplier contracts are written and managed. Traditional contracts were focused on hedging risks. Now they are moving toward the relational contract by treating the supplier as an essential part of the network. Trust becomes the basis of the supplier relationship instead of fear. This is facilitated by the transparency of intelligent supply, end-to-end integration in the digital supply network. One major enabler is machine learning.

FIGURE 8.2 **Transformation of Procurement Business Activities Through Intelligent Supply**

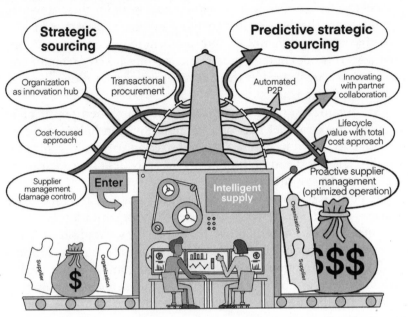

Machine learning algorithms use data from the ERP system, external systems, past orders, and invoices, along with real-time market data to predict potential failures and identify value opportunities. This system instantly suggests a supplier for a new product and manages the product flow for maximum value with existing suppliers. Alternate suppliers are identified in advance to mitigate supply shortages or quality issue predictions. This technology is used to generate the spend cube and supplier value analysis automatically by processing the data. A spend cube is the multidimensional cube of procurement costs in relation to supplier, product group, and purchase variant. This is an input to category management strategy formulation and execution. The advent of intelligent supply has eased supplier relationship management analytics and has engendered predictability in the relationship.

Transactional procurement activities like purchase order creation, shipment notification, material receival, invoice creation, invoice matching, and payment processing have been manually intensive events, consuming a significant amount of procurement professionals' time. The convergence of multiple technologies in this area, including auto purchase order generation, material tracking, autonomous material movement, material receipt, and automated invoicing and payment settlement have eliminated manual work for these activities. Organizations that have started enabling automated procurement processes have reported significant improvement in process efficiency and accuracy. This frees human procurement professionals to handle special cases that are flagged by the system, often related to compliance or service agreement issues.

An organization's ecosystem, with the combined power of its suppliers and customer network, is the innovation hub in the digital world, as shown in Figure 8.2. In the recent past, an organization was the center of the innovation, with the activities limited within its boundaries. Organizations in the digital era are creating an ecosystem of intelligent supply where a big amount of value add and innovation activities happen outside the boundaries of the organization.

Total cost of ownership is not a new term for the traditional sourcing process as part of SCM. It has been widely accepted to consider total cost with the impact of service reliability and product quality while selecting a supplier. The change with intelligent supply is to consider the lifetime value along with the total cost of ownership, as represented in Figure 8.2.

Supplier management, as the strategic part of the traditional SCM process, focuses on risk minimization, risk mitigation, and risk transfer while transacting with suppliers. This is based on the goal of damage control while protecting the firm's interest. In intelligent supply, organizations seek an end-to-end optimized operation through proactive supplier management. Through digital data and technology, risk monitoring can happen in real time. Seamless information integration minimizes the risk of the entire network.

INTELLIGENT SUPPLY CAPABILITIES

Intelligent supply seamlessly integrates the strategic, operational, and tactical source-to-pay activities through the capabilities displayed in Figure 8.3. The capabilities of intelligent supply are category management, supplier network collaboration, supplier analytics, smart sourcing execution, and intelligent contract.

Smart Sourcing Execution

By nature, traditional sourcing execution is a laborious, time-intensive, and error-prone manual process. It is typical for even leading

FIGURE 8.3 **Intelligent Supply Capabilities**

Supplier
analytics

Supplier network
collaboration

Smart sourcing
execution

Category
management

**Intelligent
Supply
Capabilities**

Intelligent
contract

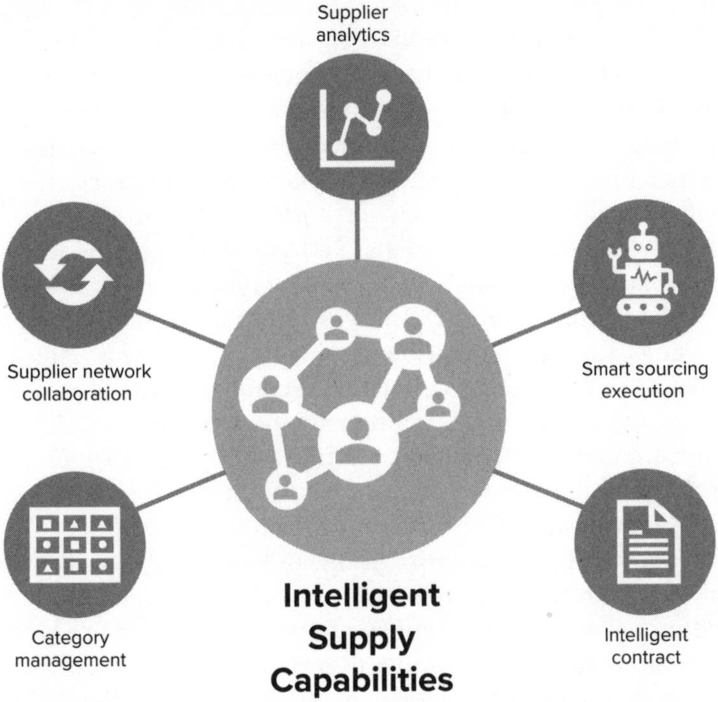

organizations to have a big team performing detailed manual transactions involving order release, quantity confirmation, material delivery notification, price matching, invoice matching, payment clearance, and settlement. Different ERP systems usually do not talk to each other, and each has different document formats, further complicating this process. A massive level of efficiency is lost here, when one calculates how much time is consumed in transactional activities by the strategic sourcing team.

With the advent of intelligent supply, most of the transactions can be automated, resulting in an immense gain in efficiency, higher accuracy, and a more motivated workforce engaged in the value-adding activities. This extends to the supplier, who can be seamlessly connected with the organization's network, gaining access to demand forecast visibility and real-time inventory. Based on the demand signal, an automated purchase order is released by the organization, the supplier's system reads this order, a warehouse order is created referring to the date and the quantity of the purchase order; then a shipment order is created automatically that is used for the transportation and sending shipment notification to the organization along with the invoice. Finally, the material is received by the organization's warehouse; the supply is matched against the requirement; and the invoice is paid automatically as per the payment term. With intelligent supply, this entire set of activities can be performed automatically. Weeks spent on order matching, invoice matching, manual payment processing, and settlement can become activities of the past.

Intelligent supply incorporates systems that accommodate multiple formats and channels to receive invoices, and systematically convert purchasing orders (POs) to invoices for touchless transaction processing. These systems use numerous electronic invoicing technologies to process all invoice types. Techniques such as automated two-way and three-way matching and streamlined exception resolution minimize invoice processing time and enhance supply chain financing and dynamic discounting capabilities. Only outlier cases flagged by the system need human attention.

For new supplier identification and onboarding, intelligent supply digitizes sourcing processes for quick screening and setup, including self-service registration for suppliers, competitive bidding, contract compliance, and online negotiations. It provides real-time ability to assess a supplier quote against decision criteria, including comparing it with cost analytics and commodity index, to select the best supplier. Intelligent supply can also leverage cognitive analytical tools to identify a best-case scenario for the award of a contract and generate insights for price negotiations, ensuring savings in time and resources. Rate validation bid analysis and compliance could be performed through software suites with artificial intelligence and robotic process automation. Once onboard, automatic demand sensing and quotes of new products/services can be enabled to add value and efficiency in the identification of the execution process.

For an end-to-end automation with strategic sourcing, a smart contract enabled with blockchain is also getting popular. It automatically executes the transactions against the predefined rules of the contract, as coded in the blockchain. Transactions like delivery, quality checking, payment, and settlement happen through smart contract rule without the necessity of a centralized authority like a bank.

Intelligent supply with connected and automated processes streamlines compliance through real-time monitoring and control.

Compliance rules in the system generate the alerts for review as soon as the system senses any noncompliant activity. Machine learning algorithms can be used to predict a noncompliance before it happens to allow preventive measures to take place.

In essence, smart sourcing execution automates the supplier selection-to-sourcing execution transactions in a transparent, connected, compliant environment.

Intelligent Contract Management

A contract is a binding agreement between the organization and its supplier. The contracts are written to detail the terms of supply, quality, and payment while hedging the risks of the relationship. The sourcing transactions like order lead time, quality parameter, payment terms, and so on are guided by the contract rules. In traditional supply chain management, substantial manual effort is involved in writing contracts, negotiating terms, and monitoring performance execution against the contracts.

Intelligent supply promotes proactive contract management by using digital tools to complete the contract and then manage it. The contract lifecycle and activities are facilitated through customized workflows. The connected, always-on system monitors the performance. With any detected deviation, an alert is generated, triggering action. Key performance indicators (KPIs) are continuously monitored in real time and are compared against the contract terms. The machine learning algorithm, along with sensors on the materials or assets in a digitally connected network, are used to predict a violation or early action.

Most traditional procurement contracts are written to minimize the risk of the involved parties. In the DSN environment, end-to-end transparency and connected data systems foster trust to build a collaborative contract in which the terms are guided by the shared vision of mutual benefits, trust, and fairness. "Formal Relational Contract" as introduced by Frydlinger et al. is recommended for understanding strategic supplier relationship management.[1] The digital technologies support contract management built on a foundation of trust and are shaped by a shared vision and six universal guiding principles: reciprocity, autonomy, honesty, loyalty, equity, and integrity. Reciprocity aims for the terms and decisions for mutual benefit; autonomy harnesses the freedom to make a decision based on value addition; honesty and loyalty are about the intention to do the right thing for the mutual long-term benefit instead of short-term risk hedging; equity is about being fair with the other party's business; and integrity is the alignment of agreement, intention, and action.

Higher automation of work activities can be achieved through a "smart contract" coded on the blockchain algorithm. Both traditional and digital contracts require a centralized institution like a bank to honor the transactions as per the terms of the contract. A smart contract decentralizes and automates the transactions based on the rules coded in the blockchain-enabled contract. Hence, as soon as an activity is confirmed, say a material delivery against a purchase order, the payment automatically gets processed as agreed by the terms and as coded in the smart contract.

In summary, writing the rules of the game, sticking to them, and monitoring them is completely changed in the paradigm of intelligent supply in the DSN process.

Category Management

A category management strategy is essential to business strategy; the category managers, while working with the business units, identify the supplier and product category for business planning and execution. Categories are generally identified for product groups or supplier groups. MRO, direct material, IT, logistics, and professional services are examples of commonly used categories. In intelligent supply, category management involves reimagined processes and digital technologies to identify the category, develop the category strategy, and execute that strategy.

Spend management tools and spend analytics are used to identify categories with reference to past actuals and future plans. These inputs inform a strategy that serves organizations through all supplier and product categories. Collaboration tools can be used to share the forecast and budget plan with the suppliers to enable synchronized planning.

Real-time market intelligence about suppliers, commodities, and other product groups supports strategy execution and monitoring results. In more advanced intelligent supply situations, a category "workbench" can be developed to serve as a control tower using sensor data, market information, pricing, and demand-supply fluctuations to make dynamic updates and take real-time actions related to category management.

Supplier Network Collaboration

Supplier network collaboration is one of the most critical capabilities of intelligent supply. This level of partnership, which was only dreamed of in the past, can be achieved now with the usage of digital tools. Supply network collaboration fosters innovation, increases revenue through a faster product development cycle and better-served customers, and reduces costs through higher efficiency of operations.

A digital platform in intelligent supply fosters collaboration and optimizes the network through real-time information exchange. Suppliers and contract manufacturers receive the demand forecast from the organization, share their capacities, and confirm the commitments against the demand. For any mismatch of the demand with the supplier commitment, the optimization engine of the synchronized planning along with the supplier collaboration portal can be used to identify the alternate supply in time. The inclusion of the supplier and contract manufacturers with real-time data and real-time collaboration (through different channels of text, voice, memo, video communication) removes waste from the system.

The supplier network is an integral part of innovation and product development strategy. The speed to market for a new product or service can be improved by using supplier networks for the technology, specialized knowledge, and end-to-end solutions of an innovation problem. A supplier connected through the organization's network plays a more active role in product development, design validation, prototype development, testing, and logistics validation.

The power to innovate can be multiplied by collaborating with other organizations to manage an innovation ecosystem. An innovation ecosystem can be viewed as the "melting pot" of different organizations in buyer-supplier relationships involved with product design, manufacturing, marketing, testing, personnel supply, and so on. These participants work on one connected network to inspire, design, manufacture, and distribute the products that serve their market. An ecosystem systematically increases the knowledge, capability, and involvement of key parties and generates success by merging R&D strategy with a supplier management strategy. Innovation work can further benefit by involving a more significant population through crowdsourcing. There are multiple technologies to support crowdsourcing and numerous successful examples in which the organizations have tapped their supplier network for crowdsourcing product and service innovation.

Intelligent supply acts as a platform to provide structured and effective collaboration between buyers and suppliers, along with real-time visibility to transactions (orders, invoices, credit memos) and performance metrics. It leads to reduced risk, improved contract performance, and higher savings. It enhances supplier partnership in mitigating risks and generating mutual value by using shared financials, forecasts, and alerts.

Supplier Analytics

The KPI metric mostly used in the SCM process is an on time in full score for a supplier. Based on this, suppliers are ranked in the context of the product and spending value categories. Intelligent supply has the capability of enabling supplier analytics, which analyzes OTIF. At the same time, the system generates and monitors multiple other indicators related to purchasing, costing, lead time, category management, and delivery performance for a holistic understanding and value generation.

Holistic supplier analytics can be represented through a "digital supplier dashboard," dynamic analytics that are generated in the cloud and shared with suppliers. Transformed supplier analytics enable predictive supplier management with early insights about risk, shutdown, catastrophes, and capacity constraints. Alerts can be generated based on the actual or predictive failure (usage of anomaly detection algorithms) at the dashboard, and workflow can also be automatically triggered for responsive action. The digital dashboard integrates the synchronized planning and dynamic fulfillment capabilities to sense the demand in real time and has complete supply network transparency as products and materials move through.

Understanding each component of cost, margins, critical design elements, technology, and process constraints enable the optimization of the network and the reduction of the total cost. This can be driven by taking waste out and by resolving constraints. The expected level of collaboration and information sharing about the cost and margin can only take place in a trusted relationship guided by the shared profit. The trust generation is fortified by transparent digital tools and technologies like the digital dashboard and smart relational contract.

Intelligent supply capabilities as explained above positively impact the organization at different performance parameters as represented in Figure 8.4. These capabilities together enhance revenue, reduce total cost, minimize risks, support innovation, and make the organization more efficient.

FIGURE 8.4   **Business Benefits Achieved Through Intelligent Supply Capabilities**

INTELLIGENT SUPPLY AUTOMATION WITH DIGITAL TECHNOLOGY

As illustrated in the preceding sections, intelligent supply is not just the addition of the digital tool into the "source" process of SCM, but is a transformed process. In the new paradigm, suppliers become partners and co-innovators, not limited to performing nonessential activities at the lowest cost. The business environment has changed in the past few decades, moving the level of in-house value-added innovation from 60 to 80 percent to less than 30 percent on average now. This shift in strategy requires the procurement team to play a strategic role as a leader of product development, innovation, manufacturing sustenance, working capital management, and customer service.

Intelligent supply is about creating an intuitively simple, yet efficient and meaningful user experience for sourcing personnel. The organization buying process can be as simple and effective as buying a product on Amazon in a guided (yet controlled) environment. Few organizations are exploring virtual assistants for tasks like finding information about a category supplier or real-time inventory tracking. We expect more innovation in this area to come, further driving process efficiency and ease.

Intelligent supply frees up the time for sourcing team members to perform value-adding strategic work by automating the repetitive, manually intensive tasks of legacy supply chain processes. Currently, a vast amount of time is spent on activities like invoice matching, making phone calls to track materials, performing calculations to generate OTIF, and entering purchase orders. Most of the repetitive, rule-based tasks can be automated and performed with higher efficiency by RPA systems, leaving human sourcing professionals to focus on the exceptions.

For intelligent supply, data is the input into the digital environment, fortified with multiple technologies. The output advantages to the firm are represented in Figure 8.5.

It has been an unfulfilled wish of most procurement managers to have actionable data at their fingertips, which is otherwise hidden in the piles of paper documents, old transactions, and local Excel sheets, across often-siloed departments of the organization. To achieve its objectives, intelligent supply needs a number of data sets: strategic data, master data, transaction data, and external data. Strategic data examples include current and previous contracts, supplier cost model, suppliers' capacity, quota agreements, and substitute supplier information. Master data refers to supplier information containing legal entity, location sites, lead times, transportation cost, lot size, quota percentage, and so on. Transaction data involves the orders and inventory for past, present, and future horizons. External data sets contain information about commodity market trends, taxes, tariffs, government regulation, market analysis, and unstructured data like social media chatter that can be scoured for analysis and decision-making processes. Digital tools facilitate moving the master and transaction data in paper form and in multiple legacy environments to easy-to-read digital format for quick reference. Through easy-to-use interfaces, many organizations are able to get their entire data set into cloud-based systems for review and calculations.

In the intelligent supply process, automation with intelligence is achieved by a set of technologies that includes AI, machine learning, robotics, quick reference (QR) code, sensors, blockchain, and RFID, as represented in Figure 8.5. These technologies allow network collaboration, platform collaboration, and crowdsourcing. Technologies like RFID, QR code, and sensors are used for real-time data capture and moving the data into the cloud for easy access that enables enhanced decision making. A network collaboration platform provides synchronized planning, demand shaping, and the ability to respond to market and operational deviations in the most optimum manner. Platform collaboration and crowdsourcing multiply the organization's capability to innovate by leveraging the power of the platform model and active

FIGURE 8.5 Intelligent Supply Process Representation

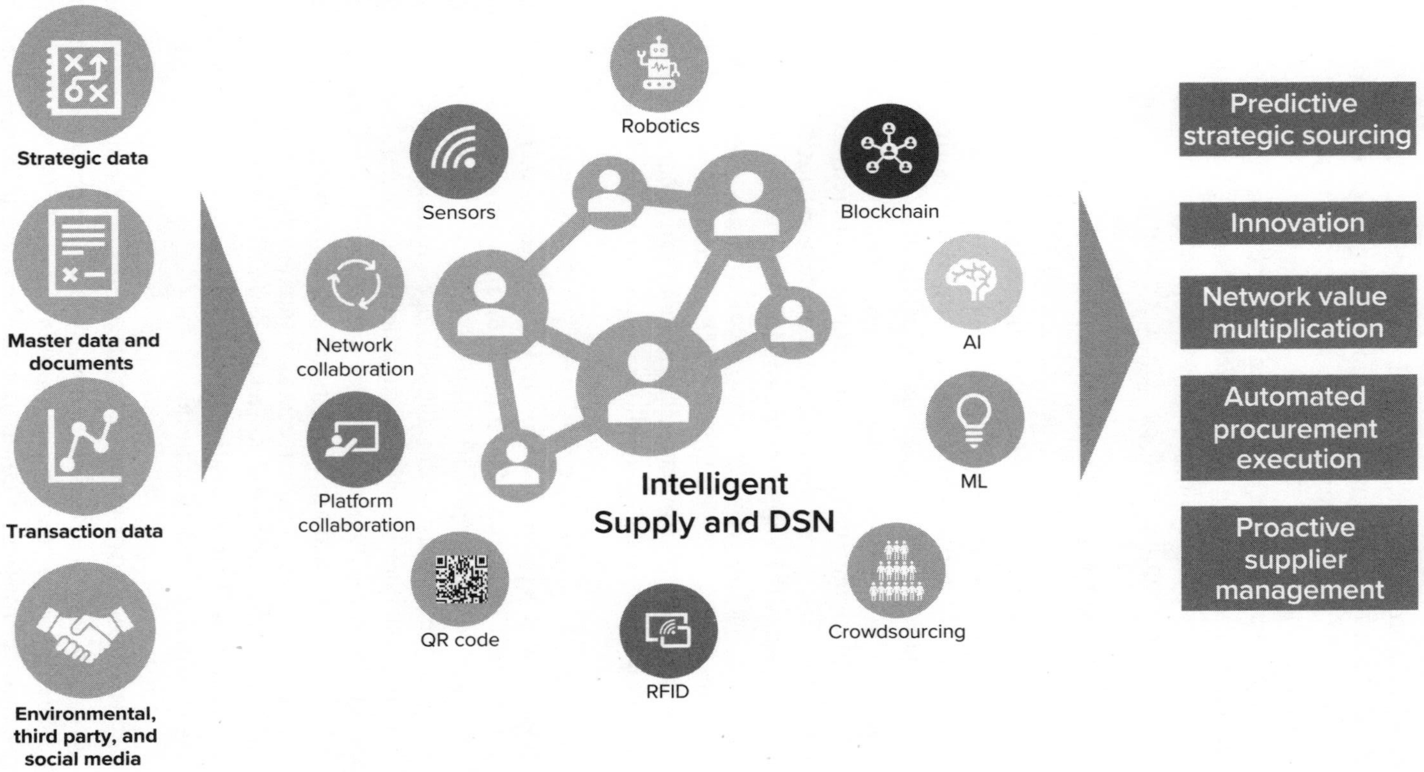

Strategic data

Master data and documents

Transaction data

Environmental, third party, and social media

Network collaboration

Platform collaboration

Sensors

Robotics

Blockchain

AI

ML

QR code

RFID

Crowdsourcing

Intelligent Supply and DSN

Predictive strategic sourcing

Innovation

Network value multiplication

Automated procurement execution

Proactive supplier management

participation of the relevant specialist to solve a particular problem. Blockchain has a unique application for the procurement process by enabling the smart auto executable contracts without requiring a centralized outside party.

As presented in the right-hand side of Figure 8.5, the benefits or output of intelligent supply are predictive strategic sourcing, innovation, network value multiplication, automated procurement execution, and proactive supplier management. Let's take a closer look at each.

PREDICTIVE STRATEGIC SOURCING enables intelligent category management and spend analytics. Category managers can visualize end-to-end information in an easy to understand format and can optimize customer service, manufacturing execution, and working capital via simulation and machine learning algorithms with rich data sets. Spend analysis in the digital age is utterly transformative. Past and present spends can be analyzed at different levels of detail using aggregation and disaggregation and by adopting different levers and scales to optimize the spend. The predictive model can consider the demand forecast from the supplier, the organization's sales and operations plans, and its future vision while predicting the spend for the short term, medium term, and long term. Total cost analysis with lifetime value and procure-to-purchase calculations can occur in an integrated approach while considering all the nodes of the DSN and associated parameters.

INNOVATION is paramount for an organization's success in the current market environment. One of the most important benefits of intelligent supply is the shift in procurement's role in the firm's innovation process. With added dependence on suppliers for the value addition, collaboration with the supplier for product and service innovation is natural. Digital tools, as part of intelligent supply, deliver this innovation through a collaborative yet controlled environment. Crowdsourcing is another recent development in this process to push innovation through gaining the ideas and intelligence of the outside networks. This innovative approach in a collaborated framework hugely impacts the network value.

AUTOMATION PROCUREMENT EXECUTION is a significant benefit of intelligent supply, as it eliminates the repetitive processes that hamper many procurement organizations today. RPA reduces the cost per invoice drastically compared to the current manual methods.

Blockchain solutions can verify and validate transactions in the P2P process and can trigger automated payments. Automated P2P transaction workflows from purchase order to shipping notification, delivery, invoicing, payment, and service settlement save significant time and greatly enhance process efficiency.

PROACTIVE SUPPLIER MANAGEMENT is the ability to respond to a potential risk before it materializes. It also enables real-time tracking of demand, supply, and product shipment in the network. With easy to access master, transaction, and other data sets related to supply, fortified by synchronized planning capabilities, supply network uncertainty can be minimized. Proactive contract management and monitoring of rules automatically achieves compliance, and compliance exceptions are identified and predicted for analysis and resolution by the relevant team.

SUMMARY

Procurement activities have been an essential part of traditional supply chain management, providing business continuity transactional support, and helping manage an organization's total cost. Intelligent supply represents the transformed purchasing, sourcing, and supplier management activities in the DSN framework. The new sourcing paradigm of intelligent supply focuses on innovation, automation, and the end-to-end value creation for the enterprise. Technologies like blockchain, AI, machine learning, sensors, RFID, QR code, and robotics facilitate the intelligent automation of sourcing activities. Intelligent supply connects physical work activities to digital collaboration and produces network-enabled insights with cutting-edge computing algorithms to enhance revenue, decrease cost, increase efficiency, and mitigate risks.

9

SMART MANUFACTURING AND INTELLIGENT ASSET MANAGEMENT

In this chapter, we will focus on smart manufacturing as an integral part of future digital supply networks (DSNs). While the notion of smart manufacturing, and Industry 4.0 for that matter, is broader than only shop floor applications and actually encompassing all areas of business along the digital supply network, we limit the scope of this chapter on the core smart manufacturing technologies, and applications related to the physical production of parts or products and predictive maintenance. The objective is to allow the reader to become familiar with smart manufacturing in general and understand the impact within the wider context of DSN.

In the past, the focus of highly efficient supply chains was on the integration in terms of delivery times (JIT/JIS), reduction of stock holding, and making sure of component and resource availability at the time of planned production. For example, in the automotive industry, probably the most efficient and well-organized supply chain thus far, one of the key achievements was the integration of all suppliers (Tier 1 to Tier n) with regard to their ERP systems—according to senior managers at Mercedes-Benz, effectively eliminating the bullwhip effect. (The bullwhip effect is a common phenomenon in supply chains where changing customer demand causes increasing swings in inventory levels, thus leading to inefficiencies.) While this is remarkable and remains a key objective, with the emergence of the new DSN paradigm, the integration of all stakeholders will be even more intense and on various levels. Not only will the exchange of data be essential, but also the insights derived from that accumulated data: visualizations of intimate data from a supplier's manufacturing operations, customer usage data, and order status of their customers' customers, just to name a few. In this brave new world, new challenges emerge, and smart manufacturing is a key component of successful DSNs. The value of data and the technologies to acquire, analyze, visualize, and share across cyber-physical systems are at the heart of smart manufacturing and thus at the heart of DSN.

This chapter is organized as follows: First, we will briefly discuss the history of smart manufacturing and Industry 4.0, cover the main terminology, and illustrate how large, medium, and small companies embrace smart manufacturing and the different challenges and barriers they may face in their journey. Second, we will holistically present the smart manufacturing paradigm based on its core governing principles: connectivity, virtualization, and data utilization. Third, we will discuss key technologies, characteristics, and enabling factors associated with smart manufacturing. Fourth, we will illustrate the distinct smart manufacturing domain of intelligent asset management and smart services. In this section, we will broadly discuss the impact of smart services before looking into condition monitoring, preventive maintenance, and untimely predictive maintenance.

SMART MANUFACTURING AND INDUSTRY 4.0

The manufacturing industry is currently going through a digital transformation that is commonly referred to as the fourth industrial revolution ("Industry 4.0") or smart manufacturing paradigm. The term "smart factory" is also used. At the core of this transformation is the merger of the virtual ("cyber") and physical worlds, and the benefits brought forth by these so-called cyber-physical systems (CPS).[1] On the shop floor level and above, smart manufacturing merges information technology (IT) and operational technology (OT) (see Figure 9.1), enabling effective and efficient operations and communication across the whole digital supply network.

Industry 4.0 and smart manufacturing are often discussed in the context of automation and robotics, and within this context the displacement of human workers is seen as a threat. However, one important aspect of smart manufacturing is the explicit focus on human ingenuity. While robotics and automation relieve human workers from repetitive, strenuous, and dangerous physical tasks,

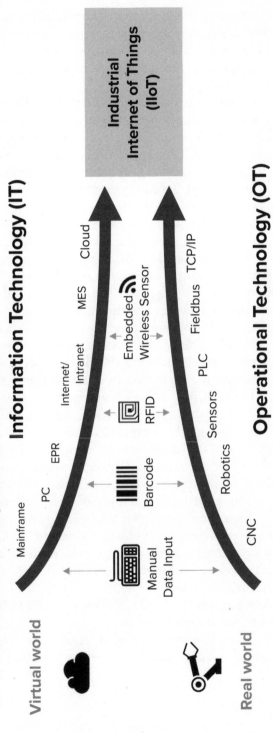

FIGURE 9.1   Smart Manufacturing at the Intersection of IT and OT

smart manufacturing aims to relieve the human operators from repetitive, strenuous, and dangerous cognitive tasks. Furthermore, concepts such as the Operator 4.0* focus on the opportunity to empower and enable human operators through the use of distinct smart manufacturing technologies (e.g., AR).

Smart manufacturing delivers higher efficiency and higher quality by connecting machines, people, processes, and data through a digital fabric. Figure 9.2 shows an example of a smart factory. Automated robots connected to the digital environment move the incoming materials to the right storage location after scanning the information on the box; the inventory is updated automatically in real time. Autonomous vehicles make the product available to the required manufacturing processes just in time and take care of the picking and inventory update. The manufacturing processes are fully automated including in situ quality monitoring based on vision systems combined with deep learning to identify quality issues as soon as they appear. Digital twins of the machine tools and physical assets on the shop floor allow an operator to monitor and simulate the material flow in real time on a handheld device. The operator gets an alert and takes action either directly on her mobile device activating sensor-actuator response, or manually if appropriate (human in the loop). When a machine tool is predicted to fail, the spare part in question is manufactured on demand just in time using additive manufacturing that has the digital files of all spare parts at its discretion. An operator reviews the plant's progress through the command center, which visualizes metrics such as OEE (overall equipment effectiveness) and manufacturing efficiency in real time; any deviation from the plan is acted on dynamically to minimize the impact on cost, quality, and efficiency.

Smart manufacturing is a truly global initiative—all major industrial and emerging economies acknowledge the importance of preparing their manufacturing industry for the digital future. While the term "smart manufacturing" is predominantly used in the United States, all of the various initiatives have similar objectives at their core despite different names, such as Industrie 4.0 (Germany), Industrial Internet (United States), China 2025 (China), Make in India (India), Smart Factory (South Korea), and many more.

Ultimately, smart manufacturing marries technology, data, and human ingenuity to access and act on new, value-adding data-driven insights.

---

* Romero et al., 2016.

FIGURE 9.2 **An Illustration of a Smart Factory**

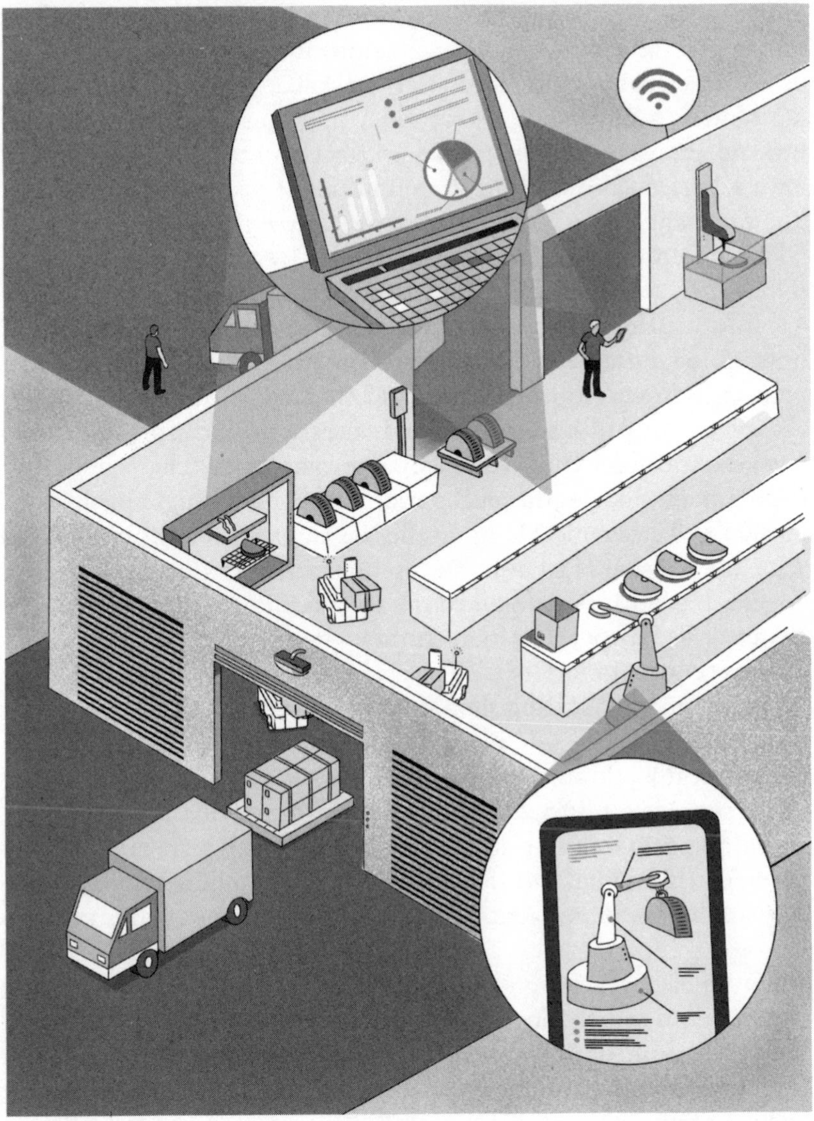

Brief History of Smart Manufacturing

Smart manufacturing is not a new concept by any means. As early as the 1990s, the term "intelligent manufacturing" was already established, and it has put forth several visions that are now becoming reality.

However, the paradigms we today refer to as smart manufacturing and Industry 4.0 first picked up traction in the early 2010s and have experienced increasing attention in the past four to five years. The catchy and now widely used term "fourth industrial revolution" (aka Industry 4.0 or I4) was coined in 2011 by a German government initiative to prepare the German manufacturing industry for the digital future.[2] The implication was that the manufacturing industry is undergoing a dramatic digital transformation that is far beyond the regular technological progress—and thus constitutes a revolution. Over the course of history, we could observe three distinct industrial revolutions before. The first industrial revolution was characterized by the dramatic changes the mechanization of labor brought forth in the form of the mechanical loom in the late eighteenth century (*industry 1.0*). The division of labor or mass production introduced in the early twentieth century is considered the second industrial revolution that changed the face of the manufacturing industry forever (*industry 2.0*). More recently, around the 1970s, automation and the introduction of IT on the manufacturing shop floor constituted the third industrial revolution (*industry 3.0*). Now, the merger of the virtual world with the physical world in the form of CPPS (the cyber-physical production system) is considered to have a similar impact on the future of the manufacturing industry and is thus named "Industry 4.0" (see Figure 9.3). This digital transformation has the potential to change the way we design, manufacture, procure, ship, and maintain products forever.

With each revolution the complexity of the manufacturing system increases and presents new challenges and barriers that companies need to be aware of and address in order to ensure their future competitiveness. Especially in the age of complex DSN, the communication and connectivity between different systems is essential to capitalize on the benefits of smart manufacturing.

Smart Manufacturing Terminology

Smart manufacturing is still a relatively new paradigm for many scholars and practitioners. Therefore, in a first step we will discuss the key terminology and define the system boundaries of the concept to provide a solid foundation for our readers.

FIGURE 9.3 Depiction of the Four Industrial Revolutions and Their Defining Technologies

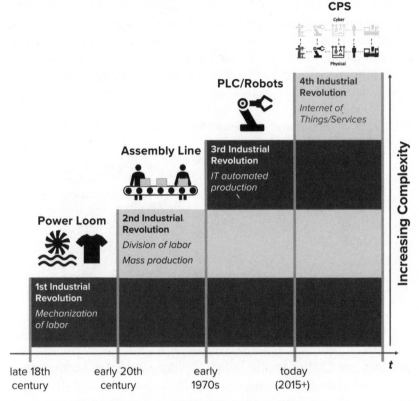

Development of Manufacturing Systems

Source: Wuest, 2019

Smart manufacturing[3] describes "a data intensive application of information technology at the shop floor level and above to enable intelligent, efficient and responsive operations,"[4] while also highlighting the data and technology focus. Smart manufacturing emphasizes the importance of including human ingenuity and the creation of manufacturing knowledge from data. In essence, smart manufacturing systems resemble complex CPS[5] with the purpose of integrating IT and OT to improve manufacturing operations through sensor systems and advanced data analytics.

We often see smart and advanced manufacturing used interchangeably. However, we argue that while there is certainly an overlap, the two terms are inherently different. Smart and advanced manufacturing describe distinct areas of the new manufacturing realities and can be seen as two sides of the same (Industry 4.0) medallion (see Figure 9.4). Smart manufacturing at its core focusses on connectivity, virtualization, and data utilization, while advanced manufacturing focuses on manufacturing process technologies, such as automation, robotics, and additive manufacturing. Nevertheless, there is no sharp dividing line between the two concepts, and in order to be successful in the future, companies need to embrace both.

FIGURE 9.4 **Smart and Advanced Manufacturing Are Two Sides of the Same Medallion**

Source: Wuest, 2019

Barriers and Challenges for Large, Medium, and Small Companies

When we talk about industrial paradigm shifts, historically, larger global companies are on the forefront when it comes to adoption. Consequently, they are the first to reap the benefits of the new technologies and methods. However, at the same time, as first movers and early innovators, they have to overcome unique hurdles and barriers in the process that the late majority can avoid to some extent. For smart manufacturing, this stands true as well. Large multinational enterprises (MNEs) such as Siemens, LG, Mercedes, and GE are heavily invested in the digital transformation and are investing significant manpower and resources.

On the other side, many small- and medium-sized enterprises (SMEs) are struggling with the paradigm shift for a variety of reasons. Mittal and colleagues compared features that have an influence on the smart manufacturing adoption of MNEs and SMEs (see Table 9.1) that provides a quick, high-level overview.[6] It has to be noted that this is a generalization and there are selected high-tech SMEs that are ahead of most MNEs when it comes to smart manufacturing, yet the majority is struggling and understanding the differentiating features helps to pinpoint causes for this struggle.

TABLE 9.1 Comparison of SME and MNE features with impact on smart manufacturing adoption

Features	SMEs	MNEs
Financial Resources	Low	High
Use of Advanced Manufacturing Technologies	Low	(Very) High
Software Umbrella (incl. data analytics)	Low (tailored solutions)	High (standardized solutions/platforms)
Research & Development Activities	Low	High
Product Specialization	High	Low
Standards Consideration	Low	High
Organizational Structure	Less complex and informal	Complex and formal
Industry Knowledge and Experience	Focused on specific area	Spread across different areas
Alliances with Universities/ Research Institutions	Low	High
Important Activities	Outsourced	Internal to the organization

Source: Adapted from Mittal et al., 2018

The question now is, why is this relevant for us as we are interested in DSNs. Well, understanding the different challenges and barriers faced by SMEs and MNEs is crucial considering that DSNs include several companies of both types in most cases. The often-postulated digital divide is a reality, and when the two extremes are working together in a digital supply network, we need to be mindful about this and understand how we can overcome the potential barriers. Otherwise, we put the performance and effectiveness of the whole digital supply network at risk. The barriers are manifold, and we cannot comprehensively discuss them all in detail. The barriers may include but are not limited to different IT/OT capabilities, employee skill levels, data analytics, and successful shop floor automation. We need to be aware and open to discuss these issues within our DSN. Then we can proactively address them and manage the risk this imposes on the whole network. Countermeasures include upskilling of underserved SMEs by other members of the DSN and/or sharing of standards, lessons learned, and expertise among the stakeholders.

SMART MANUFACTURING CORE PRINCIPLES

Smart manufacturing is a very broad and complex topic with many facets. That being said, for the purpose of this book and our readership, we broke down the complexity into three core principles: connectivity, virtualization, and data utilization. In this section we will discuss each of these core principles in more depth to provide a solid understanding of smart manufacturing.

Connectivity

Connectivity is the first of the three core principles of smart manufacturing. During the pre-smart manufacturing setting (industry 3.0), computers, programmable logic controllers, and automation were already a reality on the shop floor. The fourth industrial revolution builds on this foundation and extends it by connecting design (e.g., CAD, CAM) and production planning (e.g., ERP, MES) tools with machine tools, operators, customers, suppliers—essentially everything with everything. We will discuss the means—the Industrial Internet of Things—in a later section in more detail.

Why is this connectivity so crucial that it qualifies as one of the three defining principles? Connecting and synchronizing data gathering systems (e.g., sensors), manufacturing equipment (e.g., machine tools), and IT systems for analytical purposes is a necessary requirement to enable the development of reliable insights through advanced analytics. In order to call a (manufacturing) system truly "smart," it has to have the capability to make decisions and act on quantitative data instead of on instinct.

A second dimension of the connectivity core principle is the ability to connect across large distances. Cloud manufacturing promises to lift the manufacturing intelligence in the cloud and compose effective and efficient production plans virtually as micro-services. Without connectivity, engaging and interacting with stakeholders in a large distributed digital supply network is virtually impossible. Therefore, connectivity is a core principle and necessary requirement of a smart manufacturing system as well as of DSN, just as it is today in our private lives where we are "always on" with our smartphones, wearables, and connected cars.

Virtualization

Virtualization is the second core principle of smart manufacturing. Virtualization describes the process of replicating or bringing physical "things" into the digital, virtual/cyber environment in variating forms. Virtualization enables all advanced analytics and is the backbone of most applications of the IIoT. One of the most prominent instantiations of virtualization today is the digital twin, a virtual representation of a physical asset in the cloud. GE's digital twin of a jet engine is probably the most well-known example of such a system, but countless examples of various sophistication and scope, from component to factory level, are available and more are developed daily.

For smart manufacturing, the key traits virtualization enables are transparency and visualization. *Transparency* is essential for a variety of reasons in a digital supply network. On the technical side, it enables equipment monitoring, diagnosis, and repair as well as prediction of equipment failure (predictive maintenance). From a business perspective, with the deeper integration of stakeholders within a digital supply network, transparency is a key driver to develop the necessary trust. The partners need to understand what happens with the production at the other partners' sites to base their decision making on or define the right revenue-sharing model, just to give two examples. *Visualization* is gaining importance as it is the gateway between the ever-growing amount of data and the analytical results on the one side, and the decision makers with their limited capacity on the other. As a simple example, the sensory data collected from a production run can be presented in the form of raw data in a database. However, this representation is not very goal oriented when it comes to the plant manager, who requires real-time updates whether the system is running in a steady state or not. Nor does it provide any meaningful input to the operator working on the line itself. The insights are hidden in the data, but how we present those is key to having an effective and efficient process. In this case, the plant manager might be best served with a dashboard with a green, orange, and red lights to constantly provide the level of monitoring required. While the operator might require a customized interface that provides selected in-depth information, such as vibration data and heat curve for a manufacturing process, via augmented reality smart glasses to allow hands-free communication.

Data Utilization

The third core principle of smart manufacturing is data utilization. Connectivity enables the collection, communication, and storage of large amounts of data from the shop floor, logistics, and business operations. Virtualization enables the communication of insights from the data and is the gateway between the operations and the human operators and decision makers. Data utilization is the means that translates the unprecedented access to and contextualization of data into actionable insights through advanced analytics. Smart manufacturing is often referred to as a data-driven revolution, an accurate statement of the importance of data and data analytics within this paradigm shift.

Advanced data analytics in manufacturing are driven by both data-driven and physics-based modeling. However, in a smart manufacturing context, data-driven approaches are more prominent. Supervised and unsupervised machine learning (including reinforcement learning) are utilized at record levels (see Chapter 4 for details). New manufacturing processes, such as metal additive manufacturing, are natively digital and rely on powerful analytics to function. Manufacturing is a domain where we have the advantage that there are experts (teachers to label the data) readily available. However, the amount of data we capture today requires new and innovative solutions to efficiently but also reliably provide insights that drive quality, process efficiency, and reliability, as well as new maintenance paradigms (e.g., zero downtime). In conclusion, data and data analytics are the heart of smart manufacturing. This is reflected in the "smart" of smart manufacturing.

SMART MANUFACTURING CAPABILITIES

The smart factory capabilities expand manufacturing plants' and operators' capability by transparency, automation, and analytics, achieving optimum machine and human efficiency while upholding operation safety. The capabilities of smart manufacturing and intelligent asset management can be summarized as:

- Dynamic visibility
- Optimum operations
- Factory automation

DYNAMIC VISIBILITY. Real-time condition monitoring is facilitated in a smart manufacturing environment through the network of connected machines and sensors. A web of digital twins enables the dynamic visibility of the entire plant.

OPTIMUM OPERATIONS. Optimum operations in DSN manifests in two parts, (1) the optimum manufacturing schedule and (2) the execution of the optimum schedule with the right parameters. The optimum manufacturing schedule is achieved through the synchronized planning capability of DSN in association with smart manufacturing by considering customer demand, machine availability, manufacturing rate, setup changes, component, and labor plan. This optimization of the real execution is enabled by continuous monitoring, analytics, and simulation, as well as real-time adaptation based on identified outliers.

FACTORY AUTOMATION. The digital fabric of a smart factory has the information of machine operation (through sensors), production schedule (planning system), warehouse information (warehouse system), manufacturing (MES system), and material movement information (transport system) at its core. These integrated systems and processes can automate the factory operations of material movement, storage, and transport through robots and AGVs/UAVs. Transactions of inventory posting, delivery, and invoice generation can be automated through RPA (robotic process automation). The human workforce is essential to improve and implement automation, monitor all activities, and act on alerts and exceptional events.

SMART MANUFACTURING TECHNOLOGIES

In the previous sections we discussed the new smart manufacturing paradigm on a more philosophical level. In the following, we will dig a little deeper into the specific technologies that enable this revolution to take place. First, we will give an overview of all major technologies, characteristics, and enabling factors that define smart manufacturing and then focus on two essential ones, IIoT and cyber-physical systems.

Smart Manufacturing Technologies and Enabling Factors[*]

An important aspect of smart manufacturing for both research and industrial application revolves around associated technologies, characteristics, and enabling factors. For instance, it is important for companies to understand what technologies are relevant and might be

---

[*] Summary of (Mittal et al., 2019). If you are interested in a more in-depth analysis, please refer to the original publication, which is available open access.

worthwhile to assess or invest in. Academics and scholars can identify areas where additional research is required to develop technologies further to address current industry needs and prepare students for their future careers in manufacturing.

In this section, we briefly report on a comprehensive study that identified 38 different technologies, 27 characteristics, and seven enabling factors that were associated with smart manufacturing. The technologies ranged from machine learning to augmented reality, the characteristics from agility to decentralized control, and enabling factors from STEP standards to MTConnect. We then clustered the complete list based on their semantic similarity. The result of this clustering is illustrated in Figure 9.5. Technology clusters are highlighted in the left column, characteristics in the middle column, and enabling factors in the right column. It has to be noted that the list is derived in a transparent and methodological process from literature to provide a reflection of the experts' understanding of the field. The sometimes-inconsistent use of terminology is reflected in the results as the authors did not curate the list in order to not introduce their own bias.

FIGURE 9.5 Smart Manufacturing Technologies, Characteristics, and Enabling Factors

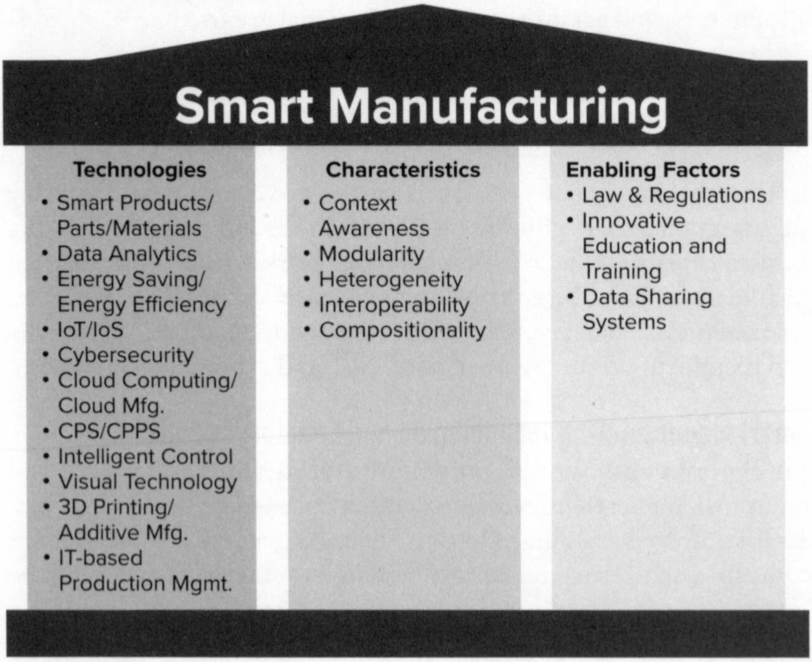

Smart Manufacturing

Technologies	Characteristics	Enabling Factors
• Smart Products/ Parts/Materials	• Context Awareness	• Law & Regulations
• Data Analytics	• Modularity	• Innovative Education and Training
• Energy Saving/ Energy Efficiency	• Heterogeneity	• Data Sharing Systems
• IoT/IoS	• Interoperability	
• Cybersecurity	• Compositionality	
• Cloud Computing/ Cloud Mfg.		
• CPS/CPPS		
• Intelligent Control		
• Visual Technology		
• 3D Printing/ Additive Mfg.		
• IT-based Production Mgmt.		

Source: Mittal et al., 2019

After focusing on two core smart manufacturing technologies, IoT/IIoT and CPS/CPPS, in more detail in the next two sections, we will briefly describe an additional novel paradigm: the Operator 4.0.

Industrial Internet of Things (IIoT)

The Internet of Things (IoT) is a global infrastructure interconnecting physical objects (*things*) with the virtual world (*Internet*). The vision of the IoT includes the complete integration of the physical with the virtual world by facilitating communication between all connected things.[7] Broken down to its core: connecting any object to the Internet. Through the IoT, thousands of smart devices in everyone's personal environments, homes, and workplaces are already connected—just think Amazon's Alexa, Apple's iPhone and wearables, and Philips's Hue.

The fourth industrial revolution is not about simply further automating the shop floor, rather a transition toward a more intelligent and connected industry across all levels of a company by means of the Internet.[8] Accordingly, the essence of smart manufacturing is the introduction and application of the Internet of Things (IoT) within an industrial setting—the so-called *Industrial Internet of Things (IIoT)*.[9] The IIoT is one of the two core technologies that are often used synonymous with smart manufacturing, at times also simply referred to as *Industrial Internet* in the United States. When we try to capture the difference between the IIoT and the IoT, we can safely say that the IIoT represents a subset of the IoT focusing on connecting industrial assets or "things" in an industrial environment, such as manufacturing equipment, machine tools, operators, IT systems, and (smart) products (see Figure 9.6). As a prerequisite for the IIoT, industrial assets have to be equipped with networking and sensing capabilities as well as Internet connectivity. Connected devices in a manufacturing environment can include mobile tablets, smart shelves, machine tools, or products.

A key trend in the IIoT space is the emergence of IIoT platforms. Multiple vendors have created platforms that allow the hosting of various generic and company-specific applications, services, and analytics. Most platforms follow certain standards that ensure interoperability and the ability to connect a variety of devices, products, and services. The ability to compose different micro-services and/or applications instead of investing in dedicated, monolithic software products is very attractive to many industrial customers. However, as the market is currently in an early phase, there is still some uncertainty about the

FIGURE 9.6 Application Areas of the (Industrial) Internet of Things

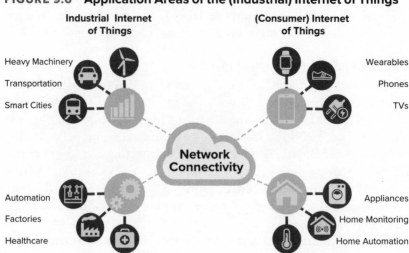

true interoperability and utility of these platforms. Figure 9.7 (see next page) depicts an overview of selected IIoT platforms with regard to their data, information, and knowledge functionalities.

Cyber Physical (Production) Systems (CPPS)

Cyber-physical systems (CPS) combine computation and communication with physical processes.[10] Embedded computers and networks monitor and control the physical processes, while feedback loops and analytics can be combined with physical processes.[11] CPS are computerized systems that are embedded in physical systems and tightly integrate the physical world with the cyber world (see Figure 9.8). Natural and physical systems are equipped with sensors, actors, and microprocessors to gather and process data. The IoT is a means to bring a CPS to life by connecting the physical instances to the virtual world through the Internet.

Through their digital representation, such as digital twins, CPS and their subsystems are able to communicate and interact with each other across virtual simulations and physical processes (such as an industrial milling process) alike. Cardenas et al. state that CPS "integrate computing and communication capabilities with monitoring and control of entities in the physical world."[12] The term "cyber-physical production systems (CPPS)" is characterized in the application within the production domain with the availability of the three main features: intelligence, connectedness, and responsiveness.[13]

FIGURE 9.7 Comparison of Selected IIoT Platforms with Focus on Data, Information, and Knowledge

Industrial Internet–based information and knowledge functionalities	GE Predix	MyJohn Deere	Bosch IoT Suite	Kaa IoT Platform	Microsoft Azure	PTC Thingworx	CyberLighting CyberVille	Industry Hack	Yammer
Data access and collection	++	++	++	+	+	-	-	++	-
Data aggregation and sharing	++	+	+	++	++	++	+	-	-
Data storing	+	+	+	+	+	-	-	-	-
Analytics and visualizations	+	+	+	+	+	++	++	+	-
Information sharing	+	+	+	+	+	+	+	+	+
Sensemaking	-	+	-	-	-	-	-	++	++

Source: Menon et al., 2018

FIGURE 9.8   CPS Connecting the Physical with the Virtual World

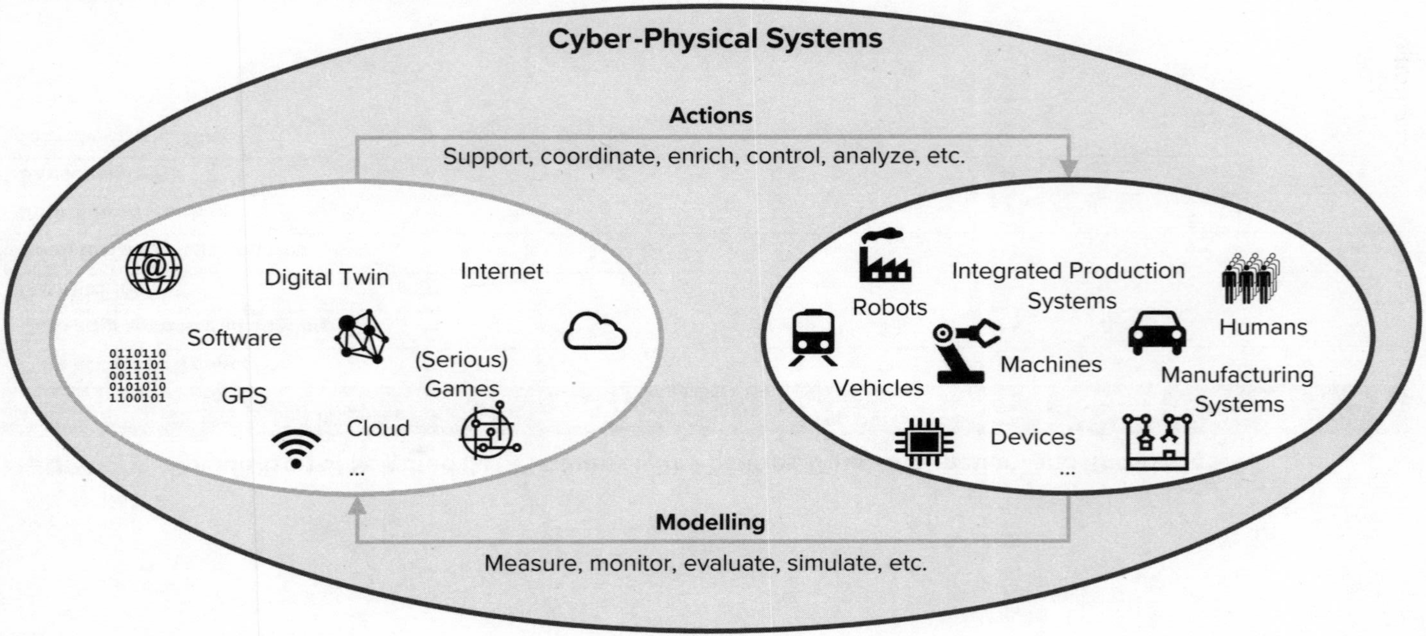

Cyber-Physical Systems

Actions

Support, coordinate, enrich, control, analyze, etc.

Humans

Manufacturing Systems

Integrated Production Systems

Machines

Devices

Robots

Vehicles

...

Internet

(Serious) Games

Cloud

Digital Twin

Software

GPS

...

0110010
1011101
1011011
0101010
1100101

Modelling

Measure, monitor, evaluate, simulate, etc.

CPPS represents the technology that connects different physical and virtual/cyber systems with each other and thus is the technical implementation of the IIoT. Together, CPPS and IIoT are the two core enabling technologies of smart manufacturing. The IIoT builds the infrastructure from a network, connectivity, and sensorial point of view, whereas CPPS builds the technical requirements to connect particular systems (see Figure 9.9).

FIGURE 9.9   Cyber-Physical Production System (CPPS) and Digital Twins

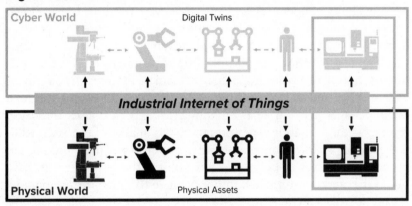

Operator 4.0

Human work and human ingenuity will play a key role within the factory of the future. A concept that utilizes technology to enhance human capabilities is the so-called Operator 4.0.[14] The Operator 4.0 is built on the premise that human ingenuity is not replaceable but is an integral part of the smart manufacturing future. Future manufacturing operators will have continuous, real-time technical support and be super-strong, super-informed, super-safe, and constantly connected. This new generation of tech-augmented human workers will emerge on factory shop floors and in offices utilizing several types of enhancements, which can be used individually or in combination to put humans at the heart of this technological revolution.[15]

The Operator 4.0 describes "a smart and skilled operator who performs not only—'cooperative work' with robots—but also—'aided work' by machines as and if needed—by means of human cyber-physical systems, advanced human-machine interaction technologies and adaptive automation towards 'human-automation symbiosis work systems.'"[16] The manifestations of an Operator 4.0 include an operator utilizing an exoskeleton to gain strength required for heavy lifting, smart glasses to enable remote maintenance, and smart wearables for safety management just to name a few. We will see many different instances where technology is actively supporting the human operator, especially with (mentally and physically) strenuous, stressful, and dangerous tasks on and beyond the shop floor.

INTELLIGENT ASSET MANAGEMENT

Manufacturing performance of a factory is based on asset availability. The reality of operating a plant is that every machine breaks down with time, and the resulting downtime causes lower efficiency, product deficiency, higher cost per unit, and customer order shortage. Minimization of downtime and optimization of plant efficiency is the most important task of a plant maintenance team. OEE (overall equipment effectiveness) and RUL (remining useful life) are relevant metrics for a plant manager. OEE, used as a manufacturing performance indicator, represents the availability, performance, and quality of the asset. RUL is the measure of how much more time, or how many more production cycles, a machine can be used before failure. The goal here is to have high OEE and consume maximum possible RUL before an upgrade, repair, or replacement.

The asset maintenance strategy can be classified as reactive, preventive, predictive, or prescriptive as shown in Figure 9.10. With the advent of the digital transformation, predictive maintenance has further matured to resemble a prescriptive maintenance strategy, though these two terms are often used interchangeable today.

Reactive and preventive maintenance strategies are widely used concepts of the traditional SCM, while the predictive approach is related to the DSN model. Let's illustrate the journey from reactive, to preventive, to predictive, and ultimately to prescriptive.

REACTIVE TO PREVENTIVE. A reactive strategy responds to the fix after the failure occurs; hence it causes costly unplanned downtime and a safety hazard that can cost millions of dollars. In addition to the losses caused by the breakdown, a machine breakage reduces total life of the machine as well as the output quality of the product possibly for a long time before failure. This happens due to the execution under nonoptimal condition. Use of a preventive asset strategy is commonplace these days to avoid the unplanned downtime and poor product quality risks. In a preventive strategy, the maintenance is scheduled periodically as a

FIGURE 9.10 **Asset Maintenance Strategy Impact on Efficiency and OEE**

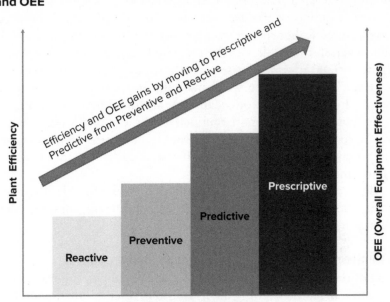

PLANT EFFICIENCY

OEE (Overall Equipment Effectiveness)

Efficiency and OEE gains by moving to Prescriptive and Predictive from Preventive and Reactive

Prescriptive

Predictive

Preventive

Reactive

Asset Maintenance Strategy

planned downtime activity. By nature, a preventive approach is highly conservative, and hence some of the useful life (RUL) is not utilized due to an earlier replacement and repair of the parts. In addition, the preventive strategy is not foolproof: the failures still happen, though with a lower rate than in a pure reactive environment.

PREVENTIVE TO PREDICTIVE. The predictive approach, aligned to DSN methodology, is based on a "predict and prevent" model to calculate when the failure is expected to take place and then combining this into the maintenance plan. It uses prior repair, past performance, and service data through a machine learning algorithm to predict the failure. The downtime and the maintenance strategy is planned for the optimal scenario using what-if simulation. This results in higher usage of parts, higher plant efficiency, a lower cost per unit, and a much safer environment.

PREDICTIVE TO PRESCRIPTIVE. In a smart manufacturing environment, sensors are used to report the operating conditions in real time, and this condition monitoring data is compared with the recommended operating parameters and past failures. Classification and predictive models are used to analyze this data to predict failure and suggested prevention activities (actions). The big difference is that not only is the failure event and the time of failure predicted more accurately, but the prescriptive system provides an automatable plan of action that addresses the predicted maintenance issue resulting in optimal uptime of assets with minimal human intervention. Since the asset is utilized with the optimum operating parameters, the machine life and product quality are maximized resulting in higher plant efficiency, more productive workers, and lower cost per unit for manufactured products. The model gets better with more data and repetitive usage resulting in a virtuous cycle of plant efficiency improvement.

The applications of predictive strategy can be further discussed as data modeling, digital twin monitoring, and intelligent spare parts management.

Predictive Modeling and Maintenance by Digital Twins

Data of the equipment operating parameters and past failures can be fed into a machine learning algorithm to predict failure. Supervised learning by application of a classification model can be used to identify an issue and alert the operator; for example, the operating parameter (e.g., vibration) of a crucial machine part from past failures is labeled and used as the safety threshold value. The regression model can be then used to predict run to failure from the current condition.

Digital twin, as introduced earlier in this chapter, is a digital representation of a physical asset with connected sensors that provide real-time operating information. This is getting adopted successfully to maximize asset uptime and optimize business performance. Real-time condition monitoring is facilitated by the digital twin; in addition to a right-time scheduled maintenance, digital twins enable asset usage at the optimum operating condition, maximizing the efficiency and profit.

A digital twin is represented in Figure 9.11. The left side of the image has the physical asset with added sensors and actuators, and the right side shows the digital replica of the same on a handheld device or a computer. An integrated circuit of sensors and actuators is used to enable communication with the digital model. In addition to the sensor data, the digital replica can be further extended with manufacturing execution system and enterprise resource planning system data. Single direction integration can be used to send the data from the machine to the digital device, and any action can be taken by the operator on

FIGURE 9.11   A Digital Twin Representation

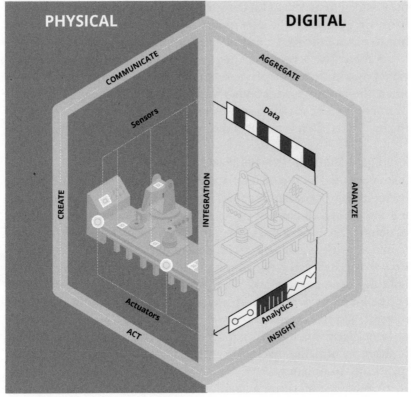

Source: Deloitte University Press, digital twin

the physical machine. Alternatively, for a bidirectional flow enabled by actuators, the signal from the digital device may directly cause an action at the physical machine without human interference. The aggregated data is analyzed with machine learning algorithms. The result is generally represented in tabular format, charts, and alerts. The alerts can create the workflow for manual intervention at the physical machine, or an action can be started through the digital twin with bidirectional flow. In this way, the physical-digital-physical loop is completed.

A group of digital twins can be applied to map an entire plant. This digital replica of the plan for real-time monitoring and control can be referred to as a command center. Both the operational data (cutting speed, displacement, torque, etc.) and environmental data (temperature, moisture, etc.) for all the machines mapped to the command center is fed to the machine learning model. Cloud computing capabilities are used to understand the process efficiency and machines' health and to predict any failure. Also, images of the in-progress products can be provided to the cloud for comparison with good and defective parts based on past data. The data modeling uses the parameters and fits a line to predict the RUL and potential failures.

A digital twin enables earlier issue identification through conditional monitoring; a negative trend will be displayed in advance even when the output product quality is in the acceptable quality range. The action taken on the trend keeps the quality consistent, mitigates the failure risks, and enhances the asset life.

Intelligent Spare Parts Management

Spares are used by the maintenance team for asset repairs and upkeep by replacing the worn-out machine parts. Shortage of a part costing less than a dollar can cause a plant shutdown costing millions of dollars. To understand the complexity, consider the fact that for a manufacturing organization with dozens of finished products, the distinct spare parts can range in tens of thousands. A network of plants, holding inventory at every plant for those thousands of the parts, takes a lot of physical space. In addition, it blocks working capital and increases the risk in case of part and machine phaseout.

Intelligent spare parts management in the digital era solves this problem by utilizing machine learning algorithms and additive manufacturing technology.

A machine learning algorithm solves the out-of-stock issue by using the predictive maintenance plan and forecasting the replacement parts demand. The right part is available at the right place at the right time with the lowest cost.

Additive manufacturing (AM) or 3D printing provides opportunity to redefine spare parts management. For parts that can be created through additive manufacturing technology, instead of holding the physical inventory, digital files are kept as the inventory (holding no physical space!) and the required parts are printed on demand either in the case of a planned repair or an unplanned machine breakdown caused by a part failure. There are special circumstances where this AM spare parts strategy provides a critical advantage. One is on board naval ships such as aircraft carriers that operate far from supply structures and have to have access to a large number of different spare parts for the ship itself and for fighter jets, helicopters, drones, and ground vehicles. Replacing the inventory with an AM shop provides significant logistical advantages. However, certification, reliability, and other issues need to be solved before this can be adopted on scale.

Intelligent asset maintenance capabilities allows a new service model called smart services, a win-win for the equipment manufacturer and users. Optimum working condition of the machine is tracked and managed by the equipment manufacturer through the connected sensors and command center. With cloud computing technology, this monitoring can happen from the equipment manufacturer's location and most of the fix can be performed through the bidirectional connection, or when manual intervention is needed, a maintenance person at the plant can do the work using the enabling technologies of VR (virtual reality).

SUMMARY

Manufacturing is changing rapidly with the dawn of Industry 4.0. Data is the lifeblood fueling the change, and companies struggle to keep up. The benefits resulting from the adoption of new smart manufacturing technologies and methods are significant, and to remain competitive on a global scale there is no question whether a company should engage—the only question is how to do it in the most effective way. Taking a problem-motivated stance with clear ROI has proven to allow companies to get the critical experience and also onboard skeptics within their ranks. However, the modern DSN is a complex system, and at some point the individual smart manufacturing solutions have to be integrated and provide scalable benefits across the network.

DYNAMIC FULFILLMENT

Dynamic fulfillment is a critical capability in the digital supply network (DSN) framework. Efficiency in fulfillment and warehouse operations has always been of great importance. As we move toward the transformation of traditional supply chains into digital supply networks, fulfillment operations must become dynamic and more intelligent, so they harmoniously support the orchestration of physical and digital aspects. In this chapter, we start with a brief discussion about significant limitations and challenges faced by fulfillment operations under traditional linear supply chain management. Next, we delve into the vision of DSN dynamic fulfillment capability, describe how it changes the game, its attributes, how it copes with the challenges and limitations faced by static supply chains, and the enabling technology supporting its development.

SUPPLY CHAIN AND TRADITIONAL FULFILLMENT

Despite attempts and much progress toward strategic supply chain process integration,[1] traditional static, linear supply chains have many constraints in planning, production, distribution, and transportation, which renders fulfillment a continuous, reactive, and sequential cycle of selling and replenishing. A typical order fulfillment cycle begins and ends with the customer.[2] The customer recognizes a need, places an order, and transmits it to the supplier. The supplier processes, prepares, and ships the order. The customer receives, accepts, and pays for the product. A traditional retail distribution channel typically involves the customer visiting the physical store or engaging an alternative setup, while the selling company uses a set of interdependent organizations to provide the products or services. However, while interdependent, that set of organizations is often siloed, and the internal and cross-channel processes are not fully connected and operate according to linear and reactive logic.

In this environment, organizations depend mostly on imprecise feedback for market intelligence and use supply-focused options to match demand by manipulating capacity levers, such as workforce utilization and scheduling,[3] and spending a lot of energy on improving the forecast. Companies then typically grapple with the very real risk of stock-outs caused by unforeseen bulk orders or related events, which ultimately leads to supply shortages and disruptions. When using demand-focused alternatives to match demand,[4] many organizations operating with traditional, static supply chains attempt to influence demand using crude price change strategies or back-ordering, achieving only limited results at best or losses at worst. To compound the issue, it is common practice to segment traditional supply chains by channels. This tendency causes duplication of inventory and infrastructure, increasing risks and costs.

Companies have attempted to virtualize inventory across the supply chain using enterprise resource planning systems to manage the process. However, e-commerce fulfillment, omnichannel services, and more demanding customers have increased the number of supply chain partners required to coordinate inventory. Under this evolving and increasingly complex market scenario, providing supply chain partners access to a company's ERP system becomes more challenging. Online orders continue to expand, and so do delivery speed expectations. As a result, picking has become more complex, and delivery timelines tighter and more challenging. The fulfillment component of a supply chain requires the coordination of various operations amid high volumes, low margins, lean asset allocation, and time-sensitive deadlines.

Also, firms have typically used traditional monthly cycles for planning in supply chains. This practice involves reviewing a set of supply and demand imbalances to make strategic decisions.[5] The challenge of this conventional process, though, is that dealing with the trade-offs involved can be time-consuming, labor-intensive, prone to errors, and often costly. While the use of connected devices and sensors is increasing in traditional materials handling logistics operations, the storage, movement, and fulfillment of goods through distribution centers and warehouses still face damages, spoilage, and incomplete shipments under traditional supply chains. Stock-outs and excess inventory are frequent, and service level and operations face frequent disruptions. In addition, organizations rely on traditional transportation methods for last-mile delivery and on the stand-alone use of GPS navigation to optimize routes, which limit the outcomes by excluding other information and often renders the process suboptimal.

DIGITAL SUPPLY NETWORK AND DYNAMIC FULFILLMENT

Dynamic fulfillment capability consists of advanced worker solutions in the distribution center and logistics operations; item tracking and visibility; autonomous, augmented, and connected processes and planning; and the ability to collaborate in real time.[6] Collectively, those elements will allow an organization to sense what its customers will need and make real-time adjustments across the digital supply network nodes to best accommodate demand signals and provide the right product to the right customers at the right time. Figure 10.1 illustrates such a notional vision. The concept is that a dynamic fulfillment network consists of an interconnected ecosystem of nodes that constantly shape the planning, production, and distribution of products[7] to deliver a seamless customer experience. The figure illustrates the underlying need to integrate across the entire user experience, from sensing a customer need to synchronizing and orchestrating all activities and assets in real time to efficiently delivering the product.

FIGURE 10.1   **Notional Depiction of DSN Dynamic Fulfillment**

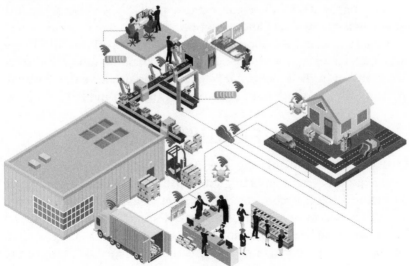

The digital interconnections illustrated in Figure 10.1 should give an organization's customers, its internal functional areas, and its network of partners superior insights, considerable agility, and a more comprehensive understanding of the costs involved. Predictive capabilities enabled by the DSN allow the fulfillment organization to sense demand based on analysis of traditional and new datasets combined with social data, visibility of customer inventories, and real-time demand. IoT sensors connecting the various assets throughout the physical network enable the organization to concentrate the complex flow of information in a traditional supply chain into a central core in the DSN for visualization, awareness, and decision making. The sensors allow an organization to monitor the location, state, and performance of its physical assets. Also, they can enable an organization to perform the same monitoring of its products deployed at a customer's facility without having to tap into the customer's ERP system to obtain information.

The DSN converts fulfillment planning from a periodic exercise into a continuous, real-time activity by supplementing integrated business planning with autonomous and smart planning. As suggested in Figure 10.1, innovative mechanisms to supply and deliver products, such as wheeled robots, autonomous stations, intelligent lockers, and drones, and their combined use support the optimization of total distribution costs and increase agility, while providing customers with superior service. Besides, those assets are connected continuously, providing real-time visibility about their location and status, which allows the organization to adjust in-transit shipment to react to unforeseen or developing events or new signals rapidly. The DSN warehouses feature automated management and execution systems, and a combination of stationary and mobile robots as well as cobots to perform fulfillment activities, changing the scope, nature, and extent of human workforce intervention in the process. DSN warehouses also have the ability to dynamically serve both online and offline, and B2B and B2C channels.

DYNAMIC FULFILLMENT ATTRIBUTES

As Figure 10.1 implicitly suggests, a DSN dynamic fulfillment prospect requires several supporting sub-capabilities, which we summarize in Figure 10.2: interconnected ecosystem signaling, supply network traceability, omni-channel competency, smart distribution operations, smart delivery operations, and smart network design. First, interconnected ecosystem signaling is the automated transmission of data across multiple aspects and entities of the network concurrently. These include signals related to supply, demand, order placement and fulfillment, authorization of returns, and product end-of-lifecycle information. This sub-capability makes the network more transparent by providing real-time visibility beyond a specific site and enables superior customer responsiveness, which can often be an elusive pursuit.[8,9] In an early example of developing aspects of this sub-capability, a leading technology company plans to integrate information from its AI-enabled customer assistant, online traffic, and previous purchase, among others, to anticipate shipping. The idea is that when the customer realizes the need for a specific product, the company has already prepositioned the item based on data signals collected through multiple means and processed by powerful analytics. The ultimate effect is that the company can fulfill the order possibly within hours and the shipping costs could decrease. The initial concept is based on prepositioning the inventory locally, so this anticipatory shipping model can evolve to include the last mile delivery by drones or autonomous ground robotics.

FIGURE 10.2 Dynamic Fulfillment Attributes

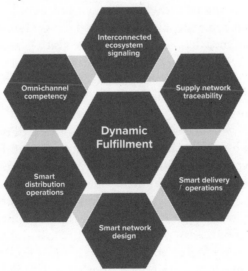

Supply network traceability is the visibility into the provenance, transfer of custody, and movement of items as they flow through the network. It provides knowledge about the location and processes of products from their origins through the end customer.[10] This sub-capability makes the network safer, more accountable, and more fitting with the increasing levels of standards and scrutiny of the market and the stringent provisions of new legislation. In an interesting example of such sub-capability, a Dutch grocery chain has connected the customers of its own brand of orange juice with the sustainable orange groves it uses in Brazil by providing traceability and provenance transparency. A single bottle of juice might contain oranges from a diverse set of growers. Using the QR code, a consumer can scan the package and see the route the oranges have traveled from farm to supermarket shelf. Besides, customers can check the percentage of oranges that come from each of the company's supplier's 25 Rainforest Alliance Certified plantations in Brazil, when they were harvested, and their degree of sweetness.

Omni-channel competency is the integration of fulfillment processes across different channels into an overarching system. It supports the confirmation, aggregation, orchestration, and fulfillment of customer orders through multiple service points. In other words, this sub-capability supports flexible fulfillment options across various channels, shorter fulfillment time and lower costs, end-to-end visibility, and better customer experience. We can illustrate this sub-capability with the use case of a leading retailer, which synchronizes order management across its e-commerce site, mobile app, and physical stores. Customers can identify online what is available before visiting stores. Employees use tablets to monitor inventory in real time to assist customers and can instantly replenish inventory based on demand, should they run out of the item. This attribute enables visibility and management of inventory across channels.

Smart distribution operations are the high-flexibility, data-driven, and balanced human-technology interconnection inside and across the various types of warehouses for efficient and adaptable services. These activities include dynamically identifying, receiving, picking, and packing orders, counting, storing, and retrieving products, among others. This sub-capability supports real-time visibility, enables the optimization of processes, provides the ability to accommodate immediate change, and reduces or eliminates errors. A leading technology company in the United States and another in China have deployed hundreds of robots that dynamically bring shelves to the pickers, have added cobots, and have experimented with drones inside the warehouse. The potential benefits include operating the warehouses during the day and night with equal costs, greater accuracy, and better use of space and human talent.

Smart delivery operations are the dynamic, data-driven, and automatic selection of the optimal modes and routes for autonomous, efficient, and fast delivery services. This sub-capability supports higher customer convenience, greater efficiency, faster delivery times, real-time visibility, and environmental regulatory compliance. For instance, an online flower retailer partnered with a technology mapping company to deal with the florist's dependence on unlimited delivery—waypoints. On special days, such as Valentine's Day, there can be potentially 1,000 deliveries in a five-hour period. The navigation system integrates multiple data sources and automatically clusters the delivery orders. The system incorporates real-time traffic conditions to optimize routes and provide tracking and communication of order status. In addition to these features, a logistics company also allows the customer to specify pickup time and location and sends this information to the navigation system to update routes dynamically.

Finally, *smart network design* is the agile and data-driven coordination and assignment of roles and capacity of flexible individual fulfillment points. In general, designing a network to serve customers better and access resources makes a lot of sense; however, executives need to decide on the configuration and how much the different operations need to work together to create customer value.[11] Smart network design sub-capability supports virtual interconnection and rapid expansion or contraction of distribution capacity and enables quick reconfiguration to augment the ability to meet customers' changing service expectations. Suppliers and logistics providers can connect virtually with the focal company and dynamically make changes in storage and processing capacity to accommodate changing demand. For instance, an e-commerce company has rapidly and dramatically scaled up its fulfillment capabilities leveraging the network of distribution centers (DCs) across the United States from an e-commerce fulfillment startup. Figure 10.2 summarizes the various formative sub-capabilities of the DSN dynamic fulfillment.

TECHNOLOGY ENABLING DYNAMIC FULFILLMENT AND ITS ATTRIBUTES

To support the DSN dynamic fulfillment sub-capabilities, executives and supply chain professionals will need to select and deploy the right smart technologies. New technologies can enable fulfillment to operate optimally and to react quickly to events, such as seasonal demand or varying product demand. Autonomous robots and drone usage in logistics operations, smart devices, IoT, and AI are the building blocks of flexible fulfillment capability. Properly combined and integrated, these technologies will support the tracking of asset and item movement, improve labor efficiency, reduce inventory levels and waste, and digitize quality defects. The use of autonomous self-learning robotics and smart devices in fulfillment operations can provide the digital supply network the ability to deal with dynamic changes in the environment in an efficient manner. More specifically, they can support omni-channel fulfillment, streamlined warehouse and transportation, real-time visibility, and adaptability to changing conditions and demand. Let's take a look at prominent categories of enabling technologies that will support dynamic fulfillment capability and its attributes.

Unmanned Aerial Vehicles

Unmanned aerial vehicles can contribute capabilities in terms of last-mile delivery, supply chain visibility, infrastructure inspection and control, and inventory picking and movement, as shown in Table 10.1. While the range of operations is still limited, the potential to increase customer service and transform last mile delivery is tremendous. Various countries, including the United States, have authorized the commercial operation of drones, and the concepts are evolving rapidly, including shipment from trucks, warehouses, and stores. Some major logistics providers are planning to have a drone fly from a vehicle to deliver the last few miles. In this general concept, some major OEMs have partnered with drone designers to explore the docking of drones on a moving vehicle. Another significant logistics provider is planning to use a station in the neighborhood with RFID tags activated by the drone and text message to the customer. Another delivery method proposes dropping packages via a controlled parachute. Some concepts integrate drone hovering with ground robots.

Internally, unmanned aerial vehicles equipped with RFID-scanning technology can produce real-time inventory visibility in warehouses. In this application, a drone navigates the warehouse and performs a physical inventory by scanning the RFID tags. In terms of inventory management, executives can use drones for inventory audits, inventory management, cycle counting, item search, buffer stock maintenance, and stock taking. For instance, a high-profile retailer has used drones to check inventory in its entire one-million-square-foot distribution center in one day. Beyond visibility, companies can potentially utilize drones to do picking and inventory movement to expand the vertical dimension. Drones could put away and pick inventory on very high shelves in distribution centers with an ultra-high ceiling. Robotic innovations incorporating the latest developments in machine vision, sensing, and learning will allow robots to work collaboratively with humans even in complex tasks such as picking and packing.

TABLE 10.1 Drone applications in logistics and fulfillment

Application	Capability	Use
External	Last mile delivery	• Delivery from truck • Delivery from DC • Delivery from store • Delivery from air
Internal	Visibility and control	• Inventory inspection • Inventory movement • Facility inspection • Yard management

Still inside warehouses and distribution centers, as the technology for indoor navigation evolves, drones have the potential to perform on-site express delivery of tools and spare parts. Some providers have started developing advanced technology for indoor navigation, combining 3D depth sensors, a 3D scanner with 360-degree wide-angle cameras, and vision-based localization and mapping algorithms. Drones will eventually be able to collaborate among themselves and with other machines. Connected systems will be able to exchange and process a massive stream of data in real time to optimally synchronize the movement of all resources. For instance, a robotic storage retrieval system can communicate with a drone or an autonomous mobile robot to dynamically retrieve goods. The items can then replenish the robot, and an outbound mobile sortation machine can communicate with a self-contained transportation management solution, such as drones and ground robotic vehicles. A solution available in the market combines drones with an automated ground vehicle with a calibration board on top to increase location accuracy. In this solution, the drone is tethered with a cable to the ground vehicle, increasing battery time.

In the intersection between the last mile and internal warehouse operations are the trailer yards. Drones can potentially assist in yard management by tracking and allowing optimal control of large amounts of transportation and inventory assets. Transportation assets can spend as much as 40 percent of their total transportation time parked idle in trailer yards at either the point of destination or origin. Drone-based surveillance can be particularly promising in congested or hard-to-access areas. Another area with potential for drone utilization is intra-logistics. Drones can potentially transfer products, components, or supporting material, such as dunnage, packaging, and shrink-wrap, from DC to DC or manufacturing to DC. For instance, drones can transport parts from warehouses located nearby to workshops in factories. In this application, a company could move materials from a remote location to shipping as needed, or suppliers can potentially deliver parts and components just-in-time to OEMs. Examples of intra-logistics use cases include the approval for automated drone flights carrying spare parts on factory premises and onsite drone delivery of laboratory samples in Europe. As autonomous drones come of age, their practical use in warehouse and distribution operations will confer flexibility and agility to the underlying digital supply network.

Collaborative Autonomous Mobile Robots (AMR)

Driverless, automatic guided industrial vehicles, popularly known in the industry as automatic guided vehicles (AGVs), have been successfully used to automate the movement of materials to, from, and through warehouses, distribution centers, and manufacturing plants for quite some time. This technology replaces non-value-added repetitive material movement and delivery. More recently, a new type of robotic vehicle based on new technologies has made this solution smarter and faster—autonomous mobile robots. AMRs are a form of AGVs that supply chain and logistics executives can implement without any supporting infrastructure, such as markers or wires or magnets implanted in the floor, or precisely located laser targets.

Similar to AGVs, AMRs support automation, but with flexibility in fulfillment operations. They are not only capable of working around the clock and handling a variety of material, but also do not require the training and learning curve of humans when they move to a new task. Executives and supply chain professionals will be able to deploy this technology to either replace human labor or to augment human efforts. Also, due to their connected nature, AMRs enable a logistics operation to capture movement data, thus supporting analytics and simulations that are not typically feasible when human operators conduct the movement. One feature that makes them promise to support dynamic fulfillment is that they incorporate collaborative capability into their designs. Another feature is that, while traditional AGVs will sense obstacles and typically stop until someone removes the obstruction, AMRs can travel the same pathways with pedestrian foot traffic and do not require a controlled environment as AGVs usually do.

AMRs incorporate several fused sensors, such as LiDAR and shorter-range 3D cameras, and powerful onboard computers that allow it to understand its operating environment. Supply chain leaders can utilize AMRs to build flexibility into fulfillment operations. There are collaborative AMRs for locating, tracking, and moving inventory in distribution centers and logistics facilities. AMRs can work jointly for several warehouse tasks, including collaborative goods-to-person tote retrieval for pickers, inventory replenishment, cycle counting, and item verification. New systems will allow warehouse automation within days as opposed to weeks and months of traditional methods. Mobile robot systems will simplify material-handling and support facility workflow to be set up and modified rapidly to accommodate dynamic environments without needing complex programing.

While many AMRs use sensors and algorithms to navigate dynamic environments safely, they are currently not yet able to utilize sensory input for advanced decision-making. However, some AMRs can utilize artificial intelligence (AI) and vision algorithms to adapt to the existing logistics environment. The addition of AI makes AMRs even more efficient, increases the range of task the robots can perform, and reduces the need for work-environment adaptations to accommodate them. The most mature AMR will have the capability to run unattended in complex environments, where there is a risk of encountering unforeseen situations. These robots can autonomously understand the situation and adequately communicate their status.

A fleet management system can select the ideal route for a delivery or pickup based on many ways produced by the mapping software used by AMRs, contributing to its flexibility. A fleet of AMRs also can communicate with each other to maximize traffic flow, avoid a collision, and increase efficiency. Decision makers can integrate AMRs with other technologies, such as programmable logic controllers (PLCs) in manufacturing plants or cloud-based analytics software in distribution centers, to produce an IoT automation solution. The data from the robotic vehicles can enable the cloud-based management system to make efficient assignments based on evolving environmental conditions. The cloud system can utilize information about the location of each robotic vehicle and progress on the current pick up to intelligently assign incoming work across the robotic fleet. The connectivity between the cloud management systems and AMRs can enable analytics on resource utilization, productivity trends, and patterns on how inventory location might be affecting picking.

We can categorize AMRs into two main types: fleet management, typically utilized for bigger payloads and routes from origin to a destination, and pick optimization, typically used to integrate the movement of machines and people in a process flow designed to increase picking throughput. Warehouses can utilize AMRs for goods-to-person picking where the robots travel flexible routes in the warehouse, moving products between workers and stations. AMRs can also monitor inventory when combined with RFID-tagged products and equipment, carrying out inventory sweeps autonomously. Forklifts are also becoming intelligent with full autonomy for some applications, mainly for operations whose load-handling processes that provide little added value, are repetitive, and involve long distances. Similarly, the capabilities, smartness, and connectivity of automatic storage and retrieval systems will continue to expand. In a nutshell, innovative robots for logistics operations are becoming increasingly flexible and autonomous. The deployment of innovative robotics in logistics operations will support executives and supply chain professionals' design to build dynamic fulfillment capability.

Ground Autonomous Last Mile Delivery

The last mile of delivery is the least predictable and most complex part of the entire journey. This characteristic is particularly so for congested urban areas full of vehicles, cyclists, pedestrians, dynamic intersections, and traffic rules, with movement in every direction and limited parking spaces. While there are many technical challenges, regulatory constraints, and societal hurdles for the widespread use of autonomous vehicles, the industry has made much progress, and many applications are now entering in the proof-of-concept stage. This technology has great potential and will be a critical component supporting dynamic fulfillment capabilities.

We can organize the many solutions in development into on-demand package delivery and retailer-to-customer delivery.[12] Let's start with a glance at the on-demand side of things. Several logistics providers and technology companies have launched concepts where retailers will be able to accept orders from nearby customers and deliver them by wheeled autonomous robots directly to customers' homes or businesses the same day. This concept aims at providing retailers' autonomous same-day and last mile delivery capability. The robot is supposed to travel on sidewalks and along roadsides and deliver smaller shipments. It will include pedestrian-safe technology and advanced technology, such as Lidar and multiple cameras. The robot will also have machine-learning algorithms to detect and avoid obstacles, plotting safe paths, and allowing the bot to follow road and safety rules.

Some conceptual use cases foresee autonomous vehicles serving as a supporting technology to cope with inefficiency caused by the need to walk long-distances when delivering parcels. This concept could be particularly useful in areas with limited parking spaces, for instance. In these circumstances, the delivery worker typically needs to park the vehicle far from the final destination and then cover the distance to the front door or mailbox on foot. The two-way walk is very time-consuming and can be strenuous for the delivery person if the parcel is heavy. The application here is to have the autonomous vehicle follow the delivery worker during the delivery of multiple packages in one area. The use of autonomous vehicles to assist delivery can take away some of the inefficiency and hazards from the urban delivery process. A related potential use case is the handover of parcels from autonomous vehicles to parcel stations set to serve multiple customers, such as a building, community, neighborhood, or campus. Here, the process would eliminate the complexities and inefficiencies of the "last yards."

A step further is to use the autonomous vehicle beyond only assisting the delivery worker. A potential use case proposes to combine the autonomous car with delivery robots. One package delivery concept consists of robot-taxis driving canine-inspired robots that autonomously bring deliveries right to the customer's doorstep. The idea behind this concept is to provide a seamless mobility chain comprised of a fleet of driverless vehicles and delivery robots to deliver packages to the customers. The goal is to eliminate the need for the customer to go out and meet the van, as the delivery robot-dogs can leave the trailer and navigate sidewalks, walk up front porch steps, go right to the door, and even ring doorbells. Yet another concept is the use of small-wheeled robots to deliver parcels. For instance, various technology companies have solutions in the proof-of-concept stage using advanced AI for navigation and interaction capabilities. On-board AI continuously senses and reacts to novel situations while navigating a dynamic and complex environment characterized by sidewalks, pedestrians, roads, and rail crossings. The use of AI here is essential, as such environments are continually changing.

Outside of the last mile, but still within the short distance segment, an example that has passed the proof-of-concept stage is a cabinless electric autonomous truck from a major manufacturer that was designed from the ground up as a self-contained solution. As the first real assignment, the vehicle is currently transporting containers with goods between a logistics hub and a port terminal on a pre-defined route along public roads. The vehicle aims at optimizing transport in highly repetitive, short distance, traffic flows with large volumes such as ports, factory areas, and logistics mega centers. The vehicle is part of a vast ecosystem concept and will operate together in a network inter-connected through a cloud-based service and management center. The system offers improved delivery precision and flexibility. Solutions such as this example will allow a company to move goods sustainably 24×7 in a seamless and predictable transport flow.

On the retailer-to-customer delivery side, several partnerships between automakers and technology companies are exploring autono-mous vehicle delivery concepts, including mobile stations. For instance, a major technology company is experimenting with a smart delivery system, in which employees can load the delivery robots with up to 30 parcels, so the robots can autonomously deliver them within a three-mile radius. The vehicles can plan routes, avoid obstacles, and recognize traffic lights. Facial recognition technology will enable users to collect their parcels. Another major automaker has a concept in which bipedal robot drives folded in the back of a self-driving vehicle. When the car reaches its destination, the trunk pops open, and the robot unfolds itself, picks up the parcel, and drops it on the customer's doorsteps.

Another use case that is entering the proof-of-concept stage in some places around the world is the autonomous stations. Here a company can dispatch standalone stations to drive toward the customer rather than requiring the customer to go to a central location. For instance, there are ongoing tests of an autonomous mobile convenience store that integrates AI-enhanced software and mobile payment systems in China. You enter the store with an app, place your purchases in a smart basket or scan the items, and an AI hologram assistant charges your purchases to your phone. The autonomous station is equipped with solar panels. The concept is supposed to eliminate the high costs of staff and rent in a major metropolitan city. While not running outside of the testing grounds yet, the idea is that it will eventually use AI to navigate city streets and will be able to drive to warehouses to restock itself.

The challenge in this segment is the last 10 yards, particularly in urban areas. As e-commerce and the "now" economy continues to evolve, investments in the "last yards" have great potential. However, deploying robots to deliver parcels to a customer's front door requires a high level of systems integration and a sizeable technological undertaking. It starts to seem that for the near future, drones may serve suburban areas, while last mile ground robots may help urban areas. We can also see different solutions for the last mile delivery, where some companies are investing in their last mile delivery robots, while others are developing solutions for those companies not interested in their own hardware.

Vision Picking and Wearable Technology

The use of technology-enabled picking is nothing new. Voice-directed warehousing has enabled streamlined DC operation processes, leading to higher productivity and efficiency. It has freed up workers' hands and has improved their flexibility by allowing them to condense tasks. This technology has helped DCs gain productivity by increasing accuracy in processes such as replenishment, processing, and loading. However, voice-directed warehousing is not very smart or adaptable, so it fits better in contexts with more standardized activities. As the need for adaptation increases, an extension of the capabilities of voice picking is vision picking. This extension is critical for an omni-channel context, which requires supply chain professionals to provide workers with on-demand inventory search and product information so they can quickly fulfill orders independent of their origin—physical store or online.

We can categorize wearables into virtual reality (VR), in which the user completely immerses in a computer-generated simulated environment, augmented reality (AR), and mixed reality (MR). Both AR and MR preserve an existing physical reality, but add a digital element to create a mix of real and virtual to create new environments. Vision picking uses AR to overlay graphical images over the worker's line of vision, adding digital information to physical objects. Besides, it frequently offers real-time user interface capability with objects and digital devices. We are starting to see smart vision applications for DC pick, pack, and shipping. These applications can improve the process of manual order picking, sorting, and packing, while contributing, albeit perhaps to a lesser extent than autonomous robots, to dynamic fulfillment capability. They can potentially be used to indicate the shortest path to the next pick and can highlight the item the worker needs to pick up.

Some vision picking systems are starting to provide real-time object recognition, barcode reading, indoor navigation, and integration of information with the warehouse management system. The use of such systems will allow workers to see the digital picking list and the best route. The barcode scanning and image recognition systems can confirm whether the worker arrived at the proper location and guide the correct item. Once picked, information about the scanned object can update the warehouse management system, producing real-time stock updates. AR can also improve the pickup process, within and beyond the boundaries of distribution centers and warehouses. Instead of manually scanning loads with a handheld device to check for completeness, AR can enable the worker to quickly perform the same check with a simple glance at the load. Such tools, combined with other technologies, such as 3D depth sensors, can enable workers to determine the number or volume of pallets and single parcels, and assess their integrity faster and more effectively.

Another use case for ARs is the optimization of the loading and unloading processes (Figure 10.3). During loading, AR can supply workers with real-time information about the sequence and location of pallets or parcels, and intuitive loading instructions. The device can perform calculations about space requirements for each volume in real time, check for suitable empty spaces inside the vehicle, and cross-reference information about the load, such as weight, fragility, and point of delivery, and instruct the worker where to place the item. This use would further eliminate the utilization of paper-based lists, speed up the process, maximize the use of space, and possibly reduce the risk of damage. During unloading, AR could eliminate the time workers typically spend searching for the right parcel or pallet.

FIGURE 10.3   Cargo Loading with Virtual Reality

Vision picking and wearable technology can assist the increasingly complex warehousing operations and contribute to dynamic fulfillment capability in many ways. They can improve quality and productivity by providing meaningful information, instructions, and documentation directly to the worker's eyes. For instance, many warehouse and logistics operations and tasks are experience-based skills. Besides, the complexity, tempo, and dynamism of logistics have continued to increase. As such, supply chain professionals can codify best practices, and then they can use those technologies to diffuse knowledge and guide workers through the learning process. Supply chain professionals can also incorporate wearables to assist with safety.

Sensors, Telematics, and IoT

Warehouse automation systems, such as conveyors and sorters, have been connected for quite some time now and frequently feed data into a warehouse control system. However, wired networks typically circumscribe automated material handling systems. While traditional automation, such as automated palletization and depalletization, has proved highly efficient, these methods have limitations in that they usually accommodate only similar product shapes and type of handling. This characteristic requires high levels of standardization and therefore restricts the potential for these technologies to streamline and improve processes.

As we move forward, managers will have the opportunity to use new sensor options and cloud-based platforms that apply machine learning for predictive analytics. Solution providers are moving toward IoT analysis of the health of critical warehouse assets as a package. For instance, a significant solutions provider has configured its offering to analyze asset health for key materials handling system components, such as motors, leveraging data from sensor options such as vibration sensors. The solution compares and correlates insights from the sensor data with control system data from the automation that provides visibility into how well the machinery is running. While providers of material handling equipment are developing an array of pretested sensor options for their equipment, executives can use sensor providers to add monitoring to many types of industrial equipment. Executives also can use the sensors of the many existing warehouse systems to feed data into cloud-based alerting, reporting, and analytics solutions.

Lift truck telematics with prebuilt reporting and alerting software is another form of IoT solution that will continue to spread into DCs. Telematics provides supply chain executives near real-time visibility into utilization and truck availability. They also provide operators the capability to perform a safety checklist digitally. Executives can use the data produced by the trucks in combination with cloud-based software for fleet analytics. Organizations can leverage telematics connectivity and analytics for decision making, such as shuffling fleet makeup.

IoT applications in warehouses and distribution centers include sensors to monitor temperature variations in cold storage areas, heat and vibration generated by motors on materials handling systems, humidity, and motion, among others. For instance, executives can use sensors to produce heat maps showing hot spot areas within cold storage, prompting adjustments to ventilation or configuration of the room. The real benefit for executives will be in the combination of warehouse control systems, a digital platform for capturing IoT data, and cloud analytics for analyzing the data. The data can come from automated material handling systems, lift truck sensors, building automation systems, and security systems.

The analytics capability is likely the most significant challenge and also an opportunity in successfully implementing connected warehouse assets solutions. Simply collecting additional or new asset data will not produce better results or contribute to dynamic fulfillment capability. The actual analyses of the data available are likely at the crux of warehouse and logistics operation digitization. For instance, a single conveyor line in a DC can generate up to five terabytes of data a day; however, the DC management may not know whether the data is from an asset that is still throughput critical for a work order or how it relates to the rest of the DC operation.

AI and Analytics

Underlying a dynamic fulfillment capability is connectivity, analytics, and smart software infrastructure. These features make the deployment of robotics and digitization of future fulfillment operations flexible by using real-time data and decision techniques to dynamically manage factors such as resource allocation, task assignment, and physical movement. The ability of AI-driven software to coordinate and optimize resources as conditions and requirements change will increasingly become a critical foundation for dynamic fulfillment capabilities. AI promises to advance automation to the point where preset algorithms programmed by software engineers no longer bound machines.[13] Instead, they will become self-learning entities that continuously monitor, add, and discard conditions salient to accomplishing a particular goal by "mapping percepts to actions."[14] For supply network application, AI falls under two categories: augmentation, where AI assists workers, and automation, where AI functions without workers' intervention.

AI will add the ability for warehouse systems to learn and adapt to the current state of the environment rather than to a collection of preset rules. For instance, a warehouse and distribution management organization will be able to utilize machine learning within its warehouse management system to determine the amount of time required to complete a given task in a given set of circumstances. The machine learning algorithm will examine past data, including the type of task, duration, and item characteristics. It will then determine which conditions will affect the amount of time needed to complete a task. The next time the task is assigned, the system will take those conditions into account when estimating the lead time to complete the job. In a current example, an autonomous picking robot captures data such as what the robot saw (camera), what it did (approach and pick method), and what happened (success or failure). Convolutional neural networks take this data and enable the robot to distinguish between adjacent items, which helps improve picking accuracy.

SUMMARY

Mobile robotics and smart technology will have a dramatic impact on how we design, build, and operate distribution and fulfillment operations. These technologies are more flexible, allowing us to achieve adaptability and dynamic capabilities. These outcomes contrast with the longstanding trade-off posed by traditional automation, which lowered costs but tended to require long lead times to install and modify. The new technology is smarter and more flexible and does not require extensive infrastructure that would make it difficult to change or reconfigure. As technology continues to evolve, we will be able to deploy robots and autonomous material handling robots to enable a zero-touch and highly efficient environment.

As the concept of digital supply network evolves, executives will be able to move their DCs from forecast-driven to demand-driven operations, building on the combined use of AI, robotics, and IoT to support dynamic fulfillment capability. IoT will increasingly provide an abundant cache of data not available previously, while AI will help micro-decisions and optimize them to a level not feasible earlier. Other robotics, warehouse management systems, and other forms of automation have improved logistics and fulfillment operations. However, those systems typically operate within bounded constraints and are mostly inflexible. Decision making is performed under established rules, capacities, and resources. As we move forward, the logistics and fulfillment environment will continue to become more dynamic and complex. Current conditions will increasingly be more critical than preset rules. Therefore, the combination of new technology and connectivity will become essential. Companies will need to implement systems that intelligently balance capacity against resources in an increasingly dynamic context.

The adaptable advanced technologies discussed in this chapter offer executives and supply chain professionals the opportunity to streamline delivery and fulfillment operations in terms of demand sensing, route optimization, and warehousing and logistics activities. Perhaps more important, they offer the possibility for organizations to transform those processes to support current and new business models entirely. We can envision a future where executives will be able to design a sufficiently smart and dynamic fulfillment process such that, for instance, an IoT signal will alert a DC of a late inbound load. AI will take that information and decide the optimal time to release and deploy a specific amount of labor to unload the truck, will schedule robotic vehicles to support the operations, determine what portion of that load should go directly to fill orders, and dynamically repurpose resources previously set to participate in the initially scheduled time. This dynamic adds an entirely new level of automation, visibility, and intelligence to the fulfillment operations. Combining machine learning, AI, and IoT to data analytics and the other capabilities discussed in this and the other chapters will support truly dynamic routing, scheduling, delivery, resource utilization, and ultimately dynamic fulfillment. May we continue living in exciting times in the development of the building blocks to support the digital supply network.

CONNECTED CUSTOMER

Customers are the key to any business, the prime reason for a company to exist! In the current digital era, customers are no longer passive buyers of products at the end of the value chain, but active partners throughout the lifecycle of the products and their associated services. The connected customer is part of the connected world through advanced technology and collaborative applications. In this chapter, we will discuss the changing customer dynamics in the current age of personalization; we will illustrate the customer connect part of traditional supply chain management (SCM), followed by the impactful changes through customer connect capabilities of the digital supply network (DSN). We will then delve into the relevant technologies impacting customer management before illustrating the capabilities of connected customers.

CHANGING CUSTOMERS IN THE AGE OF PERSONALIZATION

Customers in the current digital era want personalized products, with the convenience of acquisition whether it be online or in-store. They are ready to switch brands for a better experience, better price, or faster delivery. At the same time, customers are willing to pay a premium, forge a loyal relationship, and become brand advocates if they are connected well with the organization through a value-based association.

Technology, data, computing capability, manufacturing agility, and DSN strengths enable organizations to treat customers as individuals to be served and delighted instead of a mass of passive users. Figure 11.1 shows a few examples of products and their related service personalization in the digital era. Take, for example, an oral product manufacturer that recommends and delivers the right toothpaste and right toothbrush for a user based on the user's gum sensitivity, cleaning habits, tooth condition, and any further information shared by the dentist's office. While brushing, the mobile app shows the real-time effectiveness of the cleaning and recommends if a tooth needs more attention. In another example, a shoe company analyzes foot patterns and prompt distribution, along with exercising and usage habits, to recommend and deliver a customized shoe. The smart cap of a medicine box alerts the patient and the caretaker if a planned medicine dose is missed.

FIGURE 11.1 Examples of Product Customization and Connected Customer

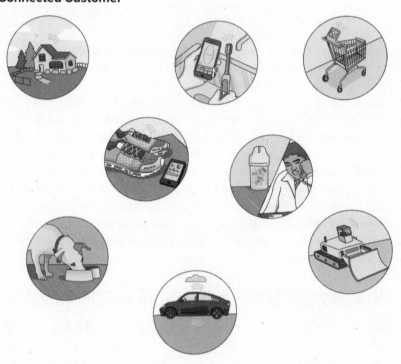

While online retailers are tracking the click and buying patterns to predict and recommend products in real time, brick-and-mortar retail stores are experimenting with ways to track customers in the store to recommend the products in real time, referring to the customer's profile, preferences, past shopping history, and current aisle location. Once a shopper scans his or her information while entering the store, a notification can be either sent to the shopper's mobile phone or displayed on a smart screen attached to the cart as shown in Figure 11.1. Retailers are also experimenting with checkout processes, testing automation and cashier-free models.

In the same Figure 11.1, a connected mining and construction digger equipment dynamically sends usage information and machine condition to the cloud. The operator is alerted for fuel replenishment, required engine tune-up, or a tire replacement. The car connected to the cloud gets required software updates automatically through the Internet, while the auto OEM or dealer monitors the performance of the vehicle for optimal usage. The smart band on a dog's neck monitors its health and eating pattern to alert the owner for any recommended action. The connected home uses digital devices to secure itself and replenish the essentials and food automatically by tracking the refrigerator shelves and other identified areas.

The examples shared here highlight the changing usage patterns, product development, delivery, and customer interaction. Customers in the current digital era behave utterly differently than in the previous period of mass market and mass communication. Figure 11.2 (see next page) shows the customer service channel used by the organization in the traditional SCM environment. The product is produced at the factory, moved to the distribution center, and then to the retail store where it is expected that the customer will walk in to purchase it. This strategy is based on standardized products for the mass market, influenced by mass one-way communication.[1] For the organization's supply chain, the retail store was considered the customer, and the SCM processes were designed and built to serve the vendor-retailer relationship, with the assumption that the consumer would buy products from the stores, influenced by marketing communication.

With the rising adoption of online shopping channels in the past decade, the convenience of same-day home delivery has transformed supply chain processes, allowing customer involvement from product design to manufacture and delivery. The customer connect process looks completely different in DSN as compared to the SCM. Figure 11.3 represents the customer service example in the digital era as part of the DSN process. Customers are no longer considered as a passive mass market; they are now active connected nodes on the digital network.[2] They use different channels to talk about the enterprise, interact with products, and connect with the manufacturer directly. The current customer talks about the brand and the product and is not shy to share her opinion, both good and bad. This information sharing is

FIGURE 11.2 Customer Service Representation in Traditional SCM

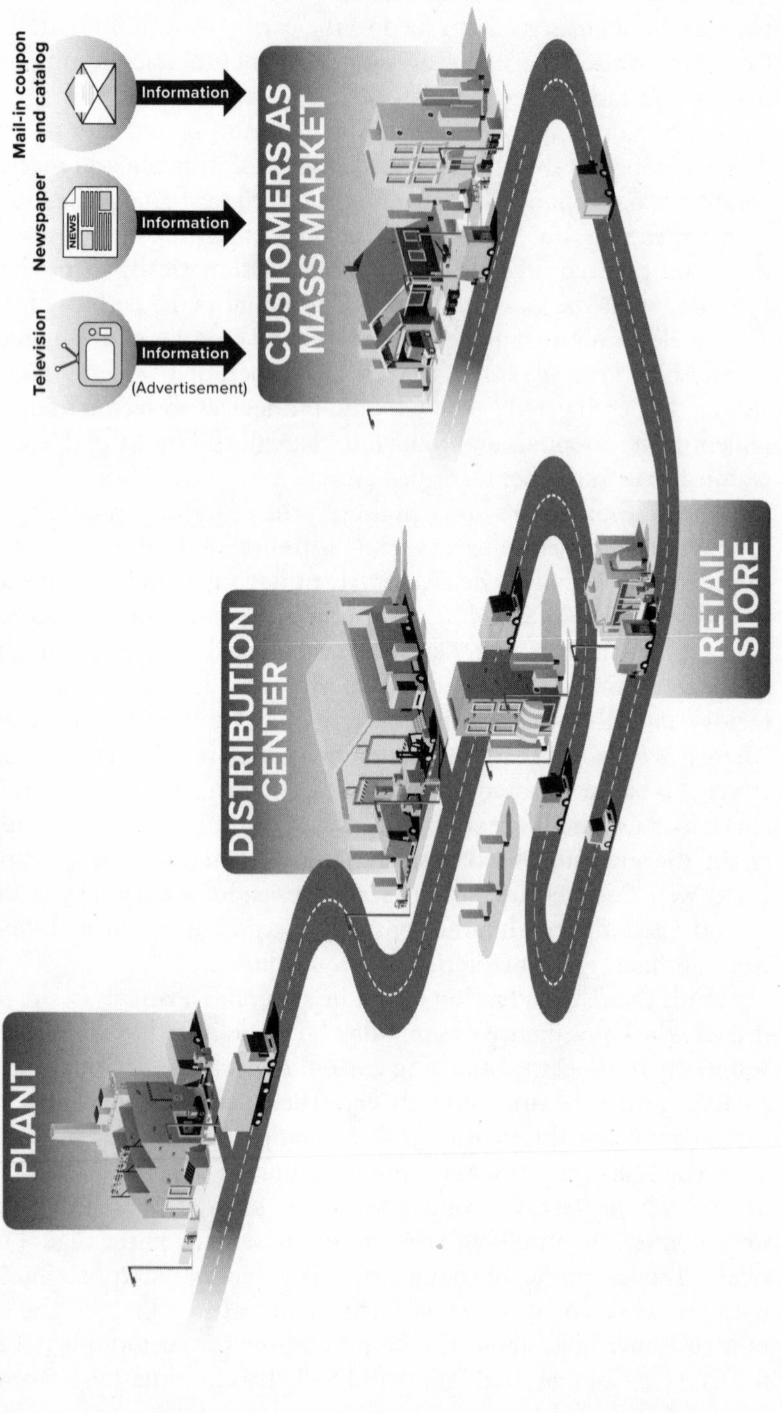

PLANT

DISTRIBUTION CENTER

RETAIL STORE

CUSTOMERS AS MASS MARKET

Television
Information
(Advertisement)

Newspaper
Information
NEWS

Mail-in coupon and catalog
Information

208

enabled by multiple digital channels, as shown in Figure 11.3. Though traditional communication channels (TV, newspaper, mail coupon) are still relevant, the market is more influenced by the actual reviews, experiences, and recommendations, often shared via social media platforms. Personalization, convenience, and a delightful experience have become the differentiators for purchase and brand advocacy decisions.

FIGURE 11.3 Customer Service Representation in DSN

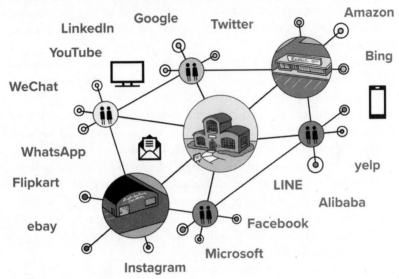

MANAGING CUSTOMER PROCESSES IN TRADITIONAL SCM

The goal of the SCM process is to make sure the product is available on the shelf when the customer walks into the store for her requirements. In the traditional "plan-source-make-deliver" process of SCM, customer service focuses on the "deliver" part, aimed at product availability. The retail store is considered as the customer, and fulfilling the replenishment order of the store has been the critical success criterion of the supply chain process.

Operation Mode and Success Criteria of Customer Service in Traditional SCM

Delivery success criteria have been measured through order fulfillment fill rates, using KPIs like "unit fill rate," "line fill rate," and "order fill rate." The unit fill rate measures the performance of the percentage of product quantity delivered on time; line fill rate measures the percentage of purchase order line items replenished in full quantity on time; while the order fill rate measures the percentage of orders honored in full amount for all items on time as compared to total number of orders.

The supply chain is then designed and managed to ensure order fulfillment parameters are met and visibility of inventory movement is available for the organization and the retail partner. Placing inventories at different replenishment locations, including distribution centers, warehouses, and factories, is done for high product availability and service reliability.

Lead time for order placement to delivery, along with the variability of the customer demand, logistics, and transportation, is the input of the safety stock calculation. Supply chain planning is then performed to fill the marked locations with the calculated safety stock. Even in a well-managed supply chain, it has been common to have 8 to 10 percent of stock-out items at the retail stores in the United States in the past five years, despite these supply chain planning processes.

The supply chain has been managed to aggregate demand at centralized plants to achieve an economy of scale for production, minimizing the unit cost of the product. The scale is optimized for transportation to place the products at the retail store for consumer access at the lowest cost.

Though it was common to solicit customers' feedback for product development through sample data of the focus market, the value flow happened in a one-way direction from the organization to the customer. The organization developed products for the big mass market, manufactured them through economies of scale, pushed them to the retail store, and performed one-way promotion through advertisement to build consumer awareness and get customers to visit the store and buy.

Challenges of Customer Service Processes of Traditional SCM

The first challenge of the sequential supply chain process is considering the customer as a generalized mass to whom products are pushed at the store level. The old methods and technologies don't enable customers to be active partners for product development and customization. "Make to order" is a regularly used term in the supply chain; however, its application is mostly limited to the B2B (business to business) buyer-seller relationship, especially for sophisticated machinery or high-cost industrial items. The supply chain process with the inherent nature of product standardization, central order aggregation, mass production–storage–transportation, and limited customer touch-points results in limited value creation and passive consumers.

Multichannel management is another reality of the current business. A customer expects the same excellent experience, irrespective of the connecting channel. It can become complicated, unprofitable, and unmanageable for an organization still operating traditional SCM processes to be able to provide the same efficiency and customer delight through a physical store, online channel, and online order with store pickup modes.

Customer issue management has been a source of adverse experience for most of the consumers who had issues with products and services in the traditional SCM. Most organizations operating traditional supply chains are ineffective in managing the customer issue. For example, it is common to get a call or email transferred to different departments of the organization when managing a customer complaint. It is commonplace to have separate helplines and resolution teams for different channels, various issues (delivery, service, price), diverse product lines, different locations, and so on. Research indicates that most consumers give up on the organization after getting transferred more than three times for their issue, and the organization loses the customer for life and risks having negative words and reviews spread across digital channels.

The complexity of multiple channels and numerous locations, with the old process and technical ability, can hugely multiply the cost for an organization aiming to maintain the same level of customer service as its agile DSN competitor. It has a massive impact on working capital because it typically requires the organization to fill high safety stock inventory levels to meet service targets.

In summary, traditional linear supply chains are not designed to solve the complex challenges of a digitally enabled, customer-centric world. The next generation of customer-focused processes, enabled by the technological capabilities to govern collaboration, communication, and operational optimization, is here, solving the issues of customer connect in traditional SCM.

CUSTOMER CONNECT PROCESS OF DIGITAL SUPPLY NETWORK

The connected customer of DSN is a shift from the transactional consumer interaction to holistic customer engagement. The customer is an active participant in the business processes and not a passive recipient of products and one-way information. With the help of data and technology, innovative ways to solve the customer's problem become the driving force of the development, manufacturing, and logistics processes.

Figure 11.4 represents the customer journey for the DSN model. The processes of awareness, acquisition, and transaction refer to the information and communication between the customer and the organization, which leads to the purchase of the products or services. In DSN format, at this stage, the organization and customer are connected in a collaborated manner and know each other through the data shared via the digital technology, platform, and channels. From the transaction stage, the next natural stage in the DSN cycle is customer engagement and value enrichment, creating a virtuous cycle. In cases where the transaction leads to an issue regarding the products or services, the "service and resolution" process, strengthened by the reimagined customer connect process and fortified with the technology, solves the problem in an efficient and effective manner, leading again to an engaged and enriched customer.

FIGURE 11.4   Customer Journey in DSN Process

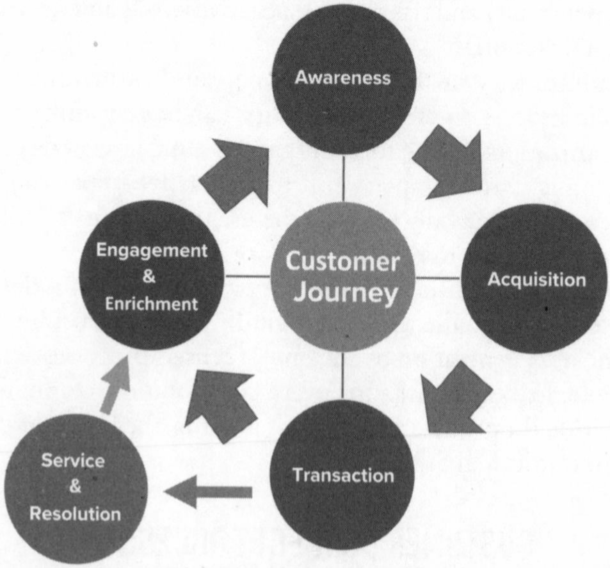

DSN processes fortified with data, computing capabilities, advanced yet affordable sensors, and IoT devices can achieve product and service personalization. Customers in the current era are ready to share personal information if it adds value to their life. People are supplying their personal data, health measurements, DNA data, and lifestyle information to organizations to get personalized products. An energy drink provider has successfully obtained the perspiration data of its consumers along with their goals (weight loss, stamina, fitness, etc.) to supply the drink aligned to their individual hydration requirements. In another example, DNA information, along with the physical data of weight, height, and age, is used to deliver individualized food. A skin cream manufacturer has partnered with medical clinics where people go to get their skin tested. The information collected is used with a machine-learning algorithm to identify the best-suited mix of active ingredients for the skin cream, a small device at the clinic mixes the ingredients in real time, and the person returns home with the personalized products. This personalization is impacting every business; it can be food, medicine, fitness, automobile, consumer products, furniture, apparel, footwear, entertainment, and so on. There is no business that is currently not impacted by personalization and digitization. Customer personalization can be enhanced through the adoption of design thinking approach. It encourages organizations to focus on the people they're creating for, which leads to better products, services, and internal processes.[3] The digital tools allow the organization to develop empathy with the customers by following the phases empathize, define, ideate, prototype, and test.[4] The phases involve understanding from the user's perspective, defining the problem and solution, ideating to create the solution ideas, prototyping the solution, and testing with the users. Further information on the design thinking and customer-centric approach are discussed in Chapter 13, "DSN Transformation Playbook."

Customer connect processes of the DSN provide the same customer delight experience across the connect channels from a physical store to an online store or mobile app. Network design and inventory management through synchronized planning take advantage of placing the inventory in a way that enables a unified channel serving the store as well as Internet customers. End-to-end visibility of the inventory supported with the sensors, a command center, and a control tower serves the need of the always-on, agile enterprise.

Product and service development in the DSN framework revolves around the customer. Instead of being product focused, the organization becomes customer focused. This topic is covered in detail in Chapter 7, "Digital Product Development."

Digital tools with reimagined processes can transform customer issue management with self-service, visibility, and an issue ownership approach. The support team is customer focused so that a support person owns the issue resolution of a customer, irrespective of department or functional area. This process is enabled by self-service automation with incorporated natural language processing and artificial intelligence. Most of the issues get resolved through an automated system, while the remaining ones are assigned to one point of contact who takes the matter to the conclusion. The result is a delighted customer!

Enhanced computing capabilities, visibility, and transparency across the network make it easier to manage the flow of the products and inventory storage for the optimum service at minimum cost. This topic has been covered in detail in Chapter 6, "Synchronized Planning." Further information on manufacturing and fulfillment in the DSN era is covered in Chapter 9, "Smart Manufacturing and Intelligent Asset Management," and Chapter 10, "Dynamic Fulfillment."

TECHNOLOGY IMPACT FOR THE CONNECTED CUSTOMER

Advanced technology is influencing customer management and enabling end-to-end automation and efficiency. Every technology discussed in Chapters 3, 4, and 5 is relevant to the connected customer process.

Following are some examples of relevant technologies that are either being used by organizations or are in the experimentation phase for commercial usage:

- Causal-based forecasting algorithms enabled by sensors at points of sale for demand shaping

- Dynamic safety stock management with advanced network algorithms enabled by machine learning and real-time demand-supply data

- Laser optical vision and sensors for inventory replenishment to the shelves at the retail store

- Product tracking technology

- IoT and machine learning algorithms for recommending the right product based on personal preferences

- Automated delivery from fulfillment centers to consumers' homes through automated vehicles and drones

- Robotic programs for self-service automation
- Beacons to enhance the in-store experience with relevant information on products and promotion sent directly to the customer's cell phone while walking through the aisles
- AI facial recognition technology as customers enter and leave the store
- Recommending a shopping list based on past purchases and lifestyles
- Guiding movement in the store according to the customer's shopping list through a smart screen attached to the cart
- Robotic shopping assistance
- Augmented reality for servicing
- Robot for moving the materials at the store
- Smart mirror with AI and VR, superimposing the outfits with selection options
- Aisle scanning robots for replenishment, pricing errors, and product placement
- Human connection, integrated with the technology, for personal support
- Scrubbing robots
- Auto payment as customers leave the store

In addition to the technologies mentioned above, there are many more experiments in progress to enhance supply network efficiency, customer convenience, and amazing customer experience.

CONNECTED CUSTOMER CAPABILITIES

There are several sub-capabilities that enable the connected customer capability. Each of the connected customer sub-capabilities spans different parts of the customer journey and can facilitate growth for its respective customer segments. The connected customer sub-capabilities, as displayed in Figure 11.5, are delightful customer experience, product as a solution and service, tracking and monitoring, and connected service network.

FIGURE 11.5 Connected Customer Sub-Capabilities

Delightful Customer Experience	• Customized Experience • Customer Issue Management
Product as Solution and Service	• Product extension as solution and service
Tracking and Monitoring	• Monitoring and Insights • Intelligent Product Tracking
Connected Service Network	• Self-Service • Connected Field Service

Delightful Customer Experience

Delightful customer experience can be defined as the seamless inter-action with companies through all channels and parts of the customer lifecycle, from engagement through purchase, service, and product end-of-life. This sub-capability covers the customized experience, self-service, and customer issue management to enable organizations to solve all customer needs.

Customized Experience

A customized customer experience allows companies to leverage their DSN to communicate, engage, and retain customers across multiple customer channels. This also allows companies to differentiate customers by utilizing targeted, data-driven actions to create tailored customer experiences from transaction to service resolution. Now, with customers shopping across multiple formats and channels, consistency in messaging is key to providing a seamless customer experience.

Digital supply networks leverage data across many different tools to tailor the customer experience—incorporating manufacturing/production and commercial aspects to recommend products, customize advertisements, and create service suggestions that enable a pleasant customer experience. A connected supply chain enables organizations to enrich experiences further and generate revenue. For example, dynamic pricing and content allow organizations to modify how they approach customers based on previous behavior and changes in demand. It requires orchestrating the interplay among inventory considerations, product design and profitability, shipping preferences, and competitor pricing while increasing the ease and speed of the transaction. Other organizations create a customized journey by deploying artificial intelligence to analyze digital footprints efficiently and at-scale to understand customer behavior (beyond purchasing history, demographics, and modeling across customer segments).

Customer Issue Management

Customer issue management sits in the final phase of the customer journey, service/resolution. This sub-capability includes the methodology, processes, and tools to enable issue resolution. When executed properly, customer issue management enables companies to process feedback in response to product issues while minimizing the risk associated with product or company reputation and maximizing and maintaining customer loyalty.

Before DSNs, companies collected unstructured and inconsistent product feedback through emails, letters, and call centers. This lack of data consistency required issues to be addressed on a customer-by-customer basis. Many times the process failed to collect and apply customer feedback to the rest of the supply network. When aggregations did occur, the efforts were manual and cumbersome and did not extract many meaningful insights.

Companies have shifted to leveraging the connected supply chain to resolve these issues via customer service representatives, digital applications, and virtual assistants that can collect normalized data. Customers can communicate their issues in real time, and organizations can process, prioritize, and respond to these issues through proactive issue management, feedback prioritization, and product quality issues. Through AI-enabled pattern recognition, organizations can build capabilities to proactively address potential issues.

Product as a Solution and Service

Traditionally, business models focus on a single customer transaction and fail to optimize long-term customer value. Product as a Service, or PaaS, enables the transformation of business models from acquisition to service/resolution and helps expand customers through new avenues of engagement and revenue. PaaS includes innovative bundling of products and services into recurring subscription and flexible-consumption offerings.

In DSN, PaaS supports an alternative business model that offers services, supported by products, with the objective to build long-term customer relationships and maximize customer lifetime value. This helps companies to create recurring revenue and implement new sales models (e.g., freemium, tiered-service offerings) and shift individual costs from capital expenditure (CAPEX) to operating expenditure

(OPEX). Additionally, companies can increase customer loyalty and engagement beyond the initial product purchase and create better aftermarket experiences. PaaS reduces the constraints on the supply chain through greater visibility on consumption patterns.

This shift from the singular transaction, short-term mindset to PaaS is marked by a few key market drivers for change. Customer preferences are shifting toward pay-as-you-go and consumption-driven pricing models. Additionally, as described earlier in this chapter, there has been an increased focus on improving customer experience by developing innovative customer engagement models. These drivers for change, paired with an improved ability to follow the customer beyond the point of sale and to monitor subscription activities, lead organizations to consider other business models outside of their traditional ones to begin meeting customer expectations.

Tracking and Monitoring

Tracking and monitoring covers the ability to track, trace, and monitor the customer experience throughout the product lifecycle.

Monitoring and Insights

In today's digital age, data is king, and organizations that can not only efficiently and effectively collect it but also drive key actionable insights from it will be able to drive higher customer satisfaction and revenue growth. This means organizations need to be able to track and understand customer behavior across the entire customer journey.

Monitoring and insights are the ability to seamlessly tie products to the customer experience through the collection of real-time product usage data in order to identify consumption patterns, define failure modes and effects, and recognize proactive maintenance opportunities across the customer journey, from awareness to connection, purchase, and service/resolution.

While customer data is traditionally derived from the transactional data generated at the point of sale, real-time product usage data is typically nonexistent. DSNs link real-time product usage with customer data to provide a contextual and more complete view of the product-customer interaction. Aided by IoT, sensing capabilities, and machine learning, this rich interaction data enables companies to deliver a more effective customer experience, identify product usage patterns and monitor product health, automate replenishment orders, provide predictive maintenance notifications and service suggestions, optimize aftermarket parts inventories, and influence new product development.

This shift from historical transactional data to real-time product usage data is the result of a few key market drivers for change. Organizations have suffered from data overload as a result of increasing volumes of unstructured customer and product data from disparate sources. Additionally, customer expectations continue to grow increasingly demanding, with asks for a hyper-now, hyper-custom experience. Finally, advancements in IoT-enabled products make low-cost, real-time product monitoring possible. Companies now have the ability to understand their customers' behaviors and purchasing decisions across the customer journey through the use of data, and customers expect the organizations with which they interact to effectively leverage this data to improve their experience. Organizations must continue to improve their monitoring processes and insight-gathering capabilities to effectively equip their DSNs to satisfy customers' ever-growing demands.

For example, using real-time product data from connected devices (e.g., washing machine, car, or television) or machine learning models can notify the customer of failure risks. Additionally, it can offer customized remedial measures such as automatically creating a replenishment order for the at-risk part or helping the customer schedule a maintenance appointment. Failure avoidance will likely result in better customer experience and reduce costs for both the customer and the service or product provider.

Intelligent Product Tracking

Previously, product tracking was conducted by manually taking inventory at each step of the production process. In today's environment, technology has enabled product tracking to enter a much more advanced state. Intelligent product tracking can be defined as the ability to track, trace, and monitor physical products and their related data in real time throughout the entire product lifecycle from initial development to delivery. Intelligent product tracking leverages RFIDs (passive or active), manual barcode scanning, Bluetooth, and GPS to track location and usage.

This technology has become more prevalent due to the decreasing cost of essential physical enablers and technology, better overall technology and use cases, and greater focus on loss prevention, theft, and damaged assets. The product tracking process is greatly enabled by the IoT examples above and helps to manage the assets in question.

As additional technology develops, sensor technologies become more advanced and reliable. This has led to the use of embedded smart sensors. These sensors improve time and proximity tracking to benefit both the customer and the company. Cloud-based IoT tracking systems can work with smart sensors to complete three goals: (1) collect, store, and analyze product and asset data, (2) generate events in real time to trigger specific actions to avoid downtime or lags, and (3) create predictive or automated decisions to drive long-term value.

Connected Service Network
The connected customer network is a differentiator to maintain ongoing customer relationships. The customer network is utilized for the organization strategy, product development, and to maintain customer relationships.

Self-Service
Self-service is the strategic capability that supports the customer's ability to (1) obtain and interact with the product or service-related information, (2) manage their customer account, and (3) resolve product or service issues without any human interaction. Aided by AI, self-service enables a seamless, highly personalized, and data-driven experience across channels from acquisition to service/resolution; this results in both higher rates of self-service resolution and greater levels of satisfaction in a cost-effective manner.

Traditionally, self-service was limited to navigation through a product's FAQ page or manual. In the context of DSN, next-generation self-service involves two key evolutions. First, companies will leverage real-time supply chain data to provide accurate product catalog information, inventory levels, substitutions recommendation, and availability/shipping dates on demand across all physical and virtual channels available in the omnichannel portfolio. Second, a new focus will be placed on the strategic use of AI technology-driven elements to quickly remedy common customer problems with no human interaction. These key evolutions provide a series of benefits, such as delighted customers and meaningful impressions that drive customer loyalty and demand stability, reduced resolution times at lower overall costs, and maintained or improved customer engagement, even during traditional "black holes" in the customer lifecycle. Additionally, companies will benefit from increased capabilities for satisfying enterprise and end-customer resupply, upselling, and cross-selling needs.

The shift from traditional FAQ pages to today's self-service experience is possible from a few key market drivers for change. First, advancements in AI technologies (virtual assistants, mobile messaging, live chat, etc.) allow self-service of customer problems with higher speed and scope. Additionally, a more effective technology infrastructure enables real-time data availability and data synchronization across the omnichannel portfolio. Finally, constant customer access through IoT, third-party customer data, and an ever-increasing number of virtual channels and platforms will continue to foster data-driven personalized self-serviced engagements. With these in mind, companies must consider how they can empower their customers to efficiently and effectively self-serve.

Connected Field Service

Traditionally, field service was a costly, yet necessary post-sales service with limited potential for generating new business. These services operated in a silo as a lower-priority arm of an enterprise with limited investments in technology and a primary focus on only performing the task requested by the customer. Today, field services management has become a key differentiator in maintaining ongoing customer relationships. Connected field service management is a holistic approach for managing end-to-end customer service activities on location aimed at managing issues and risk and reducing downtime through proactive monitoring of assets, analyzing data, predicting future issues, automating work order creation, and resolving issues correctly the first time.

Enterprises now have a suite of tools—including mobile platforms, IoT sensor-driven technology, and cloud capabilities—enabling real-time management of customer appointments/ticketing/order management, employee scheduling and route optimizations, worker activity management, service parts inventory, accounting, and other back-office integration. These capabilities further provide agents within the field with critical customer insights to ensure they are fully equipped to provide the best service as well as promote ancillary products or services that may not have originally been sought by the customer. Connected field service management provides key benefits enhancing overall customer lifecycle value, such as increasing their ability to sell premium support services by offering predictive or managed services to customers, reducing unplanned downtime from data-driven preventative maintenance, and reducing the frequency of planned downtime due to predictive analytics. Additionally, companies can benefit from improved product design by cycling asset and work order data into the R&D process and increased first-time-fix rates while reducing time-to-fix due to automation and optimization of people and parts.

The shift from costly field service activities to becoming a key differentiator in customer relationships has several causes. There has been a refocus within organizations to provide the best customer service in the market post-purchase to improve customer satisfaction and retention. Additionally, organizations have seen an increase in demand for higher productivity due to an aging workforce. Finally, the decrease in the cost of IoT coupled with cloud computing capabilities allows for better tracking of equipment patterns and health.

In summary, the connected customer is enabled by four sub-capabilities that span across the entire customer journey. Each sub-capability has a unique and essential impact on the efficiency of the DSN and the growth of customer segments within the customer journey. A series of market drivers, including changing consumer demands, advancements in technology, greater accessibility to data, and increased focus on customer experience and satisfaction for change have created a shift in how organizations should be considering these capabilities. Monitoring and driving insights, considering new business models such as PaaS, offering improved and innovative self-service, customizing the customer experience, shifting to intelligent product tracking, improving the management of customer issues, and managing connected field services are ways organizations can accelerate the connected customer vision and, in turn, move toward a more efficient and transformative DSN.

SUMMARY

Serving customers is the primary goal of any business. Customer involvement is changing in the current era of personalization. Connected customer as part of the DSN model puts the customers at the center of the decision making and dynamically connects them with all the processes of the digital supply network. Customers are at the end of the chain in traditional SCM and have limited involvement with the product design, manufacturing, and service organization structure. The communication in the conventional SCM model is one way to make the customers aware of the product and to generate the pull for the product. In the customer connect process of the DSN, the customer is involved in the product design and all the following processes. The communication is through two-way channels supported by digital capabilities and social media. The new mindset aims for continuous involvement throughout the lifecycle of the customer journey instead of a transaction-based relationship. The reimagined customer connect processes and capabilities are supported by the advanced technologies that are transforming the way products are designed, manufactured, planned, tracked, and serviced. These technologies are also changing the sales channels, both the physical stores and the online gateways.

WORKFORCE, SKILL CHANGES, AND SOCIAL IMPACT

The transformative power of artificial intelligence (AI) and the other disruptive technologies discussed in this book hold great promise. They are converting traditional supply chains into an interconnected, dynamic, and smarter system of supply chain operations—digital supply networks (DSNs). This development is overwhelmingly positive. It has the potential to improve our living standards while laying the foundation for the new nature of competition for companies in the future. However, it also poses significant challenges requiring proactive change by organizations, governments, educational institutions, and first and foremost individuals. For instance, a subtle and treacherous problem is the danger that algorithms designed by a somewhat uniform team of highly skilled professionals may disregard the needs of underrepresented groups and unintentionally enlarge the bias against them.[1]

For example, Amazon customers learned that same-day delivery was not available in zip codes comprising predominantly black neighborhoods, and computer scientists discovered that women were less likely than men to receive online ads for high-paying jobs.[2] In healthcare, AI systems can produce unreliable insights, even when we successfully implement the algorithms because social inequality affects the availability of medical data.[3] More impoverished communities have no access to digital healthcare, which creates a gap in the medical data fed into AI algorithms—and thus creates unequal representation within the predictive model. The social impact and unintended consequences of disruptive technologies can be diverse and are not yet fully understood today.

In particular, they can have disruptive effects, especially in the labor market. As supply chains become digital, jobs across all levels will go through a transformation. While some positions will disappear and new ones will emerge, the skill set required to perform existing tasks will also undergo a radical change. For instance, connected ecosystems that are transparent from end to end require workers to perform beyond their immediate teams, with stakeholders throughout the DSN, from suppliers to partners in different geographical locations to customers.[4] While the social impact of digitalization is complex and broad, we focus on this chapter on those more closely linked to the DSN and the labor market. First, we discuss what we see as potential good, bad, and ugly effects of the current wave of technological progress. We then comment on the skills gap facing industries and move to what we see as core strategic skills needed to be successful within a DSN environment. We conclude with a brief discussion of a way forward.

THE GOOD, THE BAD, AND THE UGLY

Although still evolving, the economics supporting the digitization of manufacturing and supply chain operations seem very attractive.[5] For instance, in manufacturing, estimates suggest that a welder today earns about $25 per hour, including benefits, while the equivalent operating cost per hour for a robotic welder system is about $8.[6] In the US automotive industry, the total cost of procuring and utilizing a robotic welding system has decreased from an average of $182,000 in 2005 to $133,000 in 2014 (not adjusted for inflation). By 2025, the total cost is projected to decrease to a little over $100,000. The value of systems engineering for robot welding (installing, programming, and integrating robotic systems into a manufacturing plant) has decreased from $81,000 to an average of about $46,000. Estimates suggest that a manufacturing facility should be able to amortize the costs of robotic systems over five years. As the technologies underlying digital transformation continue to progress quickly, we should expect that the payback period (ROI) will continue to decrease, significantly increasing their diffusion across industries and throughout the supply chain.

Emerging technologies will increasingly impact the competitiveness of manufacturing and supply chain activities, and possibly of national economies. As it is becoming increasingly clear, these technologies support higher productivity, but their most significant potential lies in enabling companies to reinvent their entire production and supply chain. However, leaders across multiple industries need to critically reflect on the impact of disruptive technologies and the ongoing digital transformation. Concerns about the effect of automation on jobs and fears of mass unemployment have occupied a prominent position in society since the first major wave of technological progress in the nineteenth century, from Britain's Luddite uprising in 1812 to the Triple Revolution report disseminated in various US media outlets in 1964 to the most recent debates about the threat of AI. The specter of technological displacement and rising inequality is back in the spotlight with more focus than ever.

To be sure, digital technology will continue to drive social and economic change, recasting the nature of work, and with that comes the good, the bad, and the ugly. We summarize this point in Figure 12.1, which captures significant aspects of the labor consequences from digitization.

FIGURE 12.1   The Good, the Bad, and the Ugly of Digital Technologies

The Good	The Bad	The Ugly
• New job categories • Reimagined work • More human-focused job content	• Extinction of some job categories • Some decline in the level of employment	• Broader labor market impact • Potential net job loss • Labor market divide

The *good* is that digitalization and AI have the potential to enrich jobs by removing the routine aspect from them and raising the unique contribution and value of humans.[7] In this sense, machines can augment the workforce and pay handsomely for organizations that enlarge work practices and reimagine work. As automation eliminates the dangerous, strenuous, transactional, and repetitive aspects of the labor activity, emerging more flexible positions requiring higher-level skills are joining technical skills, such as technology operations and data analysis and interpretation, with soft skills, such as communication and collaboration.[8] As these new positions continue to evolve, technology will likely change not only the nature of the skills required, but the nature of the work and the job itself, merging components of traditional positions into expanded roles that leverage value creation.[9, 10] Some proactive organizations are already reimagining the work and creating fundamentally redesigned job definitions.[10, 11] The skills needed to excel in this new environment have been shifting from manual to more cognitive-based.[12] Those new positions require well-educated professionals and command rising wages. A place that somewhat illustrates the physical-digital convergence for frontline workers is the floor of Amazon distribution centers. Amazon employs over 125,000 workers in its US warehouses, and in 2017 it brought online its 100,000th robot. Robotic palletizers are transforming the physically challenging jobs of frontline workers into more stimulating, mentally challenging positions.

The *bad* is that some job categories will naturally disappear, not unlike in previous technological leaps. In the transition from the rural economy to the industrial era, while farm labor declined, the industrial economy added positions at an even faster pace. As new farm technology improved productivity and reduced prices, demand for agricultural products increased, boosting farmers' wealth. Farmers spent a portion of their additional wealth in new industrial products, fostering the pursuit of rapid technological advancement and productivity in the new industries. As technology continued to progress and diffuse, automated looms replaced weavers; telephones replaced telegraph operators; radar replaced aircraft listeners; traffic service position systems replaced telephone switchboard operators; computers with word processing programs replaced typists; flight computers and new avionics replaced flight engineers; and so on. In the same fashion, digital technology is replacing repetitive and transactional work, and industries are investing in digitalization to improve productivity.

A justified concern and a point of meaningful debate is the relation between manufacturing supply chain digitization and the volume of employment.[13] In this regard, an interesting observation is that, historically, countries that have invested in automation more intensely do not seem to have experienced a more significant decline in manufacturing employment. Let's consider Germany, for instance. It utilizes 3 times more robots per hour worked than the United States, mostly due to its dynamic automotive sector, which employs about 10 times more robots per worker than the average industry. However, while Germany installed significantly more industrial robots between 1993 and 2007, the country lost only 19 percent of its manufacturing jobs between 1996 and 2012, compared to 33 percent in the United States. According to the Brookings Institution, if the decline in manufacturing employment were proportional to the increase in robotic systems, the United States would have lost one-third more manufacturing jobs than it did, and Germany would have lost 50 percent more.[14] Interestingly, a noteworthy cautionary tale in this context is that countries like the United Kingdom, which invested less in industrial robots but experienced faster declines in the manufacturing sector, lost five times more jobs than it should have, as per Brookings.

In the supply chain side more specifically, once again, we can use Amazon to illustrate our discussion. To be sure, the current growth of the company and the industry might play an important role here, but, at least for the moment, the increasing automation has not eliminated jobs at Amazon. This observation suggests that the use of disruptive technologies will not be poised only to eliminate jobs, but will also create new, more interesting, and better-paying ones. We can find evidence for such prediction in the previous waves of technological progress discussed in Chapter 1, which balanced the elimination and creation of positions. However, beyond the extinction of posts, natural from technological shifts, and the historical balance between job elimination and creation, the rise of AI and robotics this time has more profound and possibly ugly consequences.

The *ugly* is twofold. First, the question of whether the number of new jobs created by the current wave of digital progress, which is transforming the chain of supplies into digital supply networks, and Industry 4.0 more broadly will outweigh the number of jobs destroyed is controversial and is gaining momentum. The rise of AI and digital robotics in the current technological shift may replace entire swathes of the workforce, affecting not only routine tasks but also nonroutine and nonrepetitive tasks that were previously thought not to be automatable.[15] As indicated by some of the examples discussed in this book, the new digital technologies are not only replacing workers but will also become increasingly self-contained. Such technological developments can produce side issues, so there have been calls to reassess the fundamentals of how our economy functions. The ultimate goal is to preclude a large population of unemployed truck drivers, package deliverers, warehouse and manufacturing workers, and so on, and also the associated income inequality and eventual social unrest.

Second, the current wave of technological progress might be different from previous ones in another regard. Over the past 40 years, it seems that every single industry that has adopted technologies to increase productivity has reduced the number of jobs.[16] While industries with less productivity growth appear to have counterbalanced the loss of jobs, employment in the less productive parts of the economy offer much lower wages and prospects of advancement. Influential authors Brynjolfsson and McAfee predict that the current wave of technological progress will usher in an era of growth in productivity and wages for workers with skills complementary to the new technologies, while of declining wages or unemployment for workers whose jobs or tasks are substitutable with these technologies.[17] This point finds support in recent research and analysis suggesting that jobs have not fallen across the entire economy because less productive industries have absorbed the losses from more productive ones.[18] The consequence is that it appears that digital technology and automation may divide the job market into two camps: emerging superior jobs requiring higher-level skills and expanded roles, commanding growing wages, and commoditized jobs commanding lower salaries and prospects.

In terms of talent in the DSN environment, specifically, the broader changes and smart automation are shifting the expectations for the skills, training, and capabilities that might be most relevant for supply network roles.[19] Figure 12.2 lists some of these changes. Later in the chapter, we dive into more depth on the strategic skills required as we continue to progress.

SKILLS GAP

The caveat about the jobs that the digital transformation of manufacturing and supply chains will create is that the workforce may not be prepared to fill them.[20] Nearly 40 percent of workers in the European Union lack some critical digital skills, while 14 percent do not have any. In the United States, an estimated 60 million people cannot take jobs because of a lack of digital skills. Looking at the broader social impact of traditional value chain activities alone, cities with strong demand for manufacturing skills, and that are gaining the most workers, such as Seattle and Los Angeles, are attracting talent predominantly from across the country. Meanwhile, traditional manufacturing bases, such as Pittsburgh, are attracting workers mostly from nearby cities. This scenario is very concerning. Geographic locations that are losing a portion of their labor force will face difficulties in attracting new businesses and retaining top talent as we make inroads into the digital transformation of the value chain.

To be sure, new technologies will complement workers' skills, enable higher productivity allowing companies to produce and deliver products at a price point that is competitive globally, and create more challenging and satisfying jobs. One of the keys to the transition,

FIGURE 12.2   How Supply Network Changes Affect the Workforce

| CHANGES IN SUPPLY NETWORK | RELATED IMPACTS ON THE WORKFORCE |

Collaboration between trade partners, including both customer and supplier relationships, is being facilitated by the rise of technologies that can provide broader systemic visibility of movement of goods and materials—and is becoming increasingly important for supply chain talent to master.

Supply chain workers at every level should be able to facilitate and maintain interpersonal relationships with external partners and customers.

Increased specialization with specific tools or patterns often means that what were once single roles, such as buyer, are now often fragmented split across multiple job titles and departments (e.g., buying specialist, indirect buyer, and procurement specialist).

Current approaches to specialization and the resulting fragmentation can make it difficult to segregate tasks for automation, to define new roles accurately and to scale. The need to rationalize and refine roles could become more important as management seeks an accurate view of capacity and what can or should be automated.

End-to-end supply chain processes have allowed for greater transparency and related services to customers, such as detailed track-and-trace capability. However, this change also breaks many traditional supply chain silos.

Individual workers should have a working knowledge of, or the ability to access information across, the entire supply chain from end to end.

Customer expectations continue to change quickly, with demands for lower costs, faster response times, greater transparency into how a product is made and the origin of its raw materials, and customized products and services looming large for supply chain organizations.

These trends may demand a closer integration of customer service and fulfillment functions. It may also require faster cycle times in many departments to meet ever-changing pressures.

New technologies are improving workflows, connecting large volumes of data to improve visibility and generate more holistic insights. Advanced technologies can also complete some of the "thinking" for humans on relatively simpler tasks.

The rapid pace of technological change can also mean that workers may need to engage in continuous learning or training to keep building their skills, so they can evolve alongside technologies.

Source: Modified from Deloitte analysis.

231

however, will be better education and training.[21, 22, 23] As such, there is urgency in preparing the workforce for the digital transformation of manufacturing and supply chains, and in assisting traditional companies in making the transition. Organizations must have an effective strategy that includes a plan to reskill and upskill workers. While previous technological transformations took place over a relatively long period, the current wave of digital transformation is unfolding at a much faster pace; therefore, organizations need to move fast. Governments and organizations also must prepare to deal with and prevent the worsening of inequality and wage deflation.

For regions more heavily associated with traditional industries, a strategic, long-term view will save the day.[24] This exercise should include looking into how new technologies can potentially raise the competitiveness of existing sectors and support the diversification of the local economy. It calls for actions to retrain and upskill workers to remain relevant in current markets.[25] It should also include steps in partnership with industry, governments, and academia to prepare the workforce for the transition and to create new technology-driven businesses to include fostering entrepreneurship. In that regard, the focus of some emerging economies, such as China, may be instructive.

According to the International Federation of Robotics, China had a meager 36 robots per manufacturing worker in 2014, compared to the world average of 66 and 478 in the Republic of Korea. However, the central government and Chinese companies have focused on eliminating the gap. The internationally controversial Made in China 2025 plan, for instance, aims at transforming the country into one of the world's strongest modern technology-driven economies. Chinese regions where economies are similar to either the rust belts or the depressed areas based on traditional industries in the United States are attempting to leverage new technologies to stimulate growth, development, and competitiveness. However, investments in digitization anywhere will change the content of existing jobs and will create new ones, either of which will require a unique skill set.

STRATEGIC SKILL SETS

The rapid development of new technologies and related innovations is transforming not only the various facets of modern life and organizations but also the nature of work. Underlying the process of digitalization is the familiar concept of change—however, "change" at unprecedented blazing speed. In this context, learning must become a never-ending cycle of continuous improvement for both organizations and individuals. Organizations that do not build processes and structures supportive of constant learning will likely fail. For individuals and the labor force in general, a one-time college degree will no longer suffice to develop the skills needed to succeed in the era of digitization. Individuals at all levels will likely have different careers in their lifetime and will need to retool their knowledge and skill set frequently. As such, learning organizations and *lifelong learning* skills will become increasingly more important.

Besides lifelong learning, it could go without saying that *digital literacy* is a requirement in the process of digitalization.[26] The awareness and ability of workers to confidently and effectively use digital workplace tools to solve problems, collaborate, and be outright productive are paramount. However, leaders and decision makers need to be mindful that digital literacy should not be limited to merely using software or operating digital devices. It involves a broad set of complex cognitive, motor, sociological, and emotional skills that enable users to function effectively in digital environments. In this regard, as suggested by the World Economic Forum, there is a great need to train and reskill. Leaders should note that digital technologies are profoundly impacting how education and training themselves take place. Contemporary learners and workers are increasingly consuming short bursts of content on the go, and they are increasingly looking for learning experiences to be rapid, engaging, and immediately useful. Therefore, leaders will need to complement or replace traditional classroom or standalone online training with gamification elements, augmented reality experiences, and so on. Traditional ad hoc approaches to digital skills, such as conventional training around the launch of a specific technology, will not suffice. Organizations and leaders will need to develop a holistic approach to raise the collective digital capability of the workforce.

Creativity is another skill that will become increasingly important as digital progress opens up new possibilities to combine, recombine, and design new processes and organizational structures. This skill also enables leaders and workers alike to cope with new problems that will emerge and for which there will be no historical data or experience available to solve them. At the same time, digital technologies and digitalization open up many opportunities for outside-the-box thinking that can create value. To leverage such possibilities, workers must be able to manage innovative ventures successfully; therefore, an *entrepreneurial mindset* will increasingly become a critical skill.[27] As digital progress continues to accelerate, there will be what has been called a "Cambrian explosion of robotics"[28]—a very rapid expansion in the diversification and applicability of robotics. In such an environment, machines, digital technologies, and supply network systems will experience faster and shorter development cycles and product lifespan. Such context requires that workers at all levels continuously update their knowledge and skills, which again puts lifelong learning skills at the forefront. But they will also need to be able to creatively combine and recombine these skills to produce innovative solutions and add value.

As warehouses, distribution centers, materials handling, manufacturing equipment, and fleets become increasingly connected through the technologies discussed in this book, the exchange of data and information will grow exponentially. While digital technology will enable real-time communication in this environment, workers and leaders at all levels will need to effectively receive and convey information with both humans and technology such as AI. Workers will need to deconstruct complex problems and messages and explain them to others within or outside disciplinary and functional borders. Therefore, advanced *communication skills* with different stakeholders and diverse technologies will become a necessity.[29] And as technology continues to automate not only physical but also aspects of cognitive tasks, workers' jobs will increasingly shift toward more sophisticated tasks requiring the ability to solve problems creatively.[30] While such skill is almost bread-and-butter in traditional supply chains, the progress in digital technologies will need even sharper and systems-level *complex problem-solving* capabilities.

Tasks that must be performed in unstructured environments and require perception or manipulation are less prone to immediate changes. Humans still outperform robots at working on those tasks. For example, the packing job in a fulfillment center requires dexterity and the ability to handle many different and irregular objects. As such, even with the high level of automation in many fulfillment centers today, the last entity to touch an item is a human packer. However, new technologies such as AI and sensors are becoming better and more capable of tasks that require perception. We are starting to see technologies that can handle such tasks—for example, wheeled delivery robots that navigate streets. Therefore, robotics will perform tasks that require some level of perception in the intermediate horizon. Functions that require social and creative intelligence are not prone to changes soon. AI has made tremendous inroads in social and industrial life; however, it cannot still develop new and meaningful ideas, approaches, and products. Robotics are also still unable to comprehend the full spectrum of human social interaction, notably its subtleties. For this reason, tasks that involve negotiation and persuasion, such as handling emergencies with suppliers, will very likely not change soon with technological capabilities and will be an increasingly important *social intelligence skill.*

On the technical skills side, we will increasingly see a shift toward abstract digital skills, a greater need for interpretation of large amounts of data, and the ability to derive insights. Machines will continue to replace humans on manual tasks; therefore, workers will need fewer manual skills. Instead, they will need more *abstract digital skills,* such as understanding the state of the flow of items through a warehouse based on sensor readings to identify potential issues or bottlenecks instead of visually seeing them. However, increasing emphasis on soft skills, particularly *social intelligence,* will become more critical as we move forward. For instance, in the last decade, job listings have shied away from tasks such as scheduling, which could be performed by AI, in the more recent years, while current listings include more soft skills requirements such as creativity. So, socio-emotional skills will become critical.[31] Figure 12.3 summarizes our discussion in this section.

FIGURE 12.3 Strategic Skills for the DSN World

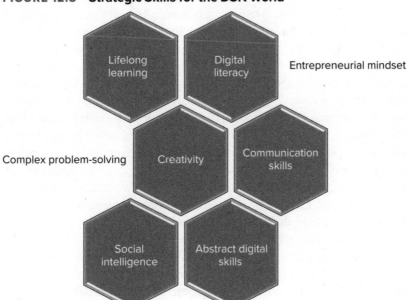

A WAY FORWARD

Digital transformation is radically changing organizational and social life. As past industrial transitions indicate, it is futile to resist technological progress. It will be more beneficial if organizations, educational institutions, and governments critically examine the broader impact of digitization and elaborate effective policies and strategies to facilitate the transformation and cope with any potential side effects. Connecting industry, educational institutions, government, and centers of excellence to create an ecosystem supportive of new businesses and small manufacturers enabled or assisted by new technologies should prove very fruitful. Traditional small organizations that do not transition their structures to plug into the emerging digital supply networks will be locked out and eventually fail.

As technology advances and we transition toward a digital supply network, productivity will continue to improve. In the process, many jobs will disappear, some will change content, and new ones will become available. Unfortunately, these developments are likely to leave a layer of the workforce in a worse-off condition. Divergence in earnings between the most-educated and least-educated might exacerbate, producing further social inequalities. The good news is that not every aspect of manufacturing and supply chain operations will necessarily replace humans. For instance, in 2019, a major athletic apparel company ended the robotic shoe production in two developed countries and moved the technology to suppliers in developing countries. Meanwhile, the world's biggest aircraft manufacturer scaled back the use of automation to make fuselage sections. These high-profile announcements are instructive—not that these episodes would suggest deceleration or reversion of the trend toward automation. As declared by both companies, effort toward automation will continue, and digital progress, in general, will not halt. However, it brings to the fore the notion that the combination of humans, technology, and superior processes will win the day. Besides, digital progress will undoubtedly require an aggressive reskilling and upskilling, with consequences for organizations, educational institutions, and future workers themselves. So, what are the implications for leaders?

Promoting the development of the skills discussed in this chapter is a starting point. A partnership between institutions of higher learning, organizations, and governments to proactively address and develop collaborative and agile solutions should prove fruitful.[32] For companies specifically, attracting and investing in the development of a highly educated workforce will lead to the creation of superior value. Also, fostering an innovative and entrepreneurial organizational mindset will provide opportunities for workers to migrate to more meaningful tasks and also produce excellent value. As the evidence provided by previous waves of technological progress indicates, benefits from implementing new technology follow only after the active redesign of processes. Thus, as we develop the digital supply network, leaders will need to fundamentally change organizational structures and ways of working to harness the power of the new concept. Creatively combining digital, human, and organizational capital will require a *learning and entrepreneurial mindset* from both corporations and workers. As such, executives will need to invest in human capital and new structures more than ever. It is critical to note that for many positions in supply chain operations, companies will start competing for the same skills and talent typically found in the high-tech industries and start-up environments. This observation is very consequential, requiring changes in hiring practices, job content, training, and organizational principles in general.

The past waves of disruptive technological progress also suggest that society, in general, is better off when organizations innovate by combining people and machines. Organizations become more competitive by leveraging the power of automation and human ingenuity to innovate. The trio of machine, humans, and creative new processes and systems should lay the basis for superior outcomes. A significant thrust behind automation is the pursuit of higher productivity. To be sure, designing humans out of many aspects of operations and supply chain processes typically has allowed tremendous gains in productivity. However, companies experimenting with "auto mates" are discovering new and innovative ways to process the work content that display entirely outside-the-box thought and will achieve truly superior outcomes.[33] Therefore, we cannot emphasize enough that building a culture of innovation in the manufacturing and supply chain organizations will assist leaders in harnessing talent and fostering productive and successful transformation. As the title of a joint report released by the MIT Sloan Management Review and Deloitte a few years back suggests, "Strategy, [and talented people, which we are adding to the original title] not technology, drives digital transformation."[34]

Better alignment of education to produce graduates with the skills and knowledge to take advantage of and foster the transformations should be equally fruitful.[35, 36] In educational settings, it will become increasingly important to assess and rethink knowledge areas that are on the verge of being profoundly transformed by disruptive technologies. Not only organizations, as mentioned above, but educational institutions will need to change the way they create value and prepare future generations of workers and leaders for the digital age. The traditional classroom lecture must give way for technology-enabled and centric training and experiential learning opportunities. Academic programs and corporate training will need a more significant focus on preparing future workers to become lifelong learners. It will become increasingly crucial that educational and training programs nurture creativity, entrepreneurship, collaboration, systems thinking, complex communication, social and emotional intelligence, and the ability to perform well in diverse environments. These are skills that new technology will not likely replace and will prepare people to work successfully alongside the new generation of machines. The role of campus-based education might become more focused on intangible skills.

Retraining programs to support more skilled jobs and knowledge transfer to support business transition will become increasingly necessary. The earlier firms engage and gain experience in this field, the better they will be prepared on the future competitive marketplace as well as in attracting future talent. As mentioned before, leaders should have a holistic view of the digital challenges and opportunities facing the various parts of their value chain. Such an approach will assist in identifying capabilities that need the most attention and in prioritizing where to focus investment. Thus, digital transformation will affect not only frontline workers in manufacturing and supply chains, but the nature and scope of managerial and leadership positions will shift as well. Entrepreneurship, innovation, and change management skills will be essential, as well as appropriate holistic administrative frameworks, tools, and mindset to manage the complexity of networked environments. If leaders heed to the calls made in this chapter, workers will have the chance to perform work that demands their creativity, imagination, and social and emotional intelligence. At the same time, these efforts should produce tremendously innovative and unbeatable DSN—and a better, more humane society.

DSN TRANSFORMATION PLAYBOOK

Disruption of the supply chain is the reality of the current age; to navigate this disruption, avoid pitfalls, and emerge with a more resilient and efficient digital supply network (DSN), organizations need to develop and follow a plan. Not actively engaging in activities will leave organizations only reacting to market changes through disconnected piecemeal responses—and losing the advantage of the bigger DSN picture.

The DSN transformation playbook presented in this chapter provides guidance for organizations to develop their own individual DSN transformation strategy and tools to harness the maximum value of the digital opportunities and prepare the organization for future success in the competitive marketplace.

Organizations need to plan the disruption through a well-defined strategy; just experimenting with new technologies is not enough. In this chapter, we will discuss a recommended playbook for the DSN strategy, how it is related to the business strategy, technology considerations, steps of the playbook, and the relevant factors that are at play while finalizing and implementing the DSN playbook.

BUSINESS STRATEGY AND DSN STRATEGY

The DSN strategy of the organization should be aligned with the organization's overall business strategy and strategic goals. Figure 13.1 shows the recommended approach of the business strategy cascade along with the corresponding DSN strategy. Business strategy formulation is represented by the five cascading choices:[1] (1) recognizing the vision of the organization; (2) identifying the customers, products/services, geographies, and channels; (3) understanding the value proposition and core competence of the organization; (4) configuring the business to harness the distinctive winning capabilities; and (5) prioritizing and execution.

Except for the first level of the business strategy (vision, goals, and aspiration to exist as an organization), the DSN strategy should be formulated for all the subsequent levels of the choice cascade to enable success of the business strategy. As represented in Figure 13.1, the alignment of the business strategy with the DSN strategy can be performed by working on the following questions for the formulation and execution of the DSN approach. The reverse arrows in the diagram represent the iterations for the strategy formulation and execution process.

- **WHERE WILL WE PLAY?** Based on the answer finalized by the business strategy, the DSN team needs to design the network accordingly. They should utilize information about the customer, product, geography, and channel for planning and execution segmentation. Synchronized planning, connected customer, and intelligent supply processes of DSN enable consistent planning and execution across the segments.

- **HOW WILL WE WIN?** DSN capabilities can enhance the competitiveness of the organization by delivering on the identified competencies related to customer service, speed, agility, cost, quality, and innovation. The speed represents how fast the products move in the supply chain, though the agility is based on the responsiveness and adaptability of the supply networks. In the previous era of traditional supply chain management, it was about selecting a preferred lever (cost, speed, service, etc.) to enhance the performance by understanding that it would have a negative impact on the other levers. For example, enhancing customer service negatively affected the cost. However, with the advanced technologies and reimagined DSN processes, we can now optimize multiple factors at the same time. This is enabled by the end-to-end transparency, advanced algorithms, and process automation of DSN.

- **HOW WILL WE CONFIGURE?** The business strategy related to people, process, and technology to deliver the distinctive

FIGURE 13.1 Business Strategy and DSN Strategy

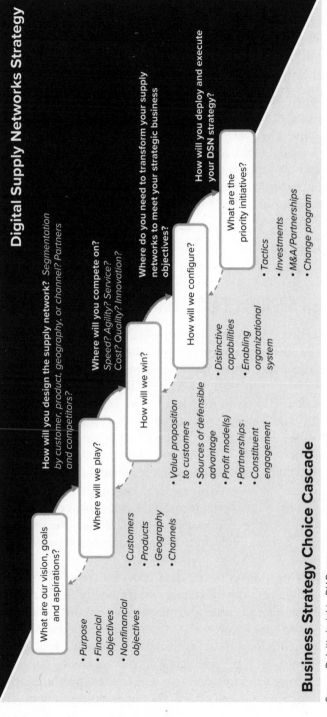

Source: Deloitte insights, DU Press

capabilities of customer service, manufacturing, and product movement is highly dependent on the DSN configuration. The reimagined DSN processes and network structure can multiply the distinctive capabilities and the competitiveness of the organization.

- **WHAT ARE THE PRIORITY INITIATIVES?** For the prioritized initiatives, the DSN is deployed and executed accordingly to deliver the maximum value. There may be a huge number of potential initiatives to add value to the firm, its customers, and the supply network. The selection and adoption of these opportunities should enhance the total value and should be collaborative with each other.

In summary, the DSN strategy of an organization should be intertwined and carefully coordinated with its business strategy for sustained success.

DSN APPROACH AND TECHNOLOGY CONSIDERATION

Organization leaders can choose to focus on many facets and areas of the supply network to begin the implementation of DSN projects. This is generally a very organization- and/or market-specific decision and varies greatly. In this playbook, we will provide the tools to support this key decision for an individual organization in a structured way. To identify the range of potential value opportunities, leaders can consider the four driving factors as visualized in Figure 13.2.

ISSUE FOCUSED. Traditional supply chain issues and the value prospects are considered for identifying the DSN work opportunities. The cross-skilled and cross-functional team analyzes the areas of speed to market, customer experience, cost to serve, manufacturing efficiency, and so on to identify the right problem to solve by considering potential values.

DATA DRIVEN. Access to big data provides tremendous opportunities to add value to the business and its supply networks, driven by the problem identification and automation opportunities. For example, access to the customer data (preference, experience, issues, etc.), manufacturing data (process deviation, real-time efficiency, schedule adherence, etc.), partner data (supplier capability, issues, etc.), and other structured and unstructured data of the supply network provides the intelligence to identify the DSN value-adding work objects.

FIGURE 13.2 Structuring the DSN Approach

Issue-Focused

Key business issues and opportunities impacting performance are identified by leveraging analytics frameworks

- Speed to market
- Product & service design
- Supply network velocity
- Customer experience
- Asset efficiency
- Cost
- Aftermarket management

Data-Driven

Internal, external, and unstructured data sets are integrated into a "digital core"

Platform-Supported

Best-in-class ERP, data processing, analytics, and visualization tools are used to arrive at smarter insights

ERP
ORACLE
SAP

Advanced Analytics
alteryx

Data Processing
Spark

Visualization
MicroStrategy
Qlik
+ableau

Science-Guided

The latest cognitive science is applied to industry-specific solutions to get to predictive answers and outcomes

Control Tower gets smarter over time through the use of advanced machine learning algorithms.

Review of the broad set of technologies for business case

Source: Adapted from Deloitte Insights, DU Press

PLATFORM SUPPORTED. Best-in-class solutions in the areas of ERP, customer service, data processing, advanced analytics, and visualization can instill new thinking and spark the ideas to gain from the digital technology and process innovation.

SCIENCE GUIDED. The basic science of the digital technologies and cognitive capabilities can be analyzed to find innovative ways of achieving the intelligently automated processes of planning, purchasing, manufacturing, storing, transporting, and delivering. The team of business users and technology specialists can brainstorm to identify how science can be used to develop technology solutions for adding value to the business stakeholders.

While formulating and delivering the DSN strategy, it is important to understand the role of the technology. It is true that the convergence of the different technologies (as discussed earlier in this book) has been a primary reason of transforming SCM to DSN based on the possibilities realized by the technologies like machine learning, AI, blockchain, robotics, and additive manufacturing. However, many past initiatives, focused on technology experimentations by various organizations did not go anywhere and were ultimately abandoned.

Few authors on this topic have recommended that the digital transformation is not about the technology; an organization should look at the business requirements and then adopt the appropriate technology (technology pull rather than technology push). However, we suggest that this can be a limited impact approach. Understanding of the technical capabilities and use cases can help an organization to better plan its unique digital transformation journey.

Many of the ever-existing business requirements are not top of mind for business executives and in customer responses because of the past era's limitations. Understanding the technology capabilities and relevant use cases helps the innovation process and enables leaders to reimagine current practices and models, assisting them in formulating their unique DSN. For example, effectively managing the spare parts inventory has always been an important business requirement for manufacturing organizations; however, without understanding of what the advance prediction algorithms, sensors, and additive manufacturing can achieve, it will be difficult for executives to consider the possibility of an innovative solution driven by these technologies.

Our recommendation is a balance between exploring the technology capability and supply network strategy for the DSN strategy, as represented in Figure 13.3. Technology understanding provides the *realm* of the possibilities, while a clear picture on the business and supply network strategy helps to select the *relevant* ones (for the individual organization) for adoption. For example, blockchain technology can provide end-to-end transparency for product movement as well as automatic execution of contracts. For a food supplier or a pharmaceutical company, the transparency of blockchain seems more promising, while for an international trading company, the automatic execution of contracts may be more beneficial.

FIGURE 13.3 **Technology Capability Consideration with Business Strategy for DSN Strategy Formulation**

Understanding the core science behind the DSN relevant technology, along with the knowledge of customer requirements, internal processes, and partner collaboration, will lead to an effective DSN strategy for selecting the right initiatives to implement. We recommend considering the cross-industry use cases such as those in Chapter 14 along with technological understanding for supply network innovation and value creation.

Now, as we understand the alignment between the business strategy and DSN strategy along with the DSN approach, let's review the playbook to transform the digital supply network.

RECOMMENDED STEPS FOR PLAYBOOK

We recommend the following four steps for the playbook of DSN transformation, as represented in Figure 13.4.

FIGURE 13.4   DSN Transformation Playbook

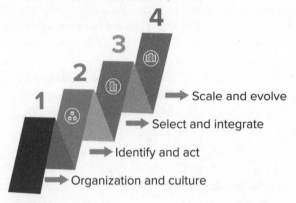

→ Scale and evolve

→ Select and integrate

→ Identify and act

→ Organization and culture

Organization and Culture

For any organization, it's the individual employees and team whose work leads to success or failure.[2] The first step toward successfully transforming an organization's supply chain into a DSN is to engage and motivate the organization, people, and culture for the upcoming change. It is important to get the transformation mindset into their hearts and minds before starting any specific project to build the DSN capabilities. Once we excite the people and create a spark, it begins a long journey to transform the organization.

The transformation readiness needs to happen from top-down as well as bottom-up for an organization with skills fortification of both leaders and individual team members.

For leaders, in addition to digital literacy, the drive to inspire the organization on the digital journey is required. It is not expected that leaders will be an expert in the core DSN technologies, but basic understanding of the technology capability and use cases is strongly recommended. The DSN journey will require new learnings for every team member; the learning readiness of the leaders will inspire the team members. Change readiness of the organization and the ability to take calculated risks are other cultural elements that a DSN leader should influence for success. The work structure is recommended to move to be product focused rather than project focused, to be delivered by the cross-functional teams.

Cross-functional and cross-skilled teams are necessary ingredients for innovation aimed at finding the right solution for customer service, partner management, and internal process automation. Open discussions and conflicting points of view should be welcomed. It is important for executives and leaders from multiple supply chains (of different organizations) to have these discussions, especially about following a rule (such as frozen periods, lot sizes, customer solutions, etc.) for which a "why so" has not been asked for a long time. Open conversation with a goal to add value might generate innovative ideas leading to successes.

Learning is a crucial factor for each team member as well as for the overall organization (organizational learning) in order to successfully plan, develop, and implement a unique DSN strategy. Organizations and executives must provide learning opportunities to every member of the DSN team in the areas of processes and technology capabilities. Digital methods can be harnessed for effective and efficient training delivery on scale, with options of "on-demand" learning. Also, we recommend that the teaching method be two-way, learning with discussion, hands-on experiences, and discovery, instead of a one-directional format.

Learning prepares the organization for the journey, but it's the drive, clear communication, and goal sharing by the leadership team that will put the entire organization on the DSN transformation expedition.

Identify and Act

Once the organization is ready for the digital transformation, the next step is to engage the cross-functional teams to identify the value-creating opportunities. This is done by exploring all the DSN processes related to customer connect, synchronized planning, digital product development, intelligent supply, smart manufacturing and asset maintenance, and dynamic fulfillment. The design thinking approach and technological capabilities should be considered in identifying the realm of the possibilities. Unorthodox ideas need to be appreciated and evaluated (thinking outside the box), and creativity methods such as design thinking are a proven way to unlock the creativity of the team. The identified opportunities should then be grouped with the DSN process alignment areas to identify any duplication or conflict and make the process collaborative.

A business case should be developed for each of the value-creating opportunities. The business case describes where the team wants to create or add value and what investment will be required for a particular initiative to deliver against the projected value. Based on our research, we have identified significant deviations (ranging from 15 to 90 percent) for both cost and value. However, the recommendation is still to create the business case as a baseline. In addition to tracking progress, developing a business case also helps in grouping and integrating the individual activities for end-to-end transformation.

In the past few years, many organizations have launched experiment-based initiatives to check that an identified technology such as robotics blockchain, AI works. We recommend getting out of this mindset where the particular technology has a strong use case proof of concept record. For many DSN technologies, there is ample support for their effectiveness. The focus of the organization should be to identify the application opportunity and work on proving that it delivers when aligned to the business case.

The agile approach is the preferred way of designing, building, and delivering DSN solutions. We recommend delivering the DSN solutions as minimum viable product (MVP) and then updating this based on the customer feedback and integration activities.

Once delivered, the value measurement for proof of value and measuring the value against the plan should be done. This activity will be an input for the further handling of a solution.

Select and Integrate

Once initial pilots have been launched and multiple DSN solutions are adding true and measurable value to the organization, it is the time to integrate.

Organizations and leaders should evaluate all the individual solutions based on the success and failure as compared to the business plan and solution goal. Successful solutions are evaluated for scaling up, extending the solution scope, and integration with other solutions. The failed ones are evaluated to identify the root cause and whether any action can be taken to turn this to success and to decide whether the business case is still valid. The solutions for which there is no longer a business case are dropped and the team is assigned to a different problem, business opportunity, or other in-progress solution.

Organizations can integrate the successful solutions identified against the DSN business processes or against the problem they solve. For example, all the solutions related to the demand-supply planning can be grouped under synchronized planning initiatives for scaling up, or all the solutions related to inventory tracking (cutting across synchronized planning, intelligent supply, and dynamic fulfillment) can be grouped together.

The integration and scaling of the initiatives with the relevant business cases (now bigger value opportunities) make the organization ready for enterprise-level DSN transformation.

Scale and Evolve

The focus of this step is on scaling at the enterprise level, transforming end-to-end process, teams, and technology into a reimagined DSN.

DSN, as an essential factor of intelligently automated enterprise, is an ever-evolving function. This transformation is not a destination to be achieved, but to get an excellent maturity and then continue the journey to further evolution. We recommend that organizations at this phase sustain momentum through a longer-term approach to digital technologies, customer service, employee engagement, and process automation to have sustainable digital capabilities.

FACTORS AT PLAY DURING THE DSN TRANSFORMATION JOURNEY

There are multiple factors that impact the outcome of the DSN transformation journey. As displayed in the Figure 13.5, these can be instrumental for the success or failure of a transformation.

FIGURE 13.5 Factors Impacting the DSN Transformation Journey

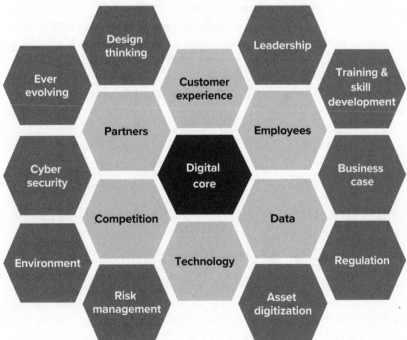

DIGITAL CORE. Digital core represents the basic operational data infrastructure of an organization. Integrated processes (consider an ERP application) of sales, finance, manufacturing, warehouse, and transport provide the elementary master and transaction data that is used by most of the DSN processes and advanced technologies. It may be difficult to perform the advanced DSN transformation without having the basic infrastructure backbone supported by the digital core of an organization. However, digital core creation and the DSN transformation activities can be performed in parallel if the digital core is still not there, and if there is a business case for the digital core and DSN opportunities.

DESIGN THINKING. A design thinking approach is recommended for the identification of the right problems to solve for value generation through the DSN capability areas. Design thinking is driven by empathy—by understanding the problems from the customer and user perspective. Understanding of the user requirements and priority is achieved through analysis, communication, role-play, observation, and research work. Design thinking for the DSN transformation can be applied for both incremental as well as radical gains.[3] Learning for faster delivery is fortified through collaboration, exploration, visualization, and prototype. A prototype represents a sketch or a rough working model of the planned final solution or product. Developing a faster prototype through digital technology helps in getting customer feedback and fine-tuning the products and services for the higher success of the finished output.

CUSTOMER EXPERIENCE. Consider the customer journey and customer experience while redefining the products, services, customer engagements, and internal processes. It is important to understand the problem that the organization is solving through the product or service. For example, an automobile company can look into transportation needs along with the experience it is creating for its customers to consider redefining its products, processes, and services.

LEADERSHIP. Like any transformation, DSN transformation needs to be driven by the leadership of the organization with a clear message and required support for the teams to succeed. The culture of learning, experimentation, and collaboration needs to be fostered, ideally leading by example. Old ideas and dogmas need to be questioned. Those that pass the test of analysis and value generation need to be retained, and others need to go away, giving space to the novel ways adding value to the firm through matured DSN processes.

EMPLOYEE. The most critical factor of success or failure of the DSN transformation is the employees. With instilled guidance, shaping, and support from the leadership, an active and engaged workforce will be able to rediscover the organization's supply chain to compete in the digital era through better service to its customers and more efficient internal processes. The culture of collaboration, a diversified team, learning from each other, support, and empathy will create the right atmosphere in the organization for enabling a successful DSN transformation.

TRAINING AND SKILLS DEVELOPMENT. Training and skill development activities are required for everyone related to the current supply chain organization. This needs to be customized and focused with respect to the role of every individual. For the leadership team, a digital literacy, technological capability, team management in the digital era, and learning from thought leaders are recommended; for the individual process leaders, digital immersion and realm of possibilities learning is required; for the individual team members, cross areas, DSN process, and technological capabilities learning is required.

BUSINESS CASE. The DSN transformation needs to be driven by a business case. It is important to understand the cost-value relationship before starting a particular transformation initiative. Though it is also important to understand that a unique initiative's cost may be more than the value opportunity, it can still be an important element for a broader digital capability and value achievement through a holistic plan. In addition to the start phase, it is advised to periodically keep track of any change in the cost and value part as the work progresses.

DATA. The "garbage in, garbage out" concept still holds true! The value creation in DSN through visualization, simulations for decision making, and process automation are entirely dependent on the input data quality. The availability of data at the right level is essential for DSN process management and automation. Data capturing, cleaning, usage, and retention should be carefully planned before designing and executing a DSN initiative. This exercise is applicable for the legacy data as well as data to be generated by the transformed processes.

REGULATIONS. Regulations and laws of the land should be input while planning the details of a DSN project. Customer data privacy, data usage, tax laws, and industry and country-specific regulations and rules must be considered while adopting the intelligence and automation in the supply network processes.

ASSET DIGITIZATION. Digitization of old generation physical assets has its own challenges. There have been incidents where adding the sensors and actuators to old mechanical devices has resulted in unexpected behavior of the machine causing operational issues. Failure on this point can have an adverse impact on the human life (operator, customer), financials, and team morale. It is strongly recommended to consider end-to-end working of the physical-digital-physical loop with the machine's capability and inherent design. Many times, adding an intelligent digital capability to the legacy dumb mechanical device is not the right answer.

TECHNOLOGY. Technology capability is one of the most essential elements of the DSN transformation. The evaluation of the technology needs to be aligned with the business goals and the possibilities generated by technology adoption. Multidimensional thinking from the customer requirements, process optimization, business vision, and technology capabilities can engender innovative and value-adding DSN solutions.

RISK MANAGEMENT. Along with the business case, it is important to have a risk management plan for DSN transformation initiatives with risk identification, impact calculation, and a mitigation plan. For most organizations, managing the current demand-supply process with the existing supply chain processes is essential while working on the DSN transformation activities. This parallel execution of activities multiplies the business risks, which must be identified, planned, and mitigated.

COMPETITION. It is important to identify who your competitor is, with the acceptance of the fact that a new disruptive competitor can evolve anytime. Hence, it is worthwhile to consider the end-to-end DSN processes to identify the value-creating opportunities and disrupt yourself, instead of being a reactive entity to the market disruptors. It may be possible to collaborate with your competitor and add value to enhance the market size while adding efficiency to the overall system. Consider if a platform impact can be generated through the organization's supply network to multiply the revenue and profit the organization and the ecosystem.

PARTNER. DSN is about optimizing and automating the holistic networks, not about being limited to the processes within the four walls of an organization. In DSN-enabled processes, partners play a crucial role in innovation and the successful execution of the transformed supply network processes. Hence, it becomes crucial to work with the partners for data sharing, overall process designing, and serving the in-process and the end customer through a well-collaborated integrated network.

ENVIRONMENT. DSN networks together create an impact on the environment and society. Factors like carbon footprints, working conditions (especially DSNs with a leg in the developing countries), and environmental impact should be considered for the benefit of all stakeholders while planning the revenue and profit maximization of an organization. The inherent efficiency gained through the DSN processes creates a positive impact on the environment by optimizing the raw materials, and process wastes. Also, the sensors and advanced tracking technologies have great potential for waste management and environmental sustenance.

CYBERSECURITY. Dependence on data, process automation, IoT devices, shared cloud, and the connected network extensively impacts the vulnerability of an organization from a cyber hacking threat. The seamless network connectivity makes the entire system vulnerable for a security breach at one device, in one process, or through just one partner. In this way, the weakest link of the network can be the strength of the entire DSN infrastructure against the malignant threats. Protection through the right tools and technologies is required to safeguard the organization against this danger.

EVER-EVOLVING. As mentioned before, DSN transformation is not a fixed destination but is a journey for an ever-evolving organization advancing on the path of intelligently automated enterprise and its supply network. Technology is changing at a fast pace, and the success achieved in an initiative creates the path of further innovation, automation, and improvement. Continuously improving the customer's life while taking care of the workforce and the stakeholders is the key to success for the right DSN transformation.

SUMMARY

For a successful DSN transformation, it is important to align this with the business strategy and plan the activities through a playbook, instead of having individual technology-focused, disconnected projects. DSN strategy influences almost every key element of the business strategy. For identification of the relevant DSN activities, four factors can be adopted, which are issue-focused, data-driven, platform-supported, or science-guided. It is important to understand the technological capability while planning the value opportunities through the DSN transformation. We recommend the four following steps for the transformation: start with changing the culture and workforce of the organization, then identify the DSN activities and act on them, select and integrate the individual initiatives to provide the right macro-level levers, and finally, scale the activities at the enterprise level for an ever-evolving organization. There are multiple factors that drive the success and failure of DSN transformation: digital core, design thinking, customer experience, leadership, employees, training and skills development, business case, data, regulation, asset digitization, technology, risk management, competition, partner, environment, cyber-security, and continuous development.

USE CASES

The transformation journey toward a DSN model is both exciting and challenging, but also full of possibilities and unavoidable. There are many examples of companies leading the way and trailblazing new innovative DSN projects and initiatives. In this last chapter, let us take a look at how a few selected firms are transforming their supply chain operating models by developing DSNs, and as a consequence removing traditional constraints, driving business innovation, and producing higher value. These firms showcase DSN initiatives at different stages of development. We present them in no particular order.

AMAZON: START-UP MINDSET DRIVEN BY CUSTOMER VALUE CREATION[1]

Amazon.com started as a book retailer back in 1994. The Seattle-based multinational technology giant has come a long way since then. From e-commerce, cloud computing, and digital streaming to artificial intelligence, and highly automated warehouses, Amazon is a front-runner in the technology space, driving many of the innovations and disruptions that we see today. The term "Amazon effect" has come to describe its success and has upended retail and supply chain practices and customer expectation, both online and offline.

Leading DSN and a Relentless Pursuit of Innovation
With a revenue upward of $230 billion, Amazon consistently invests almost 12 percent of its revenue in technological innovations yearly. The company is typically a first mover in terms of experimenting with

or adopting the latest digital technologies. Amazon displays a continuous focus on innovation. The company's vision, business model, and operating foundations focus on reimagining the traditional organizational and operating model and relentlessly pursuing platform leadership. So, rather than industry trends shaping Amazon's strategy, it is Amazon that typically drives industry trends. To accomplish such a feat, Amazon adopts an *ad eternum* start-up mindset, continuously challenging the status quo, living by the creed "everything is possible." Besides, the company pairs all of that with the principles of "delivery at any cost" and "innovation through technology."

An example of such a breakthrough innovation mindset is the Amazon Go, an artificial intelligence (AI)-powered convenience store, offering a "just walk out" facility. It promises to be a revolution in offline shopping where customers do not need to wait in queues to pay; instead, they can automatically check out their shopping carts when they walk out of the store. Using smartphones as scanning devices, customers can add the desired products in their shopping cart on the Amazon Go mobile application by scanning the item when they pick it from the shelves. Using a combination of artificial intelligence, computer vision, and data from multiple sensors, the system charges customers only for what they choose and takes care of the payment transaction digitally. So, customers can "pick up" groceries of their choice and "walk out" of the store without stopping at any kiosks or cash registers.

Amazon responds instantly to short-term changes in supply and demand through an agile digital supply network enabled by the horizontal integration of real-time information flows and analytics. It can handle external disruptions smoothly and integrate both customers and suppliers within its information platform. These capabilities help reveal detailed intelligence on customer behavior and supply patterns. Amazon uses robots, drones, sensor-based monitoring, augmented reality, and AI in its warehouses and fulfillment centers to pick-pack-ship the orders, reducing the need for human effort in low-value-added activities. For better customer experience, Amazon tries to understand customer behavior by analyzing streams of data and insights received through websites, mobile apps, and AI devices. All these features enable the company to predict future demand better and anticipate issues before they occur. Even tremendous and rapid demand shift and spike under a black swan event, such as the COVID-19 pandemic, did not ultimately compromise the system. On the contrary, Amazon's DSN initiatives and business model have not only proved the ability to adapt, but have also demonstrated the ensuing profitability of the investments.

In short, Amazon's supply network is one of the fastest and most innovative and efficient in the world. The company is committed to delivering products to customers in the shortest time possible, which pressures other retail giants across the globe to change the way they operate. It is essential to note that Amazon does not just deploy or leverage the latest technology: leaders engineer the company differently, in reimagined ways compared to traditional business models, supported by inherently unique and innovative digital supply network operating foundations.

GEORGIA–PACIFIC: STARTING THE DSN JOURNEY WITH A SUCCESFUL DIGITAL CORE[2]

Georgia-Pacific is one of the world's leading makers of tissues, paper products, pulp, packaging, building products, and related chemicals. The company has more than 30,000 employees in more than 150 locations. Georgia-Pacific's parent organization, Koch Industries, is the second-largest private company of the United States. Georgia-Pacific's Consumer Products Group produces and distributes household brands such as Angel Soft and Quilted Northern bath tissue, Brawny paper towels, Dixie tableware, and Vanity Fair napkins, as well as away-from-home brands like enMotion, Compact, and Pacific Blue that meet restroom, foodservice, and break room needs for office buildings, healthcare, lodging, and education facilities. The company started an organization-wide digital transformation and identified the reimagination of supply chain processes through digitization as key for the overall success. Specifically, executives identified the digitization of end-to-end processes involving demand planning, supply planning, production scheduling, production execution, warehouse management, and transportation as the most beneficial in terms of value.

The transformation started by building a best-in-class sales and operations planning (S&OP) process in collaboration with a consulting partner. The output of this effort resulted in an S&OP to create one version of the truth for demand and supply across the organization. The implementation of the approach made apparent the need for appropriate technology to enable connections, advanced algorithms, and seamless collaboration. Enthused with success, and after careful consideration of the cost-benefit analysis of digital transformation, Georgia-Pacific's Consumer Products Group launched a mega project, called Digital Core, with its consulting and technology partners. The goal of the project was to ready the organization for the future with accurate data, best-in-class processes, advanced technology applications, effective collaboration, and easy-to-use analytics. Digital Core was launched in 2017, is already delivering value, and is planned to continue until 2021.

The vision of Jeff Fleck, chief supply chain officer for Georgia-Pacific's Consumer Products Group, is to provide the tools his team members need to effectively drive the supply network processes. His goal is to create an integrated touchless system to calculate the demand, supply, production, and deployment, producing optimized plans for the organization. In this way, the team is performing more value-adding tasks, like acting on the opportunities and potential risks related to the demand, supply, and revenue, and are not spending a multitude of hours on repetitive manual transactions.

For the organizations embarking into DSN projects, Jeff highlights the following points:

- Data quality is crucial; digital transformation requires clean, accurate, and live data.

- People are the most important part of any digital effort, and change management is a priority.

- The journey requires resilience and may require course correction along the way.

- The right team and attitude are a must for success.

- An initial solid digital core forms the foundation for future success.

BLOCKCHAIN-BASED DSN: CREATING TRANSPARENCY BETWEEN WALMART CANADA AND CARRIERS[3]

Walmart Canada operates 8.75 million square feet of distribution center and moves more than 853 million cases of merchandise a year. It owns more than 2,100 trailers and trucks and has 70 carrier partners that transport over 500,000 loads of inventory to over 400 retail stores across Canada. Walmart Canada faces a remarkable volume of transactions and transactional data and a plethora of variable information. For instance, mileage reimbursement can be a fixed price but can vary according to the contract. Compensation for delivery times can vary between time spent on the road and time spent waiting to offload a shipment once a truck reaches its destination, and the rates differ.

With each party involved in the transaction having its own set of data, mismatches can often happen, creating a significant pain point for Walmart in terms of reconciling data and for carriers in terms of payment timeliness and clarity about data sources.

Such difficulties with invoice reconciliation are a widespread concern across the industry, with estimates suggesting about $140 billion per day tied up at US supply chains for invoice disputes, for instance, said Loudon Owen, DLT Labs CEO. The multiplicity of processes, information systems, and operating systems that each carrier utilizes, their varied level of sophistication, the sheer volume and variety of transactions involved across the interactions, and industry consolidation all aggravate the challenges from an information and data management perspective. According to Loudon, "Every single delivery has close to 200 different variable costs." All this information arrives at once and through different means (phone, fax, email). Reconciling such volume and variety of data for a huge firm such as Walmart across a high number of carriers is a big challenge. Besides, the issue touches different functions.

Blockchain, IoT, and Smart Contract: Real-Time Visibility and Accuracy

Walmart Canada started deploying an automated blockchain-based supply network for freight tracking and payment management in late 2019. The DSN initiative seeks to improve freight and payment processing and enable users to automatically trace deliveries, verify transactions, and handle payments and reconciliation. The network integrates and synchronizes all the supply chain and logistics data in real time, aggregating the data between Walmart Canada and its fleet of third-party trucks on a shared ledger. The system includes the use of IoT sensors and GPS tracking in the semitrailer trucks. It also consists of a web portal and mobile app that operators and suppliers can access manually.

Walmart Canada deployed a permissioned blockchain with 27 distributed nodes, considered as the largest of its kind worldwide. John Bayliss, Walmart Canada's senior vice-president, logistics and supply chain, asserts that the blockchain-based digital network is creating complete transparency between Walmart Canada and all of its carrier partners. He further indicates that blockchain technology has enabled tangible progress in the company's smart transportation network with benefits including expedited payments and substantial cost savings. Among the innovative elements of this blockchain-enabled DSN is the deep level of integration with existing corporate data systems. Through a set of Application programming interfaces (APIs), the blockchain ledger connects to Walmart and carrier legacy systems, such as ERP, accounting systems, and transportation management systems. The approach to invoice generation and payment is automated through the smart contract embedded in the blockchain.

The newly built system allows Walmart to track data automatically and in real time. For instance, when a freight trucker enters transport time, the information uploaded to the blockchain is automatically checked against IoT and GPS data, ascertaining the accuracy of the ledger. The DSN solution increases trust and transparency by sharing information and automating workflows and calculations. Supply network partners can effectively manage the complex shipment, invoice, payment, and settlement process. Real-time consolidation of all business rules and transactions to create a single invoice reduces waiting times and speeds up payments. Accurate, real-time data is used for enhanced analytics and predictive modeling, enabling better budgeting and planning.

LAND O'LAKES: REIMAGINING THE CREATION AND DELIVERY OF VALUE IN A TRADITIONAL SECTOR[4]

Land O'Lakes, Inc. is an agriculture cooperative listed in the Fortune 500 and based out of Arden Hills, Minnesota. The organization is a multibillion-dollar agricultural conglomerate known for its dairy products, especially butter and cheese. Its membership comprises 1,851 dairy producers, 749 agriculture producers, and 1,067 retail owners. It consists of three primary businesses: dairy foods (Land O'Lakes brand), animal nutrition (Purina brand), and crop inputs and insights (WinField United brand).

Toward a Dynamic Fulfillment System with Transparency and Multichannel Capabilities

Land O'Lakes is an excellent example of a company operating in a very traditional industry but investing in a move toward a DSN and underlying digital operating model to create, capture, and deliver value in new ways. The organization is undergoing a digital transformation to enable growers to log in and do business with the company when they want. The idea was to quickly send growers valuable ag-tech data and insights such as soil and tissue sample test result, crop models, and satellite images of their crops. Land O'Lakes/WinField United developed the ATLAS web portal to enable customer connectivity and superior customer experience. ATLAS adds value to retail owners by providing a complete digital brand experience tailoring data, insights, news, and weather information to their farmers.

WinField United Data Silo powers the ATLAS with insights. Data Silo is a data collection application that gathers, stores, and shares information between farmers, retailers, and third-party providers. It connects previously disparate systems, letting users quickly share information about crops and farm operations. With it, farmers can easily upload data to the platform, build dashboards, and search for information. In return, they receive guidance on agronomic best practices, such as which crop would provide the most profit out of their acreage. The cloud-based application developed by Land O'Lakes' WinField United brand, helps farmers make better, data-driven decisions leveraging various data and insight tools that work together to assist farmers in making a more informed decision. The tool helps farmers better predict the outcomes when it comes to in-season water, nitrogen, and potassium management decisions, for instance.

The WinField United digital platform aims at simplifying the way retail-owners order seed or crop protection products online, through a single point of data entry. The plan is to offer an integrated digital supply chain experience, from the grower through the retailer and the distributor. Dustin Braun, senior director, logistics, says Amazon is an example of what WinField/Land O'Lakes wants the fulfillment system to provide: an "incredibly simple" online ordering interface and a reliable supply chain. The platform engages customers in different ways by providing real-time critical information to assist farmers in their decision making and, at the same time, allow them to place orders for their specific needs at any time. The platform offers a comprehensive approach to omnichannel and provides retail-owners the e-business tools to make it easier and faster for their customers (growers) to do business with them. The platform offers a comprehensive experience to empower retailers to capitalize on their local knowledge, solutions for growers, and optimization and cost-saving opportunities for retailers.

T-MOBILE DIGITAL SUPPLY NETWORK[5]

T-Mobile is a global telecom leader providing wireless communication services under the T-Mobile and Metro PCS brands in the United States. T-Mobile digital transformation is based on customer-centricity and employee engagement. Besides being a telecom company, T-Mobile is like a retail organization with more than 5,000 stores and over 11,000 outlets for Metro PCS. The supply network handles the movement of delicate high-value products (cell phones) and accessories; the products flow in both forward and backward directions. The uniqueness of the supply chain is selling others' products (Apple, Samsung, etc.), with limited opportunity to influence the product design and features, though owning the customer journey and experience. The combination of T-Mobile specific device offerings and private label products further enhance the complexity of managing the flow of supplies.

End-to-End Accuracy, Visibility, and Transparency

The essential value opportunity identified in the supply chain was accuracy, visibility, and transparency. An accurate dynamic picture of inventory at the store (shelves and back-store), the location of the inventory in the network, and the precise lead time for delivering a given inventory item to the consumer's home is challenging but critical for customer satisfaction. This mandate became possible now through a robust digital supply network infrastructure.

Automation of planning, forecasting, and replenishment is another area the company identified for getting value from the digitization. Instead of the traditional macro-level forecast, the company now uses prediction at the individual product-location combination. This solution is a more robust approach, supported by a digital environment with the right data characteristics. One source of truth is available to both supply chain and finance for the planning and execution processes. The company achieved an end-to-end visibility through integration with the vendor database.

The organization started the journey by fortifying the core data and connecting the process infrastructure. Upon completing connectivity, the company started rolling out individual digital solutions based on their business value. T-Mobile has been progressing on the vision to automate to produce better data and visibility, taking the bottlenecks (both process- and human-caused) out from the operations. The company has identified RFID, sensors, and AI-based solutions for the next wave.

For other organizations planning the DSN transformation, Erik LaValle, Digital Supply Chain & Customer Experience Technology Portfolio leader, shared the following five critical points:

- Identifying and grooming the right team members is crucial. Understand the importance of change management and workforce training to support the digital transformation.

- If required, bring in the critical experience for digital delivery and envisioning the future.

- The journey cannot start without a robust digital foundation. So, do not overlook the basic data and the digital foundation; especially for the supply chain and manufacturing areas.

- Develop trust and confidence among business partners while starting the journey.

- You may have the first-mover penalty, but the journey will pay back soon.

JD.COM DSN-ENABLED BOUNDARYLESS RETAIL STRATEGY[6]

JD.com has over 500 logistics centers and 250,000 logistics vehicles across China, serving over 305 million customers. JD.com envisions a boundaryless retail future, where the organization enables customers to purchase whatever they want, whenever, and through whatever channel: online, offline, or virtual. The intent is to eliminate artificial barriers through collaboration and innovation via an agile, flexible, and fully connected retail network. For instance, near 70 percent of Chinese consumers seem to be actively using services of companies such as JD.com, which leverages big data, analytics, and other DSN technologies to deliver goods from local offline partner groceries, including Walmart, to customers in under an hour. The achievement of this vision is only possible by reimagining supply chain processes, synchronizing planning with partners, and deploying appropriate technologies to develop the formative attributes encompassing a dynamic fulfillment capability and intelligent chain.

JD.com's growing development of DSN capabilities allows the company to deliver to customers at staggering speeds all across China via its nationwide logistics network. Its DSN features the latest retail technology that JD.com is using to empower other partners, online and offline, developing a dynamic and intelligent ecosystem. The retail technology includes a drone delivery network for rural shipments to crewless delivery vehicles in dense urban areas. JD has built a massive smart logistics infrastructure to serve its 300 million e-commerce customers and is now offering that system to brand partners and other retailers. It has deployed intelligent delivery stations in the cities of Changsha and Hohhot, which use autonomous vehicles to perform last-mile delivery. The stations reportedly house fleets of delivery robots carrying up to 30 parcels each inside compartments, which are similar to lockers for parcel delivery used by Amazon on apartment buildings. However, a significant difference is that JD's cabinets are mobile instead of stationary, steering themselves to addresses within a one- to three-miles radius with smart delivery features including route planning, obstacle avoidance, and traffic light recognition. Upon arrival, the lockers use facial recognition technology to ensure the person claiming the parcel is the correct consumer. Running at full capacity, these delivery stations can deliver up to 2,000 packages a day.

Enabling New Partnerships, More Connected Customers, and Greater Customer Value

JD.com is leveraging its growing DSN capabilities to pursue partnerships that enable more connectivity with value creation for customers and additional streams of revenue. For instance, JD's partnership with hotel brands such as Sheraton allows guests to shop from their rooms and have the products delivered directly to the hotel. Another example is the innovative partnership with Walmart, which rendered DJ.com Gartner's Retail Supply Chainnovator Award 2019 "for rethinking retailer-to-retailer collaboration to deliver a unified shopping experience." The partnership includes shared coupons, real-time inventory signaling, cost-to-serve data, and unified last mile delivery offering. It leverages JD.com's e-commerce and DSN capabilities and Walmart China's physical store network to provide an integrated shopping experience to the combined customer base. The DSN capability enables customers to place an order with JD.com and have the product dynamically fulfilled from the most optimal stocking locations across the two businesses (Walmart China stores or JD.com warehouses) in terms of delivery speed, cost-to-serve, and working capital inventory investment. Independent of which company receives the order, the DSN capabilities, which include omnichannel competency and intelligent supply chain supported by an AI-driven order management system, determine not only the location that allows the faster delivery but also the most profitable. An AI-enabled delivery routing algorithm then kicks in to ascertain a consistent, on-time, and cost-effective delivery experience for the customer.

UNILEVER: FACTORIES WITH DIGITAL TWINS[7]

Consumer products giant Unilever is one of the world's major suppliers of beauty and personal care, home care, and foods and refreshment products. It is co-headquartered at London, United Kingdom, and Rotterdam, Netherlands; owns over 400 brands; has sales in over 190 countries; and boasts a turnover of over $50 billion globally. Unilever has been recognized in the exclusive Gartner Supply Chain Masters category, having topped Gartner's rankings of industry's best-performing supply chain leaders for 2019.

With the complex nature of Unilever's supply chain, the company generates massive amounts of data from across the value network. Unilever decided to leverage this data to generate insights that drive efficiencies and reduce costs. Today's customers expect customization and want products on demand, which is why Unilever chose to use the data at its disposal and complement it with the capabilities of digital technology to transform its supply chain.

Digitally Rewiring the Supply Chain

Unilever teamed up with a technology leader to build virtual versions of its factories, using data streaming from sensor-equipped machines to create digital models that can track physical conditions and enable testing of operational changes. It created a digital twin to replicate the physical requirements, capturing data from machine sensors in a digital format. Digital twin is a digital copy of inputs received from temperature and activity sensors mounted on physical assets. These inputs are modeled through software applications and are designed to monitor asset performance. Using machine learning and artificial intelligence to analyze large volumes of data, Unilever aimed to make its production more efficient and agile. The convergence of advanced technologies such as IoT sensors, cloud services, big data, ML, and AI brought this idea to fruition.

Unilever, in collaboration with its technology partner, set up a pilot at a facility in Valinhos, Brazil, in 2018, which makes products including Dove soap and ice cream. As part of the pilot, IoT devices send real-time information on temperature, motor speed, and other production variables to the cloud. Algorithms take in the data and use advanced analytics to map out the best operational conditions. Workers located on-site track product quality with handheld devices, modeling solutions to problems and sharing data with colleagues in other locations.

Unilever has saved about $2.8 million at the Valinhos site by cutting down on energy use and driving a 1 to 3 percent increase in productivity. Inspired by this success, Unilever launched eight more digital twins in factories across North America, South America, Europe, and Asia, as pilots for making algorithmic tweaks, before a broader rollout. It is now working closely with a partner, leveraging cloud services to create virtual versions of dozens of its roughly 300 global plants over the next year. Unilever engineers call this the "digital rewiring of their supply chain." Using this technology, the Anglo-Dutch company aims to make real-time changes to optimize output, use materials more precisely, and help limit waste from a product that does not meet quality standards.

CATERPILLAR: THE LIVE FACTORY[8]

Caterpillar is a Fortune 500 global enterprise with a team of more than 100,000 employees. Despite its size and history of success, in the 2000s, Caterpillar experienced a lag in growth and found the number of competitors rising and customer loyalty beginning to falter. To counter this, Caterpillar implemented a Live Factory solution by converging man, machine, and method to optimize performance and create reliable, standardized processes. This Live Factory solution tracked asset movement through a facility, digitizing the quality of defects, improving labor efficiency, and reducing the finished goods inventory using sensors and analytics. Figure 14.1 depicts the process visually.

To create this successful new "live factory," Caterpillar had to figure out how to achieve simultaneous harmony between several technological components, including location tracking, work center alert tracking and prioritization, and real-time work center analytics. The company solved simultaneous harmonization through enhanced technological tools. The enabling tools included a digital boardroom to support long-term planning, digital manufacturing insights to support tactical management reporting, and OT applications like digital delivery and predictive maintenance to help the day-to-day operational efficiencies.

These new technologies created a new digital supply network, wherein various sources of real-time data converged to inform multiple parts of the whole on how to adjust process flows. The outcome was optimized outputs and minimized waste. As goods flowed through the system, the movement, location, time spent at each station, and quality of the product were tracked. The data produced informed workers about where they needed to spend their time, and better educated the company on where it needed to spend budgets on improving the system.

The use of technologies to enhance asset tracking and movement within Caterpillar's supply chain yielded total transparency and real-time analysis. Caterpillar was also able to generate real-time simulations for "what-if" scenarios to enhance planning options. This

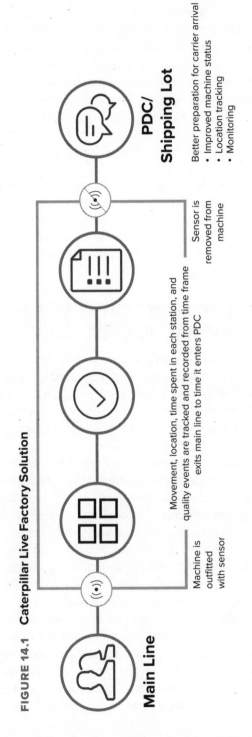

FIGURE 14.1 Caterpillar Live Factory Solution

Main Line

Machine is outfitted with sensor

Movement, location, time spent in each station, and quality events are tracked and recorded from time frame exits main line to time it enters PDC

Sensor is removed from machine

PDC/ Shipping Lot

Better preparation for carrier arrival
• Improved machine status
• Location tracking
• Monitoring

outcome created a 360-degree view of the business. And with this new 360 view, the new Live Factory model was able to identify $12 million to $18 million in savings as it reduced latency, automated activities that were previously manual, eliminated inefficient handoffs, and increased productivity and capacity utilization. Besides, Caterpillar's inventory carrying costs were reduced by $1.2 million, and labor costs were reduced by $500,000. Ultimately, this new approach saved Caterpillar time, money, and capacity. Without the power of the Live Factory, Caterpillar was at risk of losing customers and market share.

Leveraging the experience and knowledge gained years earlier, Caterpillar took its Live Factory a step further, and is now connecting its machinery to the Caterpillar cloud, enabling miners and builders to get the most out of their equipment. This initiative is done by letting users know earlier and with more precision when, for example, they need a tune-up or new tires.

NIKE INC: CONNECTED CUSTOMER AND MANUFACTURING INNOVATION[9]

American multinational sportswear conglomerate Nike Inc. is the largest global supplier and manufacturer of athletic shoes, apparel, and sports equipment. Founded in 1964, publicly traded Nike Inc. is headquartered in Beaverton, Oregon, and has over 73,000 employees and over 1,000 retail stores, and reported $39.1 billion in revenue in 2019. Nike is recognized as the industry leader.

Due to increased desirability and demand for customization and a personalized shopping experience, Nike witnessed increased demand for digital online markets and subsequent decline in in-store purchases from the average consumer in the footwear and apparel market. Nike quickly realized that to keep its consumer base, it must react proactively, adopt new innovative practices, and adapt to new technologies with an "always-on" agile approach to retain and continue to expand its consumer base. This forced Nike to reevaluate its supply chain and embrace a digitalized supply chain experience.

By utilizing data analytics to track the historical buying patterns and preferences of consumers, Nike focused on personalizing the direct-to-customer experience. Patrons now custom design their purchases, choose their desired delivery windows, and receive a unique shopping experience for every visit to the digital channels. Additionally, Nike aligned with several leading robotics and automation companies through substantial financial investments in increased manufacturing innovation to rethink the production approach of its footwear brand. The company has established partnerships to build a 3D digital design system to transform its product creation process, enabling capabilities such as digital print applications, photo-real 3D visualizations, and ultra-rapid prototyping. Another partnership aimed at reimagining the manufacturing process through 3D printing.

Nike executives understood they had to adopt new technology to build reimagined capabilities. Among them were understanding customers' individual needs while delivering on time. Nike reimagined its logistics and distribution strategy as well and included same-day delivery options. Thinking ahead and embracing innovation and change, Nike deprioritized its focus on physical store locations.

Nike has since acquired several data analytics and computer vision companies to strengthen its digital technology platforms further and has seen an increase in revenue in its brand of 4 to 8 percent year-to-year from 2017 to 2019. Continuing to embrace and adopt innovative technologies, Nike has opened two Nike House of Innovation, in Shanghai and New York, to give customers an unmatched personalized experience.

MAVEN MACHINES: REIMAGINING FLEET DISPATCH AND MANAGEMENT[10]

Maven Machines Inc. is an IoT start-up based in Pittsburgh, Pennsylvania, with a focus on the logistics and trucking industry, particularly the less-than-truckload segment. The company is a start-up reimagining carrier safety and driver compliance, and is assisting partners struggling in transitioning that aspect of the supply chain toward a DSN environment. Maven was founded by CEO Avishai Geller in 2014, and it offers an innovative and unique platform solution enabled by IoT and AI-powered optimization. The company is disrupting a segment that is somewhat traditional in terms of digital technologies and yet has a substantial economic impact. New regulations, such as the electronic logging devices (ELD) requirements recently introduced in the United States, are forcing carriers to rethink their processes. The trucking industry is facing an increasing push toward carrier safety and driver compliance, but most procedures are outdated and supported by analog systems.

For instance, traditionally, dispatchers have managed the operations and guided drivers through CB radios or phones. Maven developed a sophisticated platform to handle complex information in fleet and dispatch management. The company designed the world's first smart wireless headset for truck drivers, the Co-Pilot smart head-sets, which provide real-time driver fatigue and distraction monitoring through alerts based on cues like head motion and mirror-check rate. The company also developed a Smartsense IoT platform that makes it a full fleet management system provider that includes electronic logging device compliance. The platform gathers data on driver perfor-mance, GPS, telematics, and vehicle engine information. The platform also features a mesh network of more than 20 sensors inside the truck, which provide one-second precision for measurements including speeding, hard braking, distraction, mirror checks, and weather, along with legal compliance.

The dispatch system combines traditional dispatch with telemat-ics and added layers of information, effectively connecting previously separated data sources and presenting the information intuitively across the mobile cloud network. It enables partners to streamline their daily workflows and add critical real-time visibility, seamlessly integrating hours of service with dispatching solutions to forecast the driver's schedule ahead of time. The fleet system allows the operator to access telematics data in real time from anywhere and enables fleet leaders to visualize their entire workflow. The start-up has been work-ing closely with partners and integrating the users of the technology in the reimagining and development process, so that it can build a full understanding of requirements and gain industry knowledge to pro-vide the best solution. This use case and others in this chapter illustrate the power of reimagining processes, the value that technological part-nerships can bring when needed, and the benefits of moving toward a digital supply network operating environment.

DAIMLER: PUSH FOR PROACTIVE SENSING[11]

Daimler Trucks Asia (DTA) is an integral subsidiary within the world's largest truck manufacturer, Daimler AG. Although DTA per-formed as a leader within the logistics industry for many years, CIO Lutz Beck was looking for a way to disrupt the industry and solidify Daimler Trucks Asia as the gold standard in commercial vehicle man-ufacturing. To do this, DTA needed to reduce costs while maintaining quality and preserving brand reputation. To pull off this feat, Beck turned to the tenets of the digital supply network and began imple-menting proactive sensing techniques.

But what is proactive sensing? Proactive sensing is the implementa-tion of advanced IoT-based technology that allows companies to collect more data points and better sift through them to obtain the relevant information. They can then distill those pieces into logical and digestible flows of information. This process can be seen in Figure 14.2.

FIGURE 14.2 Proactive Sensing

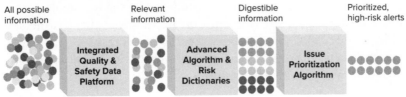

By applying advanced analytics, companies can organize their data and prioritize risks to streamline solution efficiency, resulting in a limited scope of service campaigns and reduced warranty repair costs. With considerably fewer risks going undetected, companies can also better protect customer satisfaction and brand reputation as compared to traditional issue detection. Figure 14.3 highlights the differences in these processes.

FIGURE 14.3 Proactive Sensing vs. Traditional Issue Detection

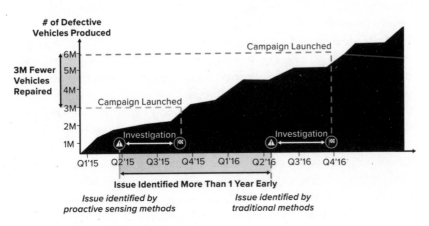

When thinking about how to transform the DTA supply chain using proactive sensing, Beck started with a focus on quality management. To solidify a future-forward foundation, Beck first implemented a new IoT-enabled system to enable real-time tracking of geographical data and vehicle system data. This proactive sensing created a predictive and intelligent stream of data that enabled DTA to anticipate previously unseen issues. After an assessment of the last 45 major DTA recalls, the company concluded that approximately 80 percent of them could have been predicted had the new proactive sensing process been in place. By applying a proactive sensing approach, DTA expects to save $8 million in warranty costs in the first 24 months and even more in recall costs. The sharper insights produced by the IoT implementation should yield a 6- to 12-month future view into the lifetime of a vehicle. And finally, thanks to this proactive sensing, DTA was able to avert thousands of trucks from being produced with a faulty part, saving money and possibly saving lives.

SUMMARY

In the current wave of technological innovation, many time-honored managerial mental models and assumptions no longer apply. As illustrated by many of the cases presented in this chapter, and others throughout the book, the creative use of disruptive technologies to "reimagine" the organization and operating processes are enabling the emergence of new ways to organize the chain of supplies. DSNs leverage a different type of operating logic and would allow companies to compete, capture value, and deliver value differently from the traditional models.

Moving toward a DSN archetype is about transforming the delivery of value by developing a new type of operating model based on data and digital technology. Shifting from electronic automation in the second wave of technological development to algorithm-enabled digital automation in the current wave brings us to the DSN stage of supply chain thought. This new digital operating model has at its core an integrated data platform, and many such platforms enable automated data-driven operational actions that gradually remove human intervention from the delivery process. This feature has good, bad, and potentially ugly sides, and executives, leaders, and governments must critically address and anticipate them. "Failure is not an option" might be less critical for some projects than "failing fast," iterating, and learning. We hope this book energized and prepared you with the foundations needed to engage in this thrilling journey. The technologies we discussed are increasingly accessible, some as a service from the cloud, and there are many competent experts and technology partners available to assist with their deployment. The challenging bit is the need for new thinking, transformation, and vision.

May you live and succeed in exciting times!

NOTES

CHAPTER 1

1. Council of Supply Chain Management Professionals. (2016). CSCMP supply chain management definitions and glossary. https://cscmp.org/CSCMP/Educate/SCM_Definitions_and_Glossary_of_Terms.aspx
2. Iansiti, M., & Lakhani, K. R. (2020, January-February). Competing in the age of AI. *Harvard Business Review.*
3. Ibid.
4. Fawcett, S., Ellram, L., Fugate, B., Kannan, V., & Bernardes, E. (2019). *Operations and supply chain management: enhancing competitiveness and customer value.* Salt Lake City: MyEducator.
5. Schwab, K. (2015, December 12). The fourth industrial revolution. What it means and how to respond. *Foreign Affairs.*
6. Schwab, K. (2017). The fourth industrial revolution. *Currency.*
7. Brynjolfsson, E., & McAfee, A. (2014). *The second machine age: Work, progress, and prosperity in a time of brilliant technologies.* WW Norton & Company.
8. Stock, J. R. (2013). Supply chain management: A look back, a look ahead. *Supply Chain Quarterly, 2*, 22–26.
9. Frohlich, M., & Westbrook, R. (2001). Arcs of integration: an international study of supply chain strategies. *Journal of Operations Management, 19*, 185–200.
10. Ballou, R. (2006). The evolution and future of logistics and supply chain management. *Production Journal, 16*(3).
11. La Londe, B. J., Grabner, J. R., & Robeson, J. F. (1976). Integrated distribution systems: a management perspective. In *Business Logistics* (pp. 3–19). Springer, Boston, MA.
12. Ballou, R. (2006). The evolution and future of logistics and supply chain management. *Production Journal, 16*(3).
13. Kirkman, M. M. (1887). *The handling of railway supplies: their purchase and disposition.* CN Trivess, printer.

14. Bernardes, E. S. (2010). The effect of supply management on aspects of social capital and the impact on performance: A social network perspective. *Journal of Supply Chain Management, 46*(1), 45–55.
15. Frohlich, M., & Westbrook, R. (2001). Arcs of integration: an international study of supply chain strategies. *Journal of Operations Management, 19*, 185–200.
16. Choi, T., Dooley, K., & Rungtusanatham, M. (2001). Supply networks and complex adaptive systems: control versus emergence. *Journal of Operations Management, 19*, 351–366.
17. Complex Adaptive Supply Networks Research Accelerator, https://research.wpcarey.asu.edu/supply-networks/
18. Mussomeli, A., Gish, D., & Laaper, S. (2016). *The rise of the digital supply network: Industry 4.0 enables the digital transformation of supply chains.* Deloitte University Press.
19. Fawcett, S., Ellram, L., Fugate, B., Kannan, V., & Bernardes, E. (2019). *Operations and supply chain management: enhancing competitiveness and customer value.* Salt Lake City: MyEducator.
20. Mackelprang, A. W., Bernardes, E., Burke, G. J., & Welter, C. (2018). Supplier innovation strategy and performance: A matter of supply chain market positioning. *Decision Sciences, 49*(4), 660–689.

CHAPTER 2

1. Global Business School (GBS). (2017, February 14). What is supply chain management, and why is it important? Retrieved from https://www.global-business-school.org/announcements/what-is-supply-chain-management-why-is-important
2. Mussomeli, A., Gish, D., & Laaper, S. (2016, December 1). *The rise of the digital supply network.* Deloitte University Press. https://www2.deloitte.com/us/en/insights/focus/industry-4-0/digital-transformation-in-supply-chain.html, p. 7.
3. Richard, C., & Kusters, J. (2019, January 1). Moving from the supply chain to the digital supply network. *Journal of Supply Chain Management, Logistics and Procurement.* https://www.ingentaconnect.com/content/hsp/jscm/2019/00000002/00000001/art00007
4. Ibid.
5. Heron, P., Walsh, T., & Umbenhauer, B. *The supply chain control tower.* Deloitte Development LLC. (n.d.). https://www2.deloitte.com/us/en/pages/energy-and-resources/articles/embracing-supply-chain-transformation.html, p. 2.
6. Mussomeli, A., Gish, D., & Laaper, S. (2016, December 1). *The rise of the digital supply network.* Deloitte University Press. https://www2.deloitte.com/us/en/insights/focus/industry-4-0/digital-transformation-in-supply-chain.html, p. 13.
7. Parrott, A., & Warshaw, L. (2017, May 12). *Industry 4.0: digital twin technology.* Deloitte University Press. https://www2.deloitte.com/us/en/insights/focus/industry-4-0/digital-twin-technology-smart-factory.html, pp. 8, 9.

8. Ibid.

9. Deloitte Development LLC. (2018, December). *Digital supply networks: our point of view*, pp. 25, 26.

10. Ratten, V. (2019). Cloud computing technology innovation advances: a set of research propositions. In *Disruptive technology: concepts, methodologies, tools, and applications* (pp. 693–703). IGI Global.

11. Deloitte Development LLC. (2018, December). *Digital supply networks: our point of view*, pp. 27, 28.

12. Ibid.

13. Fitzgerald, J., Cook, A., DeMarinis, T., & Smetana, K. (2018). *Utilizing virtual reality to drive supply chain innovation*. Deloitte Development LLC. https://www2.deloitte.com/us/en/pages/operations/articles/virtual-reality-to-drive-supply-chain-innovation.html

14. Deloitte Development LLC. (2018, December). *Digital supply networks: our point of view*, pp. 31–36.

15. Ibid.

16. Ibid.

17. Ibid.

18. Ibid.

19. Killmeyer, J., & Holdowsky, J. (2019, February 1). *From siloed to distributed. Blockchain enables the digital supply network*. Deloitte Insights. https://www2.deloitte.com/us/en/insights/topics/understanding-blockchain-potential/digital-supply-network-blockchain-adoption.html

20. Mussomeli, A., Neier, M., Takayama, B., Sniderman, B., & Holdowsky, J. (2019, June 14). *Building a cognitive digital supply network*. Deloitte Insights. (n.d.). https://www2.deloitte.com/us/en/insights/focus/industry-4-0/digital-supply-networks-cognitive-automation.html

21. Deloitte Development LLC. (2018, December). *Digital supply networks: Our point of view*, pp. 37, 38.

22. Ibid., page 47.

23. Mussomeli, A., Gish, D., & Laaper, S. (2016, December 1). *The rise of the digital supply network*. Deloitte University Press. https://www2.deloitte.com/us/en/insights/focus/industry-4-0/digital-transformation-in-supply-chain.html, pp. 4–8.

24. Ibid.

25. Ibid.

26. Ibid.

27. Mussomeli, A., Dollar, B., Laaper, S., Sniderman, B., & Mariani, J. (2017, December18). *The digital supply network meets the future of work. People, machines, and a new era of collaboration*. Deloitte Insights. https://www2.deloitte.com/us/en/insights/focus/industry-4-0/smart-automation-talent-digital-supply-network.html, pp. 7, 8, 9.

28. Ibid.

29. Ibid.

CHAPTER 3

1. Yousefpour, A., Fung, C., Nguyen, T., Kadiyala, K., Jalali, F., Niakanlahiji, A., Kong, J., & Jue, J. P. (2019). All one needs to know about fog computing and related edge computing paradigms: A complete survey. *Journal of Systems Architecture.* Volume 98, September 2019, 289–330

2. Ibid.

CHAPTER 4

1. Samuel, A. (1959). Some studies in machine learning using the game of checkers. *IBM Journal, 3*(3), 210–229.

2. Wuest, T. (2015). *Identifying product and process state drivers in manufacturing systems using supervised machine learning.* Springer Theses. New York, Heidelberg: Springer Verlag. doi: 10.1007/978-3-319-17611-6.

3. McKinsey (2017). Jobs lost, jobs gained: What the future of work will mean for jobs, skills, and wages. https://www.mckinsey.com/featured-insights/future-of-work/jobs-lost-jobs-gained-what-the-future-of-work-will-mean-for-jobs-skills-and-wages

4. Taisch, M., Casidsid, M., Despaeisse, M., Luglietti, R., May, G., Morin, T., Pinzone, M., & Wuest, T. (2019). *2019 World manufacturing forum report: Skills for the future of manufacturing.* World Manufacturing Forum. https://www.worldmanufacturingforum.org/report-2019

5. McKinsey (2017). Smartening up with artificial intelligence (AI)—What's in it for Germany and its industrial sector? https://www.mckinsey.com/~/media/McKinsey/Industries/Semiconductors/Our%20Insights/Smartening%20up%20with%20artificial%20intelligence/Smartening-up-with-artificial-intelligence.ashx

6. Moffett, B. (2018). Transform the manufacturing supply chain with Multi-Echelon inventory optimization. https://cloudblogs.microsoft.com/industry-blog/manufacturing/2018/03/01/transform-the-manufacturing-supply-chain-with-multi-echelon-inventory-optimization/

7. Gupta, C. (2017). Leveraging AI for industrial IoT. https://www.hitachinext.com/en-us/pdf/presentation/leveraging-ai-for-industrial-iot.pdf

Chapter 4 Additional References

Mills, T. (2018, July 11). Machine learning vs. artificial intelligence: How are they different? *Forbes.* https://www.forbes.com/sites/forbestechcouncil/2018/07/11/machine-learning-vs-artificial-intelligence-how-are-they-different/#729d17123521

Taisch, M., Arena, D., Gorobtcova, P., Kiritsis, D., Luglietti, R., May, G., Morin, T., & Wuest, T. (2018). *2018 World manufacturing forum report: Recommendations for the future of manufacturing.* World Manufacturing Forum. https://www.worldmanufacturingforum.org/copia-di-wmf-report

Wuest, T., Weimer, D., Irgens, C., & Thoben, K.-D. (2016). Machine learning in manufacturing: advantages, challenges and applications. *Production & Manufacturing Research, 4*(1), 23–45.

CHAPTER 5

1. Bernardes, E. (2019, January 30). Blockchain and tokenization: transforming ownership and the automotive value chain. Retrieved from https://www.supplynetworkinnovation.com/single-post/2019/01/30/Blockchain-and-tokenization-Transforming-ownership-and-the-automotive-value-supply-chain

2. Air New Zealand forms partnership for 3D printed aircraft parts. April 11, 2019. Aerospace Technology. https://www.aerospace-technology.com/news/air-new-zealand-forms-partnership-for-3d-printed-aircraft-parts/

3. Yaga, D., Mell, P., Roby, N., & Scarfone, K. (2018). *Blockchain technology overview* (No. NIST Internal or Interagency Report (NISTIR) 8202). National Institute of Standards and Technology.

4. Ibid.

5. Ibid.

6. Mussomeli, A., Gish, D., & Laaper, S. (2016). *The rise of the digital supply network*. Deloitte University Press.

7. Collak, V. (2018). Blockchain in supply chain—how to use the distributed ledger to trace products. Medium. https://medium.com/@vcollak/blockchain-in-supply-chain-how-walmart-uses-the-distributed-ledger-to-trace-products-8abf1d35b778

8. Casey, M., & Wong, P. (2017). Global supply chains are about to get better, thanks to blockchain. *Harvard Business Review, 13*, 1–6.

9. Park, T. (2018, April). Blockchain is about to revolutionize the shipping industry. Bloomberg. https://www.bloomberg.com/news/articles/2018-04-18/drowning-in-a-sea-of-paper-world-s-biggest-ships-seek-a-way-out

10. Mackelprang, A. W., Robinson, J. L., Bernardes, E., & Webb, G. S. (2014). The relationship between strategic supply chain integration and performance: A meta-analytic evaluation and implications for supply chain management research. *Journal of Business Logistics, 35*(1), 71–96.

11. Kehoe, L., O'Connell, N., Andrzejewski, D., Gindner, K., & Dalal, D. (2017). When two chains combine: supply chain meets blockchain, 1–16. https://www2.deloitte.com/content/dam/Deloitte/pt/Documents/blockchainsupplychain/IE_C_TL_Supplychain_meets_blockchain_.pdf

12. Mackelprang, A. W., Robinson, J. L., Bernardes, E., & Webb, G. S. (2014). The relationship between strategic supply chain integration and performance: A meta-analytic evaluation and implications for supply chain management research. *Journal of Business Logistics, 35*(1), 71–96.

13. Mussomeli, A., Gish, D., and Laaper, S. (2016). *The rise of the digital supply network*. Deloitte University Press.

14. Bower, J. L., & Christensen, C.M. (1995). Disruptive technologies: Catching the wave. *Harvard Business Review*, January–February, 43–53.

15. Iansiti, M., & Lakhani, K. R. (2017). The truth about blockchain. *Harvard Business Review, 95*(1), 118–127.

16. Ibid.

17. Killmeyer, J., & Holdowsky, J. (2019). From siloed to distributed: blockchain enables the digital supply network. Deloitte Insights. https://www2.deloitte .com/us/en/insights/topics/understanding-blockchain-potential/digital-supply -network-blockchain-adoption.html
18. Rogers, D., Raylor, T., Barajas, R., & Choi, T. (2018). Blockchain and supply management. CAPS Research.
19. Nanda, R., White, R. F., & Tuzikov, A. (2017). Blockchain, Cryptocurrencies and Digital Assets. *Harvard Business School Technical Note*, 818-066.
20. Delmolino, K., Arnett, M., Kosba, A., Miller, A., & Shi, E. (2016, February). Step by step towards creating a safe smart contract: lessons and insights from a cryptocurrency lab. In *International Conference on Financial Cryptography and Data Security* (pp. 79–94). Springer, Berlin, Heidelberg.
21. Ream, J., Chu, Y., & Schatsky, D. (2016). Upgrading blockchains: smart contract use cases in industry. Deloitte Insights. https://www2.deloitte.com/us/en/insights /focus/signals-for-strategists/using-blockchain-for-smart-contracts.html
22. Fawcett, S., Jin, Y. H., Fawcett, A., & Bernardes, E. (2018). Technological game changers: convergence, hype, and evolving supply chain design. *Production, 28*.
23. Ibid.

CHAPTER 6
1. Gaus, T., Olsen, K., & Deloso, M. (2018). Synchronizing the digital supply network: Using artificial intelligence for supply chain planning. Deloitte Insights.

CHAPTER 7
1. McFarlane, D., Sarma, S., Chirn, J.L., Wong, C.Y. & Ashton, K. (2003) Auto ID systems and intelligent manufacturing control, *Engineering Applications of Artificial Intelligence*, Vol. 16, No. 4, pp. 365–376.
2. Wong, C. Y., McFarlane, D., Zaharudin, A., & Agarwal, V. (2002). The intelligent product driven supply chain. IEEE International Conference on Systems, Man and Cybernetics, 6–9 October, Hammamet, Tunisia.
3. Meyer, G. G., Främling, K., & Hölmström, J. (2009). Intelligent products—a survey, *Computers in Industry, 60*(3), 137–148.
4. Wuest, T., Schmidt, T., Wei, W., & Romero, D. (2018). Towards (pro-)active intelligent products. *International Journal of Product Lifecycle Management, 11*(2), 154–189.
5. Lehmhus, D., Wuest, T., Wellsandt, S., Bosse, S., Kaihara, T., Thoben, K.-D., & Busse, M. (2015). Cloud-based automated design and additive manufacturing: A usage data-enabled paradigm shift. *Sensors, 15*(12), 32079–32122. doi: 10.3390/s151229905
6. Bosse, S., Lehmhus, D., Lang, W., & Busse, M. (eds.) (2017). *Material-integrated intelligent systems*. McGraw-Hill. doi: 10.1002/978352767924
7. Goedkoop, Mark J., et al. "Product service systems, ecological and economic basics." *Report for Dutch Ministries of environment (VROM) and economic affairs (EZ)* 36(1) (1999): 1–122.

8. Tukker, A., & Tischner, U. (2006). Product-services as a research field: past, present and future. Reflections from a decade of research. *Journal of Cleaner Production, 14*(17), 1552–1556; emphasis added.

9. Baines, T. S., Lightfoot, H. W., Evans, S., Neely, A., Greenough, R., Peppard, J., Roy, R., Shehab, E., Braganza, A., Tiwari, A., & Alcock, J. R. (2007). State-of-the-art in product-service systems. *Proceedings of the Institution of Mechanical Engineers, Part B: Journal of Engineering Manufacture, 221*(10), 1543–1552; emphasis added.

10. Khan, M., & Wuest, T. (2018). *Mapping of PSS research: A bibliometric analysis.* Int'l Conference on Industrial Engineering and Operations Management. Washington, DC, USA, September 27–29, 2018.

11. Martinez, V., Bastl, M., Kingston, J., & Evans, S. (2010). Challenges in transforming manufacturing organisations into product-service providers. *Journal of Manufacturing Technology Management, 21*(4), 449–469.

12. Vandermerwe, S., & Rada, J. (1988, December 1). Servitization of business: Adding value by adding services. *European Management Journal, 6*(4), 314–324.

13. Baines, T. S., Lightfoot, H. W., Evans, S., Neely, A., Greenough, R., Peppard, J., Roy, R., Shehab, E., Braganza, A., Tiwari, A., & Alcock, J. R. (2007). State-of-the-art in product-service systems. *Proceedings of the Institution of Mechanical Engineers, Part B: Journal of Engineering Manufacture, 221*(10), 1543–1552.

14. Porter, M. E., & Heppelmann, J. E. (2014). How smart, connected products are transforming competition. *Harvard Business Review, 92*(11), 64–88.

15. Lehmhus, D., Wuest, T., Wellsandt, S., Bosse, S., Kaihara, T., Thoben, K.-D., & Busse, M. (2015). Cloud-based automated design and additive manufacturing: A usage data-enabled paradigm shift. *Sensors, 15*(12), 32079–32122. doi: 10.3390/s151229905

Chapter 7 Additional Reference
Khan, M., Mittal, S., West, S., & Wuest, T. (2018). Review on upgradability—a product lifetime extension strategy in the context of product service systems. *Journal of Cleaner Production, 204*(2018), 1154–1168. doi: 10.1016/j.jclepro.2018.08.329

CHAPTER 8
1. Frydlinger, D., Hart, O., & Vitasek, K. (2019, October). A new approach to contract. *HBR.Org.* https://hbr.org/2019/09/a-new-approach-to-contracts

CHAPTER 9
1. Greer, C., M. Burns, D. Wollman, & Griffor, E. (2019, March). Cyber-physical systems and internet of things. National Institute of Standards and Technology; Gaithersburg, MD. Lee, E. A. (2006). Cyber-physical systems: Are computing foundations adequate? in *Position paper for NSF workshop on cyber-physical systems: Research motivation, techniques and roadmap, 2,* 1–9; Kagermann, H., Wahlster, W., & Helbig, J. (2013). Umsetzungsempfehlungen für das Zukunftsprojekt Industrie 4.0. *Abschlussbericht des Arbeitskreises Industrie, 4*(5); Thoben, K.-D., Wiesner, S., & Wuest, T. (2017, January). "Industrie 4.0" and

smart manufacturing: A review of research issues and application examples. *International Journal of Automation Technology, 11*(1), 4–16.

2. Kagermann, H., Wahlster, W., & Helbig, J. (2013). Umsetzungsempfehlungen für das Zukunftsprojekt Industrie 4.0. *Abschlussbericht des Arbeitskreises Industrie, 4*(5).

3. Kusiak, A. (2017, April). Smart manufacturing must embrace big data. *Nature, 544*(7648), 23–25.

4. Wallace, E., & Riddick, F. (2013). Panel on enabling smart manufacturing (presentation). In *APMS 2013, September 11, 2013*, State College, USA. Chand, S., & Davis, J. (2010). What is smart manufacturing? *Time* magazine, 28–33.

5. Xu, L. D., & Duan, L. (2019, February). Big data for cyber physical systems in industry 4.0: A survey. *Enterprise Information Systems, 13*(2), 148–169.

6. Mittal, S., Khan, M. A., Romero, D., & Wuest, T. (2018, October). A critical review of smart manufacturing and Industry 4.0 maturity models: Implications for small and medium-sized enterprises (SMEs). *Journal of Manufacturing Systems, 49*, 194–214.

7. Thoben, K.-D., Wiesner, S., & Wuest, T. (2017, January). "Industrie 4.0" and smart manufacturing: A review of research issues and application examples. *International Journal of Automation Technology, 11*(1), 4–16.

8. Kagermann, H., Wahlster, W., & Helbig, J. (2013). Umsetzungsempfehlungen für das Zukunftsprojekt Industrie 4.0. *Abschlussbericht des Arbeitskreises Industrie, 4*(5).

9. Thoben, K.-D., Wiesner, S., & Wuest, T. (2017, January). "Industrie 4.0" and smart manufacturing: A review of research issues and application examples. *International Journal of Automation Technology, 11*(1), 4–16; Kagermann, H., Wahlster, W., & Helbig, J. (2013). Umsetzungsempfehlungen für das Zukunftsprojekt Industrie 4.0. *Abschlussbericht des Arbeitskreises Industrie, 4*(5).

10. Lee, E. A. (2006). Cyber-physical systems: Are computing foundations adequate? in *Position paper for NSF workshop on cyber-physical systems: Research motivation, techniques and roadmap, 2*, 1–9.

11. Jones, A. T., Romero, D., & Wuest, T. (2018, August). Modeling agents as joint cognitive systems in smart manufacturing systems. *Manufacturing Letters, 17*, 6–8.

12. Cardenas, A. A., Amin, S., & Sastry, S. (2008). Secure control: Towards survivable cyber-physical systems. *The 28th International Conference on Distributed Computing Systems Workshops*, pp. 495–500.

13. Monostori, L., Kádár, B., Bauernhansl, T., Kondoh, S., Kumara, S., Reinhart, G., Sauer, O., Schuh, G., Sihn, W., & Ueda, K. (2016). Cyber-physical systems in manufacturing. *Cirp Annals, 65*(2), 621–641.

14. Romero, D., Bernus, P., Noran, O., Stahre, J., & Fast-Berglund, Å. (2016). The operator 4.0: Human cyber-physical systems and adaptive automation towards human-automation symbiosis work systems. In *IFIP international conference on advances in production management systems* (pp. 677–686). Springer, Cham.

15. Wuest, T., Romero, D., & Stahre, J. (2017, April). Introducing "Operator 4.0," a tech-augmented human worker. *The Conversation.* https://theconversation.com/introducing-operator-4-0-a-tech-augmented-human-worker-74117

16. Romero, D., Stahre, J., Wuest, T., Noran, O., Bernus, P., Fast-Berglund, A., & Gosecky, D. (2016). Towards an Operator 4.0 typology: A human-centric perspective on the fourth industrial revolution technologies. International Conference on Computers and Industrial Engineering, October 29–31, 2016, Tianjin, China. ISSN 2164-8670 cd-rom, ISSN 2164-8689 online.

Chapter 9 Additional References

Davis, J., Edgar, T., et al. (2015). Smart manufacturing. *Annual Review of Chemical and Biomolecular Engineering, 6*, 141–160.

Lee, J., Bagheri, B., & Kao, H.-A. (2015, January). A cyber-physical systems architecture for Industry 4.0-based manufacturing systems. *Manufacturing Letters, 3*, 8–23.

Menon, K., Kärkkäinen, H., Wuest, T., & Gupta, J. (2018). Industrial internet platforms: A PLM Perspective, Part B. *Journal of Engineering Manufacture*, online first, 1–20. doi: 10.1177/0954405418760651

Mittal, S., Khan, M. A., Romero, D., & Wuest, T. (2019). Smart manufacturing: Characteristics, technologies and enabling factors, Part B. *Journal of Engineering Manufacture, 233*(5), 1342–1361.

Wuest, T. (2019). Smart manufacturing builds opportunities for ISEs. *ISE Magazine, 51*(4), 40–44.

CHAPTER 10

1. Mackelprang, A. W., Robinson, J. L., Bernardes, E., & Webb, G. S. (2014). The relationship between strategic supply chain integration and performance: A meta-analytic evaluation and implications for supply chain management research. *Journal of Business Logistics, 35*(1), 71–96.
2. Fawcett, S. E., & Fawcett, A. M. (2013). *The definitive guide to order fulfillment and customer service: Principles and strategies for planning, organizing, and managing fulfillment and service operations.* Upper Saddle River: Pearson Education.
3. Fawcett, S., Ellram, L., Fugate, B., Kannan, V., & Bernardes, E. (2019). *Operations and supply chain management: enhancing competitiveness and customer value.* MyEducator.
4. Ibid.
5. Ibid.
6. Mussomeli, A., Gish, D., & Laaper, S. (2016, December 1). The rise of the digital supply network: Industry 4.0 enables the digital transformation of supply chains. Deloitte Insights.
7. Ibid.
8. Bernardes, E. S., & Zsidisin, G. A. (2008). An examination of strategic supply management benefits and performance implications. *Journal of Purchasing and Supply Management, 14*(4), 209–219.
9. Bernardes, E. S., & Hanna, M. D. (2009). A theoretical review of flexibility, agility and responsiveness in the operations management literature: Toward a conceptual definition of customer responsiveness. *International Journal of Operations & Production Management, 29*(1), 30–53.

10. Cousins, P. D., Lawson, B., Petersen, K. J., & Fugate, B. (2019). Investigating green supply chain management practices and performance. *International Journal of Operations & Production Management. 39*(5), 767–786

11. Fawcett, S., Ellram, L., Fugate, B., Kannan, V., & Bernardes, E. (2019). *Operations and supply chain management: Enhancing competitiveness and customer value.* MyEducator.

12. Bernardes, E. (2019, March 3). Last-mile and rise of on-demand autonomous delivery. Retrieved from https://www.supplynetworkinnovation.com/single-post/2019/03/03/Last-mile-and-rise-of-on-demand-autonomous-delivery.

13. Fawcett, S., Jin, Y. H., Fawcett, A., & Bernardes, E. (2018). Technological game changers: Convergence, hype, and evolving supply chain design. *Production, 28.*

14. Russell, S., & Norvig, P. (2010). *Artificial intelligence: A modern approach.* Upper Saddle River: Pearson Education.

CHAPTER 11

1. Rogers, D. (2016). *The digital transformation playbook.* Columbia Business School Publishing.

2. Ibid.

3. IDEOU blog at https://www.ideou.com/blogs/inspiration/what-is-design-thinking, accessed on April 6, 2020.

4. Interaction design foundation literature, accessed at https://www.interaction-design.org/literature/article/what-is-design-thinking-and-why-is-it-so-popular on April 6, 2020.

CHAPTER 12

1. Yao, M., Zhou, A., & Jia, M. (2018). *Applied artificial intelligence: A handbook for business leaders.* Topbots Inc.

2. Crawford, K. (2016). Artificial intelligence's white guy problem. *New York Times*, 25.

3. Hart, R. D. (2017, July). If you're not a white male, artificial intelligence's use in healthcare could be dangerous. *Quartz.*

4. Mussomeli, A., Laaper, S. & Dollar, B. (2017). The digital supply network meets the future of work: People, machines, and a new era of collaboration. Deloitte Insights.

5. Bernardes, E. (2017, October 10). Value chain transformation, competitive revitalization, and impact on the labor force. Retrieved from https://www.supplynetworkinnovation.com/single-post/2017/10/07/Value-chain-transformation-competitive-revitalization-and-impact-on-the-labor-force

6. Sirkin, H., Zinser, M., & Rose, J. (2015, September). The robotics revolution: The next great leap in manufacturing. The Boston Consulting Group.

7. Evans-Greenwood, P., Lewis, H., & Guszcza, J. (2017). Reconstructing work: Automation, artificial intelligence, and the essential role of humans. Deloitte Review, 21.

8. Sigelman, M. (2017). By the numbers: The job market for data science and analytics. Boston: Burning Glass Technologies.

9. Wellener, B., & Manolian, H. (2019). The future of work in manufacturing: What will jobs look like in the digital era? Deloitte Insights.

10. Volini, E., Schwartz, J., Roy, I., Hauptmann, M., Van Durme, Y., Denny, B., & Bersin, J. (2019). Leading the social enterprise: Reinvent with a human focus. Deloitte Human Capital Trends.

11. Hitch, J. (2019). Robots, humans, and nature of work. *IndustryWeek Best Practices Report.*

12. The 2019 World Manufacturing Forum report: Skills for the future of manufacturing. WMF. https://www.worldmanufacturingforum.org/report-2019

13. Bernardes, E. (2017, October 10). Value chain transformation, competitive revitalization, and impact on the labor force. Retrieved from https://www.supplynetworkinnovation.com/single-post/2017/10/07/Value-chain-transformation-competitive-revitalization-and-impact-on-the-labor-force

14. Andes, S., & Muro, M. (2015). Don't blame robots for lost manufacturing jobs. Brookings. https://www.brookings.edu/blog/the-avenue/2015/04/29/dont-blame-the-robots-for-lost-manufacturing-jobs/

15. Blit, J., Amand, S. S., & Wajda, J. (2018, May). Automation and the future of work: Scenarios and policy options. Centre for International Governance Innovation. CIGI Papers No 174. https://www.cigionline.org/sites/default/files/documents/Paper%20no.174lowres.pdf

16. David, H., & Salomons, A. (2018). Is automation labor-displacing? Productivity growth, employment, and the labor share. Brookings Papers, BPEA Conference Drafts. https://www.brookings.edu/wp-content/uploads/2018/03/1_autorsalomons.pdf

17. Brynjolfsson, E., & McAfee, A. (2014). *The second machine age: Work, progress, and prosperity in a time of brilliant technologies.* WW Norton & Company.

18. David, H., & Salomons, A. (2018). Is automation labor-displacing? Productivity growth, employment, and the labor share. NBER Working Paper No. 24871

19. Mussomeli, A., Laaper, S., & Dollar, B. (2019). The digital supply network meets the future of work. Deloitte Insights.

20. The 2019 World Manufacturing Forum Report: Skills for the future of manufacturing. WMF. https://www.worldmanufacturingforum.org/report-2019

21. Ibid.

22. Bughin, J., Hazan, E., Lund, S., Dahlström, P., Wiesinger, A., & Subramaniam, A. (2018). Skill shift: Automation and the future of the workforce. McKinsey Global Institute. McKinsey & Company.

23. Bernardes, E. (2017, October 10). Value chain transformation, competitive revitalization, and impact on the labor force. Retrieved from https://www.supplynetworkinnovation.com/single-post/2017/10/07/Value-chain-transformation-competitive-revitalization-and-impact-on-the-labor-force

24. The 2019 World Manufacturing Forum report: Skills for the future of manufacturing. WMF.

25. Ibid.

26. Ibid.

27. Ibid.

28. Pratt, G. A. (2015). Is a Cambrian explosion coming for robotics?, *Journal of Economic Perspectives*, *29*(3), 51–60.

29. The 2019 World Manufacturing Forum report: Skills for the future of manufacturing. WMF.

30. Ibid.

31. Organisation for Economic Co-operation and Development (OECD). (2016). Skills for a digital world. http://www.oecd.org/future-of-work/

32. Bernardes, E. (2017, October 10). Value chain transformation, competitive revitalization, and impact on the labor force. Retrieved from https://www.supplynetworkinnovation.com/single-post/2017/10/07/Value-chain-transformation-competitive-revitalization-and-impact-on-the-labor-force

33. Hitch, J. (2019). Robots, humans, and nature of work. *IndustryWeek Best Practices Report.*

34. Kane, G. C., Palmer, D., Phillips, A. N., Kiron, D., & Buckley, N. (2015). Strategy, not technology, drives digital transformation. *MIT Sloan Management Review and Deloitte University Press, 14*, 1–25.

35. The 2019 World Manufacturing Forum report: Skills for the future of manufacturing. WMF.

36. Bughin, J., Hazan, E., Lund, S., Dahlström, P., Wiesinger, A., & Subramaniam, A. (2018). Skill shift: Automation and the future of the workforce. McKinsey Global Institute. McKinsey & Company.

CHAPTER 13

1. Mussomeli, A., Gish, D., & Laaper, S. (2016.) *The rise of the digital supply network*. Deloitte University Press.

2. Kane, G. C., Phillips, A. N., Copulsky, J. R., & Andrus, G. R. (2019.) *The technology fallacy*. MIT Press.

3. Lockwood, T., & Papke, E. (2017). *Innovation by design*. Career Press.

CHAPTER 14

1. Sources for Amazon use case:
   - Calvo. J. (2019, July 26). The miracle of Amazon's digital supply chain. Global Insights. https://e.globis.jp/tech-innovation/the-miracle-of-amazons-digital-supply-chain/

2. Sources for Georgia-Pacific use case:
   - Interview with Jeff Fleck, chief supply chain officer, GP CPG, conducted by Amit Sinha on January 30, 2020.
   - Georgia-Pacific website: https://www.gp.com/product-overview/consumer-products

3. Sources for Walmart Canada use case:
   - Interview with Loudon Owen, CEO DLT Labs, conducted by Ednilson Bernardes.
   - Mearian, L. (November 19, 2019.) Walmart launches world's largest blockchain-based freight-and-payment network. *Computerworld*.
   - James, C. (November 20, 2019). Walmart Canada introduces blockchain-based supply chain. *Deli Market News*.

4. Sources for Land O'Lakes use case:
- Interview with Scott Nieman, expert enterprise integration architect, Land O'Lakes, conducted by Thorsten Wuest and Amit Sinha.
- Land O'Lakes CEO Beth Ford: The *60 Minutes* Interview. Broadcast October 6, 2019.
- Land O'Lakes website: https://www.landolakes.com/

5. Sources for T-Mobile use case:
- Interview with Erik LaValle, digital supply chain and customer experience technology portfolio leader, and Bhanu Sistla, principal product manager and digital supply chain and customer experience, T-Mobile.
- T-Mobile. Forbes. Retrieved on January 5, 2019, from https://www.forbes.com/companies/t-mobile/#6fc4194b3fb4
- Lawrence, M. (2019, March 2.) T-Mobile drives customer centricity through digital transformation and customer first culture. Gigabit. Retrieved on January 5, 2019, from https://www.gigabitmagazine.com/company/t-mobile-drives-customer-centricity-through-digital-transformation-and-customer-first?amp

6. Sources for JD.com use case:
- Choudhury, S. R. (2018, August 8). Walmart and JD.com invest $500 million in a Chinese online delivery company. CNBC.
- DC Velocity Staff. (2019, January 7). JD.com says its fulfillment technology will support "boundaryless" shopping for other retailers. DC Velocity. https://www.dcvelocity.com/articles/20190107-jd-com-opens-its-fulfillment-network-to-other-retailers/
- O'Connor, T., Suleski, J., Enright, T., Pradhan, A., & Becker, K. (2019). Retail Supply Chainnovator 2019: JD.com wins for rethinking retailer-to-retailer collaborations to deliver a unified shopping experience. Gartner.

7. Sources for Unilever use case:
- Smith, J. (2019, July 15). Unilever uses virtual factories to tune up its supply chain. *Wall Street Journal*.
- Digital twins concept gains traction among enterprises. (2018, September 12). *Wall Street Journal*.

8. Source for Caterpillar use case:
- Digital supply networks: Our point of view. (n.d.). Deloitte Development LLC.

9. Sources for Nike Inc. use case:
- Statista.com. (2019, March 29). Nike—statistics & facts. Retrieved from https://www.statista.com/topics/1243/nike/
- MacDonald, C. Harvard Business School Digital Initiative. (2017, November 15). Getting personal: What digitization and customization mean for Nike's supply chain.

10. Sources for Maven Machines use case:
- Interview with Avishai Geller and Jonas Kohls, Maven Machines, conducted by Thorsten Wuest.
- Maven Machines website: https://mavenmachines.com

11. Sources for Daimler use case:
    - A deeper perspective: How Daimler Trucks Asia utilized data-driven insights to proactively change the course of the entire organization. (2017). Deloitte.

INDEX

Page numbers followed by *f* and *t* refer to figures and tables, respectively.

Intelligent spare parts management,
182–183
Intelligent supply, 141–157
automation in, 153–157
capabilities of, 146–152, 153f
and digital procurement, 144–146
as DSN capability, 26f, 27
in DSNs, 155f
impact of digital transformation on, 8
and traditional procurement concepts,
141–144
Interconnected ecosystem signaling,
188–189
Internal synchronization, 112, 113f
International Data Spaces Association, 61
International Federation of Robotics, 232
International trade, 96–97
Internet of Things (IoT), 39, 40f, 173,
174f
and Daimler Trucks Asia, 271
dynamic fulfillment, 201–202
and Maven Machines Inc., 269
used by Walmart Canada, 259–260
Interoperability, 63, 103
Intranet infrastructure, 65–66
IPSS(industrial product service systems),
136
ISO 10303, 63
IT (see Information technology (IT))

JD.com, 263–264
Jet engine production, 139

Koch Industries, 257

Lakhani, K. R., 99, 100
Land O'Lakes, Inc., 260–261
Large multinational enterprises (MNEs),
166–167, 167t
Last mile delivery, 196–199
LaValle, Erik, 262–263
Laws, related to data, 61–62, 62t
Leadership, in DSN transformation,
246–247, 250–251
Learning, lifelong, 233, 246
Learning mindset, 237
Leverage suppliers, 143f
Liability, with AI, ML, and robotics, 85
Lifelong learning, 233, 246
Line fill rate, 210
Linearity, of traditional SCM, 18–19
Live Factory, 266–268, 267f
Local computing, 65–66

Logistics, 13
Loyalty:
in contract management, 149–150
of customers, 217–218

Machine learning (ML), 72–78, 82–87
algorithms for (see Machine learning
algorithms)
application process for, 77f, 78
applications of, 83–84
and artificial intelligence, 72–75, 74f
artificial intelligence vs., 73f
benefits of, 86
challenges for, 85
as enabling technology, 36
levels of, 79f
predictions about, 82–83
Machine learning algorithms, 75–78
in intelligent spare parts management,
182
in intelligent supply, 145
Machine teams, 48
Made in China 2025, 232
Maersk, 96, 102–103
Manufacturing innovation, 129f
Manufacturing resource planning (MRP
II), 14
Manufacturing systems, 165f
Mass production, 11, 164
Master data, in intelligent supply, 154
Master production schedule (MPS), 108
Material requirements planning (MRP
I), 14
Maven Machines Inc, 269–270
McAfee, A., 229–230
Mechanization, 10–11
Metcalfe's law, 70
Meyer, G. G., 131
Middle-of-life (MOL) applications, 130
Minimum viable product (MVP), 248
MIT Sloan Management Review, 237
Mixed reality (MR), 40f, 199
ML (see Machine learning (ML))
MNEs (large multinational enterprises),
166–167, 167t
Model-based manufacturing, 129f
Model-based product definition, 129f
MOL (middle-of-life) applications, 130
Monitoring, of customer experience,
218–220
Moore's law, 70
MPS (master production schedule), 108
MR (mixed reality), 40f, 199

ABOUT THE AUTHORS

Amit Sinha

Amit Sinha is an accomplished leader, consultant, trainer, author, and researcher in the areas of digital supply network, supply chain management, operations management, and enterprise technology. A Production and Industrial Engineer and an MBA by education, Mr. Sinha has more than 16 years of professional experience in integrated business planning, sales and operations planning, production scheduling, manufacturing, logistics, order management, data strategy, and technology applications.

Mr. Sinha is currently serving as a leader in the Enterprise Performance practice of Deloitte Consulting, helping leading organizations with digital transformation, supply network design, value creation, change management, and technology and data strategy. He started his professional career with a manufacturing firm learning production processes, quality control, new product development, and customer management. Driven by the impact of value creation through process transformation and technology adoption, he joined Accenture, where he architected and delivered supply chain solutions for business transformation projects. Later he moved to Deloitte, leading the internal organization building and external consulting assignments. Mr. Sinha has worked extensively for industry leaders in manufacturing, consumer products, life sciences, and technology sectors while living in different cities of USA, Europe, and Asia.

Mr. Sinha is the leader of training and skills development for his team at Deloitte, helping consultants to broaden the cutting-edge skills for solving the challenges of the current and future business problems related to supply chain and technology. He has helped multiple leading organizations with the supply chain training strategy and organization readiness to adopt the changes brought through digitization and automation.

Mr. Sinha has been a speaker in numerous leading conferences and business and technology events. He has authored textbooks and professional books on supply chain management, integrated business planning, sales and operations planning, and intelligent enterprise. His research papers on supply chain, and education and talent development have been published by leading international journals. He has delivered guest lectures at many leading business schools in US, Denmark, and India. Apart from work, his other interest areas are travel, tennis, yoga, meditation, writing, teaching, and spending time with family and friends.

Ednilson Bernardes

Dr. Ednilson Bernardes is an award-winning researcher and a Professor of supply chain management. He started his post-secondary education and career with the Brazilian Air Force, where, upon graduation, he worked in air transportation as an air crewmember and led quality control and process improvement initiatives. His responsibilities also included inventory management, project management, material management and relationships with suppliers, directing maintenance, operations and monitoring activities, and aircrew training.

He later joined the aerospace conglomerate Embraer, the world's third largest aircraft manufacturer, under their Young Talents Program, a fast career track program aimed at training and developing selected employees to ascend to critical leadership roles. In this position, he experienced many aspects of global supply chain design and operation, from product development to global strategic sourcing, product certification, compliance, and delivery. He led process innovation and digitization projects as well as quality and performance improvement initiatives, and served as a liaison between engineering departments.

Dr. Bernardes holds a PhD in Operations and Management Science from the University of Minnesota and a Master's Science degree in Operations, Innovation, and Technology Management from the Universidade Federal do Rio Grande do Sul. His research focuses on competitive dynamics and innovation in supply network operations and integration and innovation in buyer-supplier relationships. He has served as a guest speaker and delivered talks, seminars, and training to various organizations and countries in the Americas, Europe, and Asia. He started the Global Supply Chain Management Program at West Virginia University (WVU) and has served as its inaugural Program Coordinator. He also founded the WVU Supply Chain Advisory Council, recruited its initial cadre of members, and has led the interactions and work between the Chambers College and the council. He was a member of the team charged with reimagining the vision and mission of the John Chambers College of Business and Economics at West Virginia University and of selected graduate programs.

Besides research, Dr. Bernardes has interacted with and led or facilitated innovation and performance improvement initiatives in large organizations, such as Toyota, WVUHospital, and the DEA, including quality, logistics, and process flow issues. He has also served on the Boards of government authorities and other organizations, as well as advised government organizations in supply chain issues. He is a member of the Editorial Boards of the *Journal of Operations Management*, *Journal of Supply Chain Management*, *Journal of Business Logistics*, and *Journal of Purchasing and Supply Management*. He has coauthored various other books. He is passionate about flying, cycling, technological innovations, reimagining processes and operating models, and learning about and experiencing different cultures.

Rafael Calderon

Rafael Calderon serves as the Global Synchronized Planning and Fulfillment market offering leader at Deloitte. In his role, he helps leading organizations across the globe with their supply chain strategy, organization transformation, and digital supply network enablement. Working as a close ally to senior executives and CXOs, he helps them with the value realization and problem resolution in the supply chain, logistics, and associated business functions.

Mr. Calderon holds an MBA from the University of North Carolina at Chapel Hill and BS in Industrial Engineering from Purdue University. He has 20 years of industry and consulting experience, helping global companies drive operations performance through large-scale growth and efficiency initiatives. His experience encompasses a wide range of supply chain topics including digital supply networks, end-to-end supply chain transformation, integrated business planning, demand-driven supply chain, merger integration, working capital reduction, operational cost reduction, and network optimization. He has been a critical part of helping his clients identify and deliver more than $1B in benefits. He has led and been part of cross geography teams in large scale, complex global transformation efforts across North America, Asia, Europe, and Latin America.

Mr. Calderon is a frequent speaker at business schools and industry conferences. His multi-lingual capability (English, Spanish, and French) allows him to interact with students and professionals across the globe. Being the "US Consumer Products National Talent and Learning Leader" at Deloitte, he helps the consultants across the levels for cutting edge skills development. He is involved in generating eminence through writing, researching, and leading the team at his firm as "US Supply Chain Eminence Leader." His work has been published through business articles and research papers.

Mr. Calderon complements his work with an active role as a devoted husband and father of five who loves good food, travel, essential oils, reading about people, and most importantly spending quality time with his extended family and friends network.

Thorsten Wuest

Dr. Thorsten Wuest serves as Assistant Professor at West Virginia University and J. Wayne and Kathy Richards Faculty Fellow in Engineering at the Benjamin M. Statler College of Engineering and Mineral Resources. Dr. Wuest holds a PhD in Production Engineering (summa cum laude) from the University of Bremen as well as two Master's degrees in Industrial Engineering (University of Bremen) and International Business (Auckland University of Technology).

Dr. Wuest received the Statler Outstanding Teacher of the Year 2019 award and was selected as an IDEA Fellow in the office of the Provost of West Virginia University to further entrepreneurship across campus. His research, funded by federal and international agencies as well as industry, focusses on Smart and Advanced Manufacturing, Machine Learning and AI, Hybrid Analytics, Industry 4.0, Servitization with a focus on manufacturing systems. In his research, he puts an emphasis on an interdisciplinary and holistic approach toward analysis and optimization. He is a recognized Smart Manufacturing thought leader, listed among the 20 most influential professors in smart manufacturing by SME.

In addition to publishing his work in the premier academic outlets of the field, he was featured by *Forbes*, Futurism, the World Economic Forum, CBC Radio, and World Manufacturing Forum, etc. He is involved in several professional societies, among others he is a member of IFIP Working Group 5.7 and 5.1, IFAC TC 5.3, SME, senior member of IISE, and research affiliate of the CIRP.

Dr. Wuest has given invited talks in seven countries and published three books and over 120 peer-reviewed articles in international archival journals and conferences gathering over 1,600 citations to date, and serves as a reviewer for many. He serves as Vice-Chair Americas for the IFIP WG 5.7, is a member of the Editorial Board for the *Journal of Manufacturing Systems (JMSY)* and an Associate Editor for the *ASTM Journal Smart and Sustainable Manufacturing Systems (SSMS)* and the *International Journal of Manufacturing Research (IJMR)*. He was a member of the Strategic Core Transformation Team at WVU, served on the Statler College Glen H. Hiner Dean search committee 2019, and is a member of the WVU Statler College Research Council. He is working closely with industry and the startup community, among others, he is a member of the advisory board of Maven Machines Inc. and Veepio.